AF847240

Information Security

Thomas Liedtke

Information Security

Opportunities and Limitations

Springer

Thomas Liedtke
Remseck, Germany

ISBN 978-3-658-45710-5 ISBN 978-3-658-45711-2 (eBook)
https://doi.org/10.1007/978-3-658-45711-2

Translation from the German language edition: "Informationssicherheit" by Thomas Liedtke, © Springer-Verlag GmbH Deutschland, ein Teil von Springer Nature 2022. Published by Springer Berlin Heidelberg. All Rights Reserved.

This book is a translation of the original German edition "Informationssicherheit" by Thomas Liedtke, published by Springer-Verlag GmbH, DE in 2022. The translation was done with the help of an artificial intelligence machine translation tool. A subsequent human revision was done primarily in terms of content, so that the book will read stylistically differently from a conventional translation. Springer Nature works continuously to further the development of tools for the production of books and on the related technologies to support the authors.

This Springer imprint is published by the registered company Springer Fachmedien Wiesbaden GmbH, part of Springer Nature.
The registered company address is: Abraham-Lincoln-Str. 46, 65189 Wiesbaden, Germany

Preface

Information security is always and everywhere … *"It won't happen to me"* …

For years/decades, the topic of **information security** has been gaining in importance. Every day, new (bad) news about information security, cybersecurity, exploitation of security gaps, vulnerabilities, misappropriated (personal) data in connection with the use of technical systems becomes known. Efforts and negative effects hit every industry equally, a golden general "solution" to the topic does not (yet) exist.

As long as the increase in **networking** and **complexity** of new products continues (an end is not in sight), and attackers can keep up with ever more sophisticated attack scenarios, it will remain so.

Events and incidents are increasingly making it into the daily news, we directly feel the adverse effects of successful attacks.

The socially accepted level of risk in relation to information security has not yet been explored. Many "successful" attacks remain without medium-term consequences, attackers are not caught, known insecure products/applications continue to be used. Perceived advantages and comfort on the part of the users appear to be more important characteristics.

Manufacturers only care about information security up to a necessary minimum. Information security means additional **costs,** which usually cannot be recouped. Customers and users take their presence for granted. Information security is merely one of many attributes of trustworthy systems.

How the issue of attack security is to be legally assessed (e.g., analogous to product safety?) has not yet been conclusively clarified. It seems that as long as health is not directly affected, the presence of security gaps is accepted, and potential attacks are accepted as a natural part of technical systems. However, the technical possibilities of the attackers are far from being exhausted. Much will still happen (have to) and lead to the fact that procedures and standards will gradually be improved (have to).

We are still in the midst of the "hare and hedgehog game" between attackers and manufacturers/service providers. In particular, we must fear **scalable attacks,** attacks with impacts on **critical infrastructures** or life and limb, as well as public effects on trust or reputation (keyword **trustworthiness**).

This book is intended to provide an overview of technology, terms, efforts, and regulations. Each of us is affected, both privately and professionally.

What can be done about it? What are the possibilities, where are the limits?

This book explains principles, strategic, methodological approaches for organizational and technical design. The identification and evaluation of risks are central points of any approach to achieve more security. Identification of values, security objectives, and risks, analysis of attack paths, modeling of threats, specification of security measures to reduce security risks and close security gaps, are core pieces.

The book was created based on the experience of applying a variety of methods in numerous real projects over many years and is intended to describe both an introduction and an overview.

Thomas Liedtke

Contents

Glossary of Abbreviations

AA	Airworthiness Authorities
ABC	Attribute-Based Credentials
ADAS	Advanced Driver Assistance Systems
AES	Advanced Encryption Standard
AI	Artificial Intelligence
Auto-ISAC	Automotive Information Sharing and Analysis Center
BCMS	Business Continuity Management System
BDSG	Federal Data Protection Act (national law for Germany)
BSI	Federal Office for Information Security (german "ENISA")
CAN	Controller Area Network
CC	Common Criteria
CCPA	California Consumer Privacy Act
CEM	Common Methodology for Information Technology Security Evaluation
CEO	Chief Executive Officer
CERT	Computer Emergency Response Team
CIA	Protection goal attributes: Confidentiality, Integrity, Availability
CISO	Chief Information Security Officer
CMMI	Capability Maturity Model Integration
COBIT	Control Objectives for Information and Related Technology
CRC	Cyclic Redundancy Check
CRF	Common Regulatory Framework
CRS	Cybersecurity requirements
CSD	Center for Secure Design
CSIRT	Computer Security Incident Response Team
CSMS	Cybersecurity Security Management System
CVE	Common Vulnerability Enumeration
DAST	Dynamic Application Security Testing
DC	Data Confidentiality

DPA	Data Processing Agreement
DPbD	Data Protection by Design
DSB	Data Protection Officer
DSP	Digital Service Provider
EDV	Electronic Data Processing
EECC	European Electronic Communication Code
ENISA	European Network and Information Security Agency
ENX	European Network Exchange Association
EU	European Union
EU-DSAnpUG	EU Data Protection Adaptation and Implementation Act
EU-GDPR	European General Data Protection Regulation
EVG	Evaluation object (see IoI)
EVITA	E-safety vehicle intrusion protected applications
FAA	Federal Aviation Administration
FDE	Full Disk Encryption
FHE	Full Homomorphic Encryption
FIP	Fair Information Practice
FIPP	Fair Information Practice Principle
FIPS	Federal Information Processing Standards Publication
FMEA	Failure Mode Effect Analysis
FPE	File Preserving Encryption
FSE	File System-Level Encryption
GG	Basic Law (Germany)
GHDB	Google-Hacking Database
GoBS	Principles of proper computer-aided accounting systems
GPS	Global Positioning System
HARA	Hazard Analysis and Risk Assessment
HDSG	Hessian Data Protection Act (Germany)
HGB	Commercial Code (Germany)
HIPAA	Health Insurance Portability and Accountability Act
IAC	Identification and Authentication Control
IACS	Industrial Automation and Control Systems
IEEE	Institute of Electrical and Electronics Engineers
ICT	Information and Communication Technology
intacs	International Assessor Certification Scheme
InVeKos	Integrated Administration and Control System
IoI	Item of Interest (see ToI)
IP	Intellectual Property Internet Protocol
IPSec	Internet Protocol Security
IR	Internal Report
ISA	International Society for Automation
ISACA	Information Systems Audit and Control Association

ISMS	Information Security Management System
ISO	International Organization for Standardization
IT	Information Technology
ITGI	IT Governance Institute
ITIL	IT Infrastructure Library
ITSM	IT Service Management
KPI	Key Performance Indicator
KRACK	Key Reinstallation AttaCK
KRITIS	Critical Infrastructure
NFC	Near Field Communication
NHTSA	National Highway Traffic Safety Administration
NIS	Security of Network and Information Systems
NIST	National Institute of Standards Technology
NONCE	Number used only once
NSA	National Security Agency
OASIS	Organization for the Advancement of Structured Information Standards
OBD	On-Board Diagnosis
OCTAVE	Operationally Critical Threat, Asset, and Vulnerability Enumeration
OEM	Original Equipment Manufacturer
OGC	Office of Governance Commerce
OLA	Operational Level Agreement
OT	Operational Technology
OTA	Over-the-air
OTR	Off-the-Record Messaging
OTT	Over-the-Top
OWASP	Open Web Application Security Project
PAM	Process Assessment Model
PbD	Privacy-by-Design
PCI DSS	Payment Card Industry Data Security Standard
PDCA	Plan—Do—Check—Act
PET	Privacy Enhancing Technologies
PGP	Pretty good privacy
PH	Privacy Homomorphisms
PIA	Privacy Impact Analysis
PII	Personally Identifiable Information
PIMS	Privacy Information Management System
PIR	Private Information Retrieval
PKI	Public Key Infrastructure
PKSE	Passive Keyless Entry and Start
PMRM	Privacy Management Reference Model and Methodology
PP	Protection Profile

Introduction 1

"It's not about predicting the future, but about being prepared for the future."
(Pericles, around 500 – 429 BC; Athenian politician and general)

1.1 Motivation

Not least due to the increasing number of corresponding press releases, awareness and knowledge about the topic of information security and everything associated with it are increasing: Cyber attack, Hacker, Cyber Army, Malware, Blockchain, credit card numbers on the internet, publication of passwords, unauthorized data outflow to third countries, insecure communication in messenger services, unauthorized eavesdropping, unauthorized use of private data from third parties for unwanted purposes, Ad-Blocker, Profiling, personal penetration with unwanted advertising. This raises questions like:

- Can you surf the internet without being observed at all?
- How secure are assistance functions in the car?
- Does everyone know what you write in messenger services?
- Who is monitoring whom in the background?
- Which data has already been misappropriated?
- Who can you turn to in case of incidents and events when you discover unexplainable "strange" connections (e.g. personal data in places where you do not suspect/want them)?
- How can you protect yourself against eavesdropping/profiling by third parties?
- Which controls are effective if you want to protect yourself?
- What needs to be done in the development of technical systems to remain compliant with the law (e.g. according to EU General Data Protection Regulation requirements)

T. Liedtke, *Information Security*, https://doi.org/10.1007/978-3-658-45711-2_1

and to be up to date with science and technology (e.g. according to current cryptography)?

"Safety" (in the sense of functional safety) and "Security" (usually in the snese of information security) are equally "felt" at their corresponding (usually negative) effects when they are no longer given.

This book is intended to help bring order and light into the darkness of various aspects of ***security*** (information, product, process, cybersecurity, …) In particular, many examples of practical applicability of the described are shown.

1.2 Chapter Structure

The structure of the book is given in the following summary of its chapters.

Chapter Structure

Chapter 2 introduces the concept of information security (i.e. of "Security") and defines various aspects and areas. What is generally understood by security, how do you notice it, what mainly constitutes it. The word security in this book is mainly about:

- **Information security**: Security of electronic or analog data/information, e.g. in organizations and
- **Product security**: Security of mostly electronic data, referred as ***Cybersecurity***.

Security in processing is the keyword here for technical as well as organizational security measures.

Chapter 3 describes the topic of privacy and its relationship to information security. The topic of privacy (in English: ***Privacy***) experienced a real hype, not least because of the activation of the new EU General Data Protection Regulation (EU-GDPR) [EU-GDPR] on May 25, 2018. Since privacy is an important component for possible damage scenarios in information security, this chapter explains commonalities, intersections, and differences to information security. It mentions essential articles of the EU-GDPR and effects on product development, as well as ***Privacy Engineering*** and ***Risk Management*** for privacy explained. ***Privacy-by-Design*** [Cav10], ***Privacy-Enhancing-Technologies*** are further terms that are examined.

Chapter 4 shows that safety in the sense of the functional term ***Safety*** is very similar to ***Security***. However, there are fundamental differences both in the definition and consideration in the development of technical systems. Even if the methodical approach seems quite similar and known analyses seem to be transferable with appropriate abstraction, there are significant differences regarding mindset and basic consideration. In this book, Safety particularly refers to ***functional Security***. It too is to be considered for possible damage scenarios in information security. Furthermore, for autonomous systems or systems equipped with artificial intelligence, the term SOTIF (***Safety of the Intended Functionality***) is increasingly gaining importance.

In Chap. 5 various standards, guidelines, and regulations in the field of information security are described. The connection with development lifecycle models is viewed from different perspectives. This also includes the topic of Information Security Management System (e.g., NIST SP 800-39 [NIST800–39] or ISO/IEC 27001 [ISO27001]).

Chapter 6 shows that in connection with information security, terms such as ***hackers, hacking, attacks, threats, kill-chain*** are used. This chapter explains what these terms mean individually and why it is so important to be able to see the world through the eyes of an attacker in order to successfully (confidently) deal with information security.

Chapter 7 describes the essential components (and at the same time the most challenging) of information security, the so-called ***threat analysis,*** the ***risk assessment,*** the ***risk treatment*** etc. Depending on the standard, the terms are differently assigned. At its core, it is about a very similar approach: Identification of the values to be protected, identification and evaluation of possible damages in case of compromise, connection to vulnerabilities, attacks on values to be protected followed by risk assessment, prioritization and definition of measures and selection of controls. This chapter aims to describe the general approach step by step, considering different standards (e.g., NIST SP 800-30 [NIST800-30]).

Chapter 8 explains as an essential part of information security, organizational aspects of IT management. There are also corresponding standards and guidelines for this (known examples: COBIT [COBIT], ITIL [ITIL]), which are applicable to support a systematic approach. These are presented and explained in terms of their areas of application.

Chapter 9 contains an overview of control families and their assigned individual controls from the NIST SP 800-53 [NIST800-53]. With the appropriate objective, this can serve as a source for the selection of possible implementable controls.

A glossary at the end of the book explains essential terms related to the topic of information security, especially different types of attacks.

References

[Cav10] ***"Privacy-by-Design – The 7 Foundational Principles – Implementation and Mapping of Fair Information Practices";*** Ann Cavoukian. Published, May 2010. Link: https://www.ipc.on.ca/wp-content/uploads/resources/pbd-implement-7found-principles.pdfaccessed: 10.04.2021

[COBIT] ***"COBIT"***; Link: https://www.isaca.org/resources/cobit accessed: 10.04.2021

[EU-DSGVO] ***"EU-General Data Protection Regulation***"; Link: https://eur-lex.europa.eu/legal-content/EN/TXT/PDF/?uri=CELEX:32016R0679 accessed: 10.04.2021.

[ISO27001] ***"Information security management systems – Requirements"***; ISO/IEC 27001

[ITIL] ***"ITIL";*** Link: https://www.axelos.com/best-practice-solutions/itil accessed: 10.04.2021

[NIST800–30] ***"Guide for Conducting Risk Assessment"***; NIST SP 800–30; Link: https://www.nist.gov/privacy-framework/nist-sp-800-30 accessed: 10.04.2021

[NIST800–39] ***"Managing Information Security Risk: Organization, Mission, and Information System View"***; NIST SP 800–39. Link: https://www.nist.gov/privacy-framework/nist-sp-800-39 accessed: 10.04.2021

[NIST800-53R5] ***"Security and Privacy Controls for Federal Information Systems and Organizations"***; NIST SP 800-53 Revision 5. Link: https://csrc.nist.gov/publications/detail/sp/800-53/rev-5/final accessed: 18.04.2021

2 Basics of Information Security

> "It's time for cybersecurity to no longer have to sit at the kids' table, but to be allowed to sit at the table of the big kids."
>
> (expanded quote, based on a tweet from the GDPR Coalition)

This chapter introduces the topic of information security. The first Sect. 2.1 motivates the topic. This is best done by realizing what is already happening in terms of security today and where negative effects on our daily life exist.

Important terms are ***protection goals, security*** and ***security goals,*** which are explained. Attack and defense options are listed (Sect. 2.2). The section on security in processing (Sect. 2.3) is intended to introduce the topic of (cyber)security controls. Here it becomes clear that information security is not only a topic for technology, but that organizational security controls also play a crucial role in achieving security. The nature of security is attempted to be captured from different perspectives. In this context, the mindset with which the topic can be successfully approached plays a role.

The two following code examples, Variants A and B, are supposed to be semantically equivalent in our imagined environment. Nevertheless, there is a significant difference between the two variants

```
// Variant A

c := 7
if a == 42
c := 13
```


T. Liedtke, *Information Security*, https://doi.org/10.1007/978-3-658-45711-2_2

```
// Variant B

c := 7
b := (a == 42)
c := (1-b) * c + b * 13
```

One might consider the difference and the impact towards cybersecurity. Later in the book, we will return to this example. Being able to anticipate, find, recognize and deal with such differences is part of dealing with information security/cybersecurity.

Another part is the **process view.** Even though one might believe to have done everything correctly, there is an unconsidered "loophole" (later called vulnerability), which leads to systems believed to be secure no longer being so due to known vulnerabilities they possess. The fact that this can take many years is demonstrated by the example of a successful KRACK (**K**ey **R**einstallation **A**ttac**k**) attack on the **WPA2** protocol [MV17] (a protocol for securing all modern Wi-Fi networks). After 14 (!) years, it became publicly known that the protocol, which was believed to be secure until then, can be made to use a **NONCE** (a number or letter combination to be used only once) a second time, thereby compromising the security of the protocol. We will also return to this example later.

Although the fear of direct threat from attacks on (information) security is still low compared to other threats, the topic is experiencing strong growth and is gaining importance in society. Questions like *"is it really secure?"* when installing a financial services app on the smartphone, *"who actually gets to see my data?"* when creating a social media account, or *"what happens when the autonomous vehicle is hacked?"*, are being asked more and more frequently and want to be answered.

In relation to the **European level,** guidelines are relevant that are examined exemplarily in the following sections in relation to the topic:

- EU General Data Protection Regulation [EU-GDPR] (see Sect. 3.2.2)
- ENISA as an organization
- NIS Directive [EU-NIS21] (see Sect. 2.4)
- EU Cybersecurity Act [EU-CA19] (see Sect. 5.2.10)

Chapter Overview
The introductory chapter first motivates the topic fundamentally.

- After a motivation in Sect. 2.1, the
- concept of information security and security objectives are defined in Sect. 2.2.
- Sect. 2.3 deals with security in processing.
- A summary in Sect. 2.4 and one
- bibliography round off the basic chapter.

2.1 Motivation

"Happiness often arises from attention to small things, unhappiness often from neglect of small things"
(Wilhelm Busch)

What exactly does information security mean? What are its characteristics? Strictly speaking, it is only really recognized when the impact of an (unexpected) incident shows that it is no longer (was) given. Two prominent and frequently cited examples are:

Example

Attack on the SCADA (**S**upervisory **C**ontrol **and** **D**ata **A**cquisition) of the ***"Australian Maroochy-Water-Breach"*** (2000) [SM08]: In March 2000, the Maroochy water service in Queensland (Australia) was attacked by exploiting a security vulnerability in its sewage pump stations via radio. The pumps no longer worked properly. The attacker managed to hack into the system remotely. Over a three-month period, 150 pumps were controlled from a laptop in such a way that a million liters of sewage entered a retention basin and from there into local waterways. ◀

Example

The ***"Jeep Hack"*** **attack** (2015) [VM15] was an attack carried out remotely by Charlie Miller and Chris Valasek on a vehicle (Jeep Cherokee) in St. Louis. Via an air interface, a laptop could access a (previously determined) car driving on the highway and send commands such as *"windshield wipers on"*, *"radio volume up"* to *"engine stop"* via its communication control unit to the CAN bus. (see Chap. 5). ◀

▶ Insights from information security-relevant events:

- **Attacks can** possibly be very **simply motivated,** see example motive revenge of a dissatisfied employee in the case of the Maroochy-Water-Service-Breach.
- **SCADA systems** are **extremely vulnerable;** especially when they communicate unprotected (e.g., via unencrypted radio traffic).
- Successful attacks show possible impacts and especially the **high motivation** on the part of **the attackers.**
- Upon closer observation, one realizes that **attacks are not isolated incidents** (even if they are often kept quiet).
- **Impacts** can, as indicated in the Jeep Hack, potentially be fatal and pose a **danger to life and limb.**
- The **impact** on different categories such as Safety can be **directly** and **indirectly** triggered.

- **System architectures** (such as in vehicles) are becoming **increasingly vulnerable** to attacks due to their **increasing complexity** and increasing number of interfaces.
- Due to the **increasing networking,** more and more attacks can be carried out "at rest" from a (almost arbitrary) distance.

2.1.1 Information Security

Information security is always directly related to individual personal behavior. Train passengers briefly leave their seats and forget to activate the password-protected screensaver of their laptops, on which they had just been editing confidential emails or documents. As a consequence, attackers have immediate unauthorized access with the same rights as the owner to information worth protecting. And if the brief absence of the owner is sufficient to quickly install a ***Trojan*** as a backdoor in order to carry out the actual attack through this created security gap at a later time, for example, to "take over" the laptop using this backdoor.

► Information security is:

- always also a question of individual **personal behavior**
- **not just the collection** of technical measures

The stream of news about information security incidents, which result in the unintended disclosure of confidential information, does not stop. Information security also means collecting information and observing what happens: Which attacks are successful in what way? It is therefore important to analyze successful attacks in order to estimate the frequency of occurrence for future attacks on further (own) systems, and to take appropriate countermeasures if necessary. The occurrence of attacks cannot be calculated in advance and cannot be captured with a mathematical probability.

Example

Popular examples of information security breaches:

- An iMessage bug allowed the decryption of photos and videos. Through a ***brute-force attack*** by communicating with the smartphone, digits of the key could be guessed [ZDNet16].
- The largest ***cyber attack*** in Switzerland [Gen16]: In 2015, mail customer servers were periodically paralyzed, making them unreachable by their users. This had an impact on companies that used the same service provider.
- Using an ***illegal transaction***, unknown individuals withdrew approximately 4.6 million euros from a Ryanair bank account [Hei15].

- An XSS vulnerability in the eBay messaging system allowed fraudsters to record sessions and take over accounts [IM14].
- Fraudsters stole 40 million euros from the automotive supplier Leoni [Cap16]. By using forged documents and identities and utilizing electronic communication channels, confidentially classified emails were sent from a fake account of the CEO instructing money to be transferred to foreign accounts. This scam is known as ***Fake-President*** or ***CEO-Fraud***. The aircraft supplier FACC from Austria was hit even worse, with the same method even 50 million euros were stolen [OÖ16].
- Hackers paralyzed a German blast furnace through computer manipulations [SO14]. Using a so-called ***spear-phishing attack*** through fake emails specifically tailored to employees, attackers gained access to office computers of the plant. From there, they could penetrate the plant's network until they had access to control computers of the production plant.
- That cyber attacks can also have effects on human life and health became clear in an English hospital service [NHS16]. After a **Ransomware attack** (Crypto-Trojan Locky), all IT systems had to be shut down initially. Planned surgery appointments were put on "hold". Despite this experience, it only took half a year until the same hospital service provider was hit again by the next ransomware using the same method [NHS17] (Crypto-Trojan WannaCry).
- There were also victims in Germany in the medical field: The case of the Neuss hospital became known, which could only treat a reduced number of patients for weeks and initially had to handle many processes exclusively on paper [Hei16] (Crypto-Trojan: TeslaCrypt 2.0). A detailed report on this was given in a special broadcast on WDR. The case even made it to television (which is not very common) …
- Ransomware like ***Crypto-Trojans*** (e.g., Locky, Petya, …) can infect several thousand computers per hour and now "speak" perfect German.
- That ***Ransomware attacks*** can have "curious" effects was shown by the attack on the payment terminals of the Muni city train in San Francisco [PCW16]. Until the ransomware was removed (extortionists demanded $73,000), all passengers could ride for free [Hei16a]. ◀

Even from these few examples, some basic **patterns** and **lessons** can be derived:

- Attackers make great efforts to appear credible after appropriate research. For the attacked, fake addresses/emails from well-informed attackers are indistinguishable from real ones.
- If vulnerabilities are not remedied in the short term, they offer a permanent security gap that can be exploited multiple times subsequently.
- Critical networks must be separated at least logically, better physically. Production facilities accessible from the internet are highly endangered.
- Even institutions that have been affected once are not immune to being successfully attacked again in the near future, even if the same scam is attempted.

More and more (new) external interfaces, such as the internet, increase the attack surface and thus enable additional attacks. On the one hand, there is comfort and flexibility for the use of known interfaces, on the other hand, the danger of being able to use them unintentionally for malware.

Examples of attack targets range from software in pacemakers that can be updated via a radio interface [SOP13] to car washes accessible via the Internet of Things [Kas17, 20], which are inadequately secured with researchable standard passwords. By now, everything seems to be networked, even the unthinkable, as the ransomware attack with ***WannaCry*** (WanaDecrypt0r 2.0) 2017 showed, when both passenger information screens of the German railway and payment terminals at Berlin Tegel airport were paralyzed at the same time [Hei17].

Increasing criminal energies of the attackers cover two dimensions:

- **Own advantage** of the attackers, especially Bitcoins/Euros extorted through blackmail.
- Disadvantage/**damage to others** such as a successful ***Denial-of-Service*** attack in critical infrastructures.

Often a successful attack is accompanied by a previously carried out ***identity theft.*** The knowledge about weaknesses and the associated vulnerabilities, that can be exploited, enable all kinds of attacks.

2.1.2 Study Findings

Conducted studies unanimously come to the conclusion that attacks on information security now cause considerable damage to the economy. Several studies report from different domains on the situation of information security. Some findings will be listed as examples.

In a study on **industrial espionage** 2014, Corporate Trust reports [CTS14]:

- In 2013 and 2014, **every second company suffered a spy attack** or suspected case. Specifically, 26.9% in Germany were affected by a concrete incident. Another 27.4% had at least a suspicion.
- The annual financial damage caused by **industrial espionage** amounts to 11.8 billion euros in Germany.
- 77.5% of the affected companies suffered a **financial loss** due to the espionage attacks. For a large part of the companies, the damage was between 10,000 and 100,000 €. 4.5% had to complain about a damage of over 1 million euros.

In a 2018 study by the Ponemon Institute [Pon18a], practices related to **automotive and cybersecurity** were recorded and the following was found:

- **Main factors** leading to vulnerabilities in developed automotive technologies are:
  - Pressure to meet product deadlines,
  - Lack of understanding/training on secure coding practices,
  - Unintentional coding errors,
  - Lack of quality assurance and testing procedures (e.g., vulnerability tests that take place too late in production)
- Proposed **countermeasures:**
  - More focus on cybersecurity,
  - Training on secure coding for key employees,
  - Use of automated tools to detect errors and security gaps in the source code,
  - Use of software composition analysis tools to identify third-party components that may have been introduced by suppliers
- The most common **security activities** in the industry are (all used at a higher level):
  - Security patch management,
  - Penetration testing,
  - Dynamic Application Security Testing (DAST).

Another study from 2018, also by Ponemon, titled **Global Megatrends in Cybersecurity** [Pon18] deals with information security across domains and comes to the following conclusions, among others:

- **The Internet of Things is an open door:** 82% of respondents predict that unsecured IoT devices are likely to cause a data breach in their company. 80% fear that such a breach could be catastrophic.
- **More ransom demands are coming:** 67% believe that cyber extortion, such as ransom demands, will increase in frequency and resulting payouts.
- **Cyber warfare is becoming more likely:** 60% predict that attacks by nation-state actors against the government and commercial companies will worsen and could lead to a cyber war. 51% of respondents believe that cyber warfare will pose a high risk in the next three years, compared to 22% who think so today. Similarly, 71% believe that the risk of breaches involving high-value information will be very high, compared to 43% who rate this risk as high today.
- **Trust is dwindling:** Less than half of the surveyed IT security experts believe they can protect their organizations from cyber threats. This is a decrease from 59% three years ago.
- **Cybersecurity takes a backseat among executives:** Only 36% of respondents say that their leadership views cybersecurity as a strategic priority, which means less investment in technology and personnel.
- **Company boards are not engaged:** 68% of respondents say that their boards are not informed about what their organizations are doing to prevent or mitigate the consequences of a cyber attack.

- **IT professionals are pessimistic about progress:** 54% believe that their organization's cybersecurity situation will either remain the same or decrease. 58% believe that staffing issues will worsen, and 46% predict that artificial intelligence will not reduce the need for cybersecurity experts.
- **The stress level of CISOs will increase:** When asked to rate their stress level today and in three years on a scale of 1 = low stress to 10 = high stress, it is expected that the stress rating of respondents will rise to a new high of 8.08.
- **Direct impact on shareholder value:** 66% believe that data breaches or cybersecurity misuse will seriously affect their organization's shareholder value.

In the automotive sector, there are also studies: The Upstream Report of 2020 [Ups20] analyzed more than 600 attacks in the automotive sector and came to the following conclusions:

- Connected vehicles are already here and have inherent risks that cannot be ignored
- 99% growth in the number of incidents since 2018
- 94% annual growth since 2016
- 57% of all incidents in 2019 were Black-Hat attacks (carried out by cyber criminals)
- Uber currently has over 1,300 resolved reports with a total sum of awards of $2.3 million since its launch in December 2014 with Bug Bounties
- Vulnerabilities in key fobs were exploited in 38% of all incidents in 2019
- In 2019, cyber criminals (Black-Hat) were responsible for 75% of all keyless attacks
- 25% of the incidents in 2019 involved server attacks
- In a connected world, cybersecurity is as important for safety as brakes are for the car
- 13% of the incidents in 2019 involved attacks via mobile apps
- 82% of the attacks in 2019 were carried out remotely
- 66 CVE entries (MITRE databases [CAPEC]) were added for the automotive industry by the end of 2020
- 36% of the incidents in 2019 involved car thefts and/or break-ins
- 16% of the incidents in 2019 involved control over vehicle systems
- 22% of the automotive incidents in 2019 involved data breaches
- 20% of the incidents in 2019 led to a disruption of business operations
- Ransomware often leads to business interruptions, which can result in financial losses and can affect the safety of citizens.

In an automotive study by Kugler Maag Cie and the University of Stuttgart [KMC20], the following results were found, among others:

- Only 50% of companies are already conducting risk analyses.
- 50% of companies expect that cybersecurity will account for 10 – 20% of project effort in the future.
- Only 50% of companies feel well prepared regarding cybersecurity issues.

So there is still a lot to do …

All studies show the importance of taking care of information security and cybersecurity to make it more difficult for attackers in the future and to keep damage away from the economy.

Principles are important for information security and serve as a guide. Renowned large companies, together with the Federal Office for Information Security (BSI), have created a Charter of Trust [CoT19], which defines principles to achieve the following three goals:

1. **Protection of data** of individuals and companies
2. **Avoidance of damage** to individuals and companies
3. Establishment of a **reliable association,** on which trust in a network-based digital world can be anchored and grow.

To best achieve these goals, the following 10 general principles have been established. They can be found in varying degrees in all security-relevant domains, standards and guidelines:

1. **Ownership** of cybersecurity and IT security: Responsibilities must be defined at the highest level of governments and companies, measures and goals as well as the right mindset must be established in all organizations.
2. **Responsibility** over the **entire supply chain:** Companies and governments must establish risk-based rules for adequate protection with clearly defined requirements across all levels. Protection goals such as confidentiality, integrity, availability, and authenticity must be ensured.
3. **Security-by-Default:** Security must be pre-configured in product design, functionalities, processes, etc.
4. **User-centricity:** Acting as a trusted partner, based on customer security needs, impacts, and risks.
5. **Innovation** and **Co-creation:** Continuously innovate and adapt cybersecurity measures to new threats, drive and promote, combining domain knowledge.
6. **Education:** Incorporation of special cybersecurity courses into curricula to maintain the skills and job profiles needed in the future.
7. **Certification** for critical infrastructures and solutions: Companies and—if necessary—governments establish binding independent certifications by third parties (based on future-proof definitions),
8. **Transparency** and **Response:** Participation in an industrial cybersecurity network to share new insights, information about incidents, etc.; reporting of incidents beyond today's practice, focusing on critical infrastructures.
9. **Regulatory Framework:** Promotion of multilateral cooperation in regulation and standardization to create a level playing field that corresponds to the global reach of the WTO.
10. **Joint Initiatives:** Driving joint initiatives involving all relevant stakeholders.

2.2 Security and Security Objectives

"The value of security is only recognized when it is no longer there."
(unknown)

In February 2019, it was revealed that scooters with electric drive can have drastic security gaps [Tre19]. Scooters can be remotely controlled via Bluetooth. Functions such as theft protection can be activated or deactivated, the speed can be regulated, the firmware can be replaced.

This example once again makes it clear how diverse security can be: Information for control can unintentionally fall into unauthorized hands. An attacker can exploit information for attack scenarios to cause damage. Possible damages in this example can be both

- a **lower availability** (scooter no longer operates as planned),
- a **financial loss** (scooter is stolen despite theft lock),
- as well as **danger to life and limb** (scooter suddenly switches off at full speed).

Before one can delve into the technology, we look at the in German versatile used term ***"Safety/Security"***, as it can be defined in its different possibilities meaning can be defined. To identify the different meanings, Fig. 2.1 provides an overview with the usual terms.

Fig. 2.1 Conceptual relationships "Safety/Security"

Term definitions for "Safety/Security"

Safety (functional safety):	When technical systems are designed that are subsequently to be put into circulation (cars, locomotives, chemical plants, medical devices), and there is a risk to life and limb despite proper use, this is referred to as Safety s.a. Chap. 4
Information Security (Information security):	The protection of information and information systems against defined protection goals/categories such as confidentiality, integrity, availability, …
IT-/Data Security (IT and data security):	Security and protection of security controls (e.g., a firewall)
Cybersecurity:	concerns the security of electronic data/information
Privacy (Data protection/Privacy):	concerns the security of personal data against defined protection goals/categories such as predictability, unlinkability, manageability
Risk management:	concerns the control/management of risks in all areas
Compliance:	concerns legal requirements ◀

Another possibility of separating individual aspects is shown in Fig. 2.2:

- **Electronic product safety:** the safety that a product possesses when it is in operation in the field. Example: Used methods of cryptography for remote access possibilities to a vehicle (keyword Keyless-go)

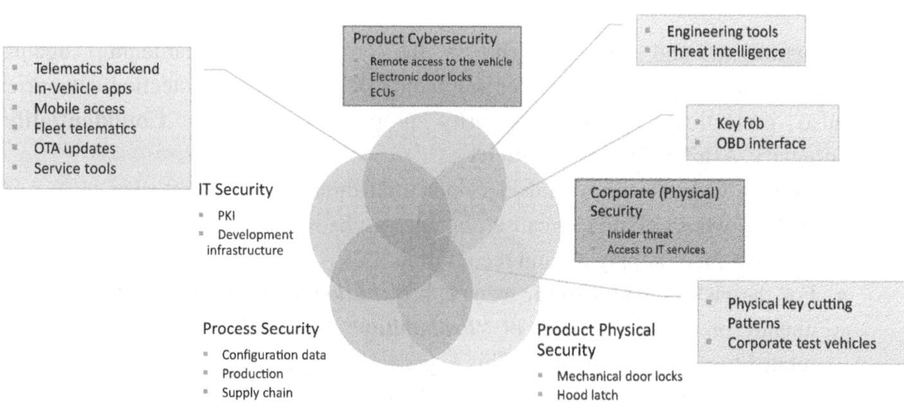

Fig. 2.2 Manifestations of Security with examples from the automotive sector

- **Physical corporate security:** Security in the organization. Example: Regulation and enforcement of access rights to confidential data in an organization
- **Physical product security:** Physical security. Example: Security of physical access possibilities (doors) or protection against side-channel attacks by installing control units at accident-safe or inaccessible locations
- **Process security:** Safety in the execution of processes. Examples: It must be procedurally ensured that the correct configuration and calibration data are loaded at the end of a production line (according to the correct vehicle type) or also the safety in logistics processes, ...
- **Information technology security:** Securing standard IT devices, such as virus scanners, firewalls, networks, ...

Depending on the unit of observation, different manifestations of security may become relevant

Example

Development tools: the security of tools plays a crucial role in the development of systems (software and/or hardware). Unintentionally or intentionally remaining debug options, backdoors, etc. can lead to security gaps in the product. In the company, tools must be protected against manipulation and unauthorized access. ◀

2.2.1 Information Security—Characteristics—Protection Goals

In the following section, the term **"security"** is described in terms of its characteristics and properties:

> Information/Cybersecurity—Characterization
>
> **Information**- and **Cybersecurity** is the protection (the hardening) against (intentional) attacks (incl. accidents/coincidences) related to protection categories (also protection objectives, security properties), such as **Confidentiality**, **Integrity**, **Availability**, **Authenticity**, ...:
>
> - **System Cybersecurity** considers potential threats from an attacker to a system, whose goal is to cause damage or chaos, gain financial or other advantages, or simply to gain recognition.
> - For the **risk consideration,** we speak of ***"Likelihood"*** (plausibility, frequency of occurrence) not of ***"Probability"*** (probability of occurrence related to a total population). This is generally not the case in information security, as attackers cannot be mathematically modeled.
> - **Vulnerabilities** arc intentionally sought, exploited or sold when found.

- Information security must not **Safety** (danger to life and limb) impair:
  - Performance: the use of cryptographic methods costs computing time and power, which one may not have (securing emergency brake).
- Additional **organizational measures** must be taken: authentication, key management, behavior training, ...
- Computer-controlled security functions increase possible **attack vectors** (e.g., CAN-Bus Injection)
- Systems must be **constantly updated** to be able to fend off new (known) threats.
- Security requirements can conflict with other requirements such as functional safety, performance (e.g., doors: lockable? only openable with authorization?).
- Information security is an inductive "bottom-up" topic. Each component must be considered individually. A single insecure component can destroy the entire security.
- Information security must be able to anticipate. One must not only be immune to threats today, but also tomorrow against threats unknown today (e.g., virus scanner).

> It is not enough to just make fragile robust, it must be made "antifragile" [Tal14]. One must anticipate, one must be "fit for the future".

Weaknesses that contain vulnerabilities can be found at all levels of an application, making securing them correspondingly difficult and complex. One will not be able to achieve one hundred percent security. In the case of applications or use-cases, we speak of an end-to-end security. While a customer usually only sees the "surface" of an application he uses, there may be many applications, functions, services, platforms, infrastructures, companies, buildings and rooms behind it. An attacker may only need a single exploitable security gap in one of the associated levels to penetrate other levels.

The criticality of a business process determines the protection requirement and the level of information security to be achieved. Security measures must be considered from the outset in the development of technical systems to prevent costs from skyrocketing. Standardization is intended to help reduce the complexity and effort required to implement security measures.

The **core values** of information security or also protection objectives must be defined and considered individually depending on the environment and application used. The most frequently used are listed in the following definitions.

Protection Objectives

Confidentiality the non-publication or non-disclosure of confidential information, the denied access for unauthorized individuals; access control

Integrity the correctness, completeness, authority to change, non-falsifiability
Availability the availability of information at the right time for authorized instances, redundancy

In German, the three best-known protection objectives are often abbreviated with VIV, in English with CIA. Examples of values and corresponding protection objectives are given in the next example.

Example

- **Confidentiality:** personal data in the HR department, secret construction plans, intellectual property, classification of documents: internal, confidential, secret, ...
- **Integrity:** messages arrive unaltered at the recipient (message security with CRC, hashes, ...), In a database, only authorized instances can change data, tax data are correct, ...
- **Availability:** lost data can be restored in time, authorized persons have access to needed data. What use are secret files if no one has access anymore ... ◀

Corresponding threats (thus possibilities of attack) can be assigned to the protection objectives:

- Confidentiality: **Espionage**
- Integrity: **Manipulation**
- Availability: **Loss of access**

If needed, further (additional) protection objectives can be used:

- **Authorization:** Ensuring that people who want to perform actions have the corresponding rights (keyword role and authorization concept).
- **Authenticity:** Actions can only be performed by people who have appropriately authenticated/identified themselves.
- **Non-repudiation:** Processes are recorded in a legally secure manner and cannot be falsified (e.g., by appropriately certified tools). After an attack, it can be proven who carried it out, without this being able to be denied.
- **Repudiation/Non-traceability:** This protection objective, which is in contradiction to non-repudiation stands, is often needed in privacy: Ability to deny having performed an action that other parties can neither confirm nor refute (keyword anonymization) (see Sect. 3.6.2).
- **Controllability:** no processing of data without the knowledge of the responsible person.

For privacy, the following specific privacy objectives can be considered (see also Chap. 3):

- **Transparency** and **Predictability:** Important protection objective for personally identifiable information (personal data). The intended processing of personal data is transparent for the affected person, they are aware of what is being done with their data.
- **Interveneability:** An affected person can intervene against processing, edits can be undone.
- **Manageability:** Ability to administer personal data granularly (modify, delete, read, …).
- **Disassociability:** Different data are stored in such a way that they cannot be linked to each other. Example: Electricity consumption values at a provider with the water consumption in the municipality.
- …

Achieving (data) protection objectives is in the interest of every company. There are a number of legal requirements (Federal Data Protection Act, Social Security Code, Telecommunications-Telemedia Data Protection Act, …) from which the protection objectives can be derived.

In order to focus on the areas with the highest benefit (e.g. in terms of effort), the restriction for the respective development of the application or system to the protection objectives to be achieved must be defined in advance and, for example, a balance must be struck between repudiation and non-repudiation.

Important building blocks for achieving the protection objectives are provided by information security management systems (Sect. 5.2).

> The three most important protection objectives in information security are **Confidentiality, Integrity** and **Availability.** These must always be considered. Others should be defined as required.

Table 2.1 provides a possible classification of the initiation of information security losses.

2.2.2 Foundations of Information Security

Contents and purpose of **information security** are:

- the **information technology** itself: It includes all technical facilities to process and transmit information.

Table 2.1 Classification of the initiation of information security losses

	Direct	Indirect	Publicly motivated
External	Viruses, Trojans, Malware, Botnets, Script-Kiddies	Anonymous industrial espionage, Sabotage, Social Engineering, Denial-of-Service	NSA affair, Stuxnet & Co., China, …
Internal	Unknowing or negligent employees, loss; Drive-by, Malware	Disgruntled employees, unauthorized use, theft, industrial espionage, sabotage	Dependent on location and industry

- the **security within information technology:** It includes compliance with security standards related to confidentiality, integrity, and availability of information through appropriate …
  - secure **equipment**
    - Information technology systems (security devices like firewall, access controls, intrusion detection systems, intrusion prevention systems, …)
    - secure components: software, hardware, …
    - secure processes: business processes, emergency plans (Business Continuity Management); …
  - appropriate **application** of information technology systems, components, and processes.

▶ **Information security:** Connection of all relevant information/data (analog or digital) of an organization or enterprise including personal data.

Information security is part of IT corporate management and affects an entire organization and its processes. Everyone is responsible for information security in the company. An effective information security management system must be correspondingly comprehensive—from information security, IT security, compliance with standards, and risk management.

A number of laws provide guidelines for information security in a company:

- **TTDSG Telecommunications-Telemedia Data Protection Act**
  - new basic law combines the Telecommunications Act (TKG) and Telemedia Act (TMG). It affects, for example, the private use of company communication tools
- EU-GDPR: **European General Data Protection Regulation**
  - affects the rules with which the processing of personal data (PII) is standardized for most responsible parties across the EU.
- BDSG n. F.: **Federal Data Protection Act** (new version)
  - affects, among other things, clarifications on opening clauses of the EU-GDPR, such as the appointment of a company data protection officer

- **BSI Compendium**
  - affects the minimum security measures/controls to be taken in a company
- IT-SIG: **IT Security Act**
  - affects guidelines for operators of critical infrastructures, such as energy supply
- HGB: **Commercial Code**
- UWG: Act against **unfair competition**
  - affects the use of communication channels
- GoBS: Principles of proper computer-aided **booking systems**
  - affects, for example, rules on retention periods
- FPG: **Driver Personnel Act**
- …

Table 2.2 provides an overview of this.

Table 2.2 Protection of information through laws and standards

Data group	Date	Law	Objective
Personal data	Name, IP address, telephone number, email, address, …	EU GDPR, BDSG n. F.	– Protection of personal self-determination rights – from unauthorized access, – access and permission to access to personal data
Accounting relevant data	Incoming and outgoing invoices	GoBD: Principles for proper DV-based management and storage of books, records and documents in electronic form as well as data access	– Criteria for entrepreneurs – Accounting documents when using a computerized accounting system – capture, process and archive. – Prevent manipulation possibilities
Credit card holder data	Credit card number, CVV, name	PCI DSS: Payment Card Industry Data Security Standard	Protection of credit card transactions
Driver data	Driving times, steering and rest times	FPVO, FPG Professional Drivers Act	Compliance with steering and rest times according to the StVO
Tax relevant data	Accounting, booking receipts and invoices	GDPdU: Principles for data access and auditability of digital documents	Archive data so that it can be made electronically available at any time during a company audit

Well-known standards for information security can be found at:

- **NIST** (National Institute of Standards and Technology) SP 800 family (Sect. 5.2.3);
- **ISO 27** series (Sect. 5.2.5);
- **COBIT** (Sect. 8.2.2), **ITIL** (Sect. 8.2.1); **OWASP;** …
- **SANS** (System Administration Networking and Security Institute)
- …

Less known:

- **PCI DSS** (Payment Card Industry Data Security Standard) for handling credit cards
- **HIPAA** (Health Insurance Portability and Accountability Act)/ Kennedy Kassenbaum Act: for handling electronic health data

Roles in the organization of information security:

- **CISO** (Chief Information Security Officer): Member of the board, responsible for a company's information security
- **IT Security Officer:** operationally responsible for information security (Sect. 8.5)

2.2.3 Definitions Related to Information Security

Depending on the area and domain terms are defined differently. Following a list of the most common terms and their meaning.

Clarification of terms related to information security

Hazard:	Situation/fact without specific temporal, spatial or personal reference, which can lead to a negative impact (people, things, companies, environment, …) (Example: storm/ flood, …).
Threat:	Serious danger with specific temporal, spatial or personal reference with the mere possibility of causing damage (human, company, legal good, …) (Example: flood river area; attackers exploit a vulnerability, …).
Attackability/: Vulnerability/Security gap	Specific weakness that can be exploited for an attack to cause damage.
Weakness:	Characteristic that promotes or enables the occurrence of a security event (Example: use of software).

Exploitation of a weakness:	by using a vulnerability.
Risk:	qualitative/quantitative assessment (frequency of occurrence) of the – relevance of a – threat (by exploiting a weakness) of a protectable good (causing damage) (Example: confidentiality, availability, integrity etc.) ◀

In context, this means that an attacker exploits specific vulnerabilities in weaknesses of a system to cause damage. The exploitation of weaknesses represents a threat to the system.

Further terms like attack potential, attack surface, attack vector, cyber attack, cyber security, hacker, incident/disturbance, malicious attacker are often domain-dependent. This will be discussed in connection with specific standards.

2.2.4 Social Engineering

"The trash can is full" or "Why hack a password when you can get its owner to give it up?"

▶ Under **Social Engineering** one understands the interpersonal influence with the aim of inducing certain behaviors in people. The "attacker" tries to get a person to disclose confidential information, to release financial resources or similar.

As a rule, the negative variant of the term dominates the concept.

Social Engineers spy on the personal environment of their victim, pretend identities or exploit behaviors such as obedience to authority or helpfulness to obtain secret information or unpaid services. **Often, social engineering serves to penetrate a foreign computer system to view confidential data;** one then also speaks of **Social Hacking**.

The exploited patterns of action are always similar:

- **Stereotypes:** *Fight-or-flight* reaction. Most efficient decision-making behavior
- **Culture:** *"Expensive is good", "One hand washes the other"*
- **Impulses:** Being *"helpful"*

One of the first cyber criminals to exploit this was Kevin Mitnick. As early as 1992, he was able to access the source code of a mobile phone with a call and "simple" internet access. He started with a call to Motorola's 1-800 service number and worked his way up to the Vice President. In the end, he managed to be forwarded to someone who provided him with the sought-after source code of a Motorola mobile phone for download [Mit18].

In 2009, the spectacular case of an art figure became known, for whom a fictitious profile (**fake profile**) was created on a social network [Sch19]:

Robin Sage, 25, attractive graduate of a prestigious university (MIT), cybersecurity analyst at the US Navy, 10 years of professional experience. Her name was taken from a training exercise of the United States Army Special Forces. Accounts were published under the name Sage on several popular social networks. About 300 (some high-ranking) military personnel, NSA employees, industrialists, and politicians sent her friend requests and were only too willing to transmit confidential information to her, including military secrets.

▶ One must be careful when dealing with social networks.

2.2.4.1 Social Engineering—Examples

Below are situations in which social engineering attacks can be promising (all have already worked).

Example

- **Business trip:**
  - In the evening at the hotel bar/in the sauna, secret carriers (executives, IT administrators, …) are engaged in a conversation to get information that is officially not accessible in other environments. Under the influence of alcohol, business goals, system architectures, responsibilities in the company, personnel responsibilities are revealed, which would otherwise be kept confidential.
  - On the train/flight, a seat neighbor gets insight into the unprotected laptop screen. The neighbor presents himself as a trusted colleague/expert, a conversation ensues and confidential information is inadvertently revealed.
- **Application:**
  - An "applicant" sends an application to a company on Friday. On Monday, he appears at the gate and asks for admission, referring to his application, naming the correct contact persons, and the fact that he lives far away but is "coincidentally" nearby.
  - In a job interview, an "applicant" can easily obtain many interesting insider information, such as organization, company structure, responsibilities, etc.
  - A "headhunter" quickly gets insider information told carelessly by a potentially willing to change employee of a company (salary level, contract conditions, responsibilities, …).
- **Vishing** attack [RF16] with the following situation: A stressed playing caller reports to a telecommunications provider. In the background, faked baby crying

sounds from a running audio file. With an excited voice, the caller wants to know her husband's user access data on his alleged behalf. Her husband would have instructed her to set up her own user access. Of course, she does not know the credentials of "her husband", but can gain necessary trust through the empathy of the extremely helpful call center assistant and finally gets the additional access set up. Why should a stressed mother with baby crying in the background want evil?

- Through the **professional networks,** project employees can be easily found from outside. Developers are usually proud of what they have achieved and like to write about what they are working on. A correspondingly seductive approach (e.g., from "colleagues") can easily lead to further insider information being elicited.
- Dismissed or **dissatisfied employees** are often willing to share information about their former employer and its projects with others (e.g., new colleagues at their new workplace). They can be easily identified and specifically contacted via the internet.
- A **USB stick** found and left on a parking lot with the label "private" easily tempts curious individuals to plug it into their computer to see what "private" means in this case. And if that doesn't work, malware-prepared USB sticks with personal addresses can be "trustingly" handed over on appropriate occasions (trade fairs, events) without the recipient suspecting anything.
- **Clothes make people:** disguised as craftsmen or cleaning staff, it's easy to get past security services and gain access to companies.
- At **parties** (especially in the family circle), personal and/or trade secrets are often carelessly revealed, which, if they fall into the wrong hands, can cause harm to others.
- Even in **"secure" believed harmless environments,** information can be easily extracted. Be it through a designed "game", conversation with strangers, etc. Someone claims to be able to guess a party-goer's password with a high hit rate due to his long professional experience with security. To do this, the password owner must answer 10 personal questions, e.g.: What is his partner's name? What did he eat yesterday? When was he born? When did he get married? … The interviewee is curious to see if the interviewer can actually guess his password and answers willingly (and honestly). In the end, the interviewer reveals himself: In fact, he can't guess passwords, but he has now been able to collect a lot of personal data in a simple way, which the interviewee might not have revealed so willingly in a casual normal conversation with a stranger.
- What can happen when those responsible pass an **open-source project** on to a (new) development group is shown by the following case: Hackers managed to damage a JavaScript module that is used as part of Copay's Bitcoin wallet application [Law18]. They had gained control of an open-source project and exploited it. These social engineering hacks target the software packages that developers use to create JavaScript applications. The common way of creating modern apps

today—hundreds of individual software libraries, packages or modules—is an easily attackable vulnerability.
- CEO-Fraud attacks (see Leoni, FACC in Sect. 2.1.1) are also to be classified under this category. ◀

Often it is not a single approach alone, but the combination of information from different sources, so that the individual does not recognize the value of the embezzled information, as it only enables an attack in combination with other information. It can be assumed that the attackers proceed extremely perfidiously, prepare very well and behave professionally and cold-bloodedly. A "faked" call cannot be distinguished from a "real" call by the person called. The caller can come up with confidential information that only the "real" person should know. This immediately builds trust in the person called and suppresses the possibility that the call could be faked.

When employees find themselves in unusual situations, they are often not brave enough to want to clarify them. An unknown face in the office, possibly disguised as a craftsman, who has already passed so many people, seems unsuspected, it may also be uncomfortable to address the stranger for this reason, one does not know how they will react in the end.

A target person can assume that they will not recognize the purpose for which information is being extracted from them when they are approached by an attacker:

- The **high degree of networking** simplifies the exchange of information and the acquisition of information (e.g., social networks as a data source).
- The **trade in information** is a lucrative business model (for example, data collected by Google, profile data, access data from the Deep Web or Darknet, …).
- The **value of the information determines the need for protection of processes,** people and the systems used.

Conclusion

Social Engineering is something to describe methodically. Giving the impression that something else is wanted than what is directly desired. The statement "the trash can is full" vs. "please empty the trash can" has the same goal despite different semantics. Conversely: From an innocuous statement/question/ statement, the goal is not immediately recognizable.

Examples of information that have a "value" and have a potential for damage if they fall into the hands of unauthorized persons include, among others:

- illegal actions
- competitive data
- personal data

- trade secrets
- information from research and development
- access data
- strategic decisions
- system vulnerabilities
- ...

2.2.4.2 Social Engineering—Targets of Attack

Even if information appears harmless to one person, it can be an important component of a planned attack for another (an attacker).

Targets of attack include, for example:

- **Information takeover:** Information can be sold and further attacks can be carried out using the compromised data
- **Identity theft:** Activities can be carried out or concealed in the name of a person with their identity
- Triggering **financial transactions** (e.g., **CEO Fraud**)
- **Industrial espionage** (customer data, patents, development secrets, ...)
- Image/**Reputation loss:** the aim is to inflict damage to someone's image
- **System access:** to be able to carry out ongoing attacks, unauthorized system accesses are spied out
- **Blackmail** (e.g., using malware): The aim is to extort money with the threat of publishing confidential data. In the sense that if the money is not paid, the confidential data will be published.
- **Dumpster-Diver** (Trash Diver): Searching through "waste" to easily gain information that is obviously intended to be disposed of.
- **Phishing/Spear Phishing:** Electronic communication fraud targeting specific individuals, organizations, or companies. Although the main purpose is to steal data for criminal purposes, cybercriminals may also intend to install malware on the attacked computer. They are very difficult to detect. A small mistake by an employee can have dramatic consequences for a company.
- **Whaling:** While phishing targets random people and spear-phishing targets specific people, whaling is a particularly intense attack on individuals. The fraudulent messages sent appear to come from someone who is particularly high-ranking or influential in their company. The "big fish" or "whales" in the company in question are targeted, e.g., the CEO or the financial manager.

To defend against social engineering attacks, a corresponding risk assessment can be carried out, comparing the complexity of an attack (e.g., expertise, equipment, knowledge, opportunity, ...) with the complexity of appropriate countermeasures (e.g., expertise, equipment, feasibility, costs, ...). Usually, the best method of choice is to conduct awareness and training sessions.

With open eyes and a healthy dose of skepticism, the actions of others should always be observed.

2.2.5 Bug Bounty Programs—Honeypot

Q: "Why do you rob banks?"
A: "Because that's where the money is"
(Sutton's law)

Two ways to *"harden"* systems, i.e., make them more resilient or to obtain information about attacks/attackers (in addition to technical measures), are shown below:

> Bug Bounty (Sect. 2.2.5.1) and
> Honeypot (Sect. 2.2.5.2).

2.2.5.1 Bug Bounty Program

"Every technology has weaknesses, and if you don't create an incentive for hackers to tell you about the weaknesses in a legal way, you will learn about the vulnerabilities through attacks from the black market."
(Alex Rice, former Facebook security chief)

Essentially, a "bounty program" for program errors, **Bug Bounty** is an initiative to identify, fix, and publicize errors in software by offering material or cash prizes for the discoverers. Prominent examples of initiators are Microsoft, the Pentagon, US Air Force, "Hack the Air Force", Facebook, Tesla, and others. In some cases, several thousand euros or, as in the case of Facebook, a permanent position are offered if a new, previously unknown security gap is found and reported.

The advantage for companies is obvious: a concentrated community finds more security gaps in a shorter time than one would find with one's own testing methods. Security gaps were identified and documented in a very short time. The disadvantage is the risk that a discovered security gap will actually be passed on/sold to others instead of being reported [Gor20].

Background Information
The principle of bug bounties is based on the fact that people are basically good—or at least the majority of people. Dan Kaminsky, a star of the scene or "security researcher", as many hackers call themselves, says: *"When the first such programs were introduced, I was afraid people would blackmail the companies. I am amazed at how civilized it has been so far. Bug bounty programs are particularly helpful to small companies that can't afford their own security department and can now access a global talent pool."* [be15]

2.2.5.2 Honeypot

A **Honeypot** is a facility designed to distract an attacker or enemy from the actual target or to draw them into an area that would otherwise not have interested them—e.g., in the form of a decoy. They are designed to attract attackers and hackers deliberately and specifically. This allows attack methods and system weaknesses to be discovered before an actual attacker targets similar real targets through appropriate observation and analysis.

Honeypots can be seen as security solutions for networks. They mislead attackers and store their actions. The attackers are offered false or nonsensical data. The attacks can be analyzed to draw conclusions about the hackers and take appropriate countermeasures. During the attack, details are recorded to determine afterwards how the attackers penetrated the network and what actions they carried out:

- Researchers can use honeypots to find out how malware spreads and how attackers proceed.
- Security teams operate honeypots in their customers' IP address space to find out if attacks are taking place there.

Honeypots can be distinguished by the type of resources and the degree of interaction.

A prominent example is Honey Train [KOR15]. A signal box with industrial components was simulated and made accessible via the Internet. Within six weeks, there were 2.7 million accesses. The analysis of the accesses provided insights into origins, attack methods, and other findings.

Fake profiles (see Sect. 2.2.4) in networks, from whose calls and addresses corresponding insights can be gained, can also be understood as a honeypot.

> You don't have to use illegal tricks to get suitable (unauthorized) information.

2.3 Processing Security

The EU-GDPR[EU-GDPR] defines in Article 32 requirements for the security of processing. These requirements can be adopted 1:1 into information security. The following parameters play a role in the assessment (Sect. 3.3.3):

- **State of the art**
- **Implementation costs**
- Type, scope, circumstances and **purposes of processing**
- **Probabilities of occurrence/Frequencies of occurrence** of risks
- **Severity** of risks (risk level, risk value, …)

Based on an appropriate analysis, suitable technical and organizational measures must be taken to ensure a level of protection appropriate to the risk.

Essential components here are:

- Use of **encryption techniques**
- Ability to ensure **protection objectives** such as **confidentiality, integrity** and **availability** (and others) of the systems and services in connection with processing
- Ability to maintain the **availability even in case of attacks**
- Procedures for **regular review,** assessment and evaluation of the **effectiveness** of technical and organizational measures to ensure the security of processing

Background information
On the **state of the art**, the Federal Association for IT Security e.V. has a ***"Guide to the state of the art"*** of technical and organizational measures [TT20]. The state of technology must be clearly and measurably distinguished from conceptually similar technology standards such as the "generally accepted rules of technology" and the "state of science and research".

2.3.1 Technical security measures

Technical security measures/controls are primarily aimed at system crashes, hard disk crashes, ...)

- **Hardening** of systems through technical precautions (Firewall, Antivirus protection, Network segmentation, ...)
- **Deactivation** or **Blocking** of **interfaces** and/or features of hardware components that are not absolutely necessary for the performance of the intended tasks
- Increasing the security of the IT system by **reducing** the weaknesses and possible **attack methods**

2.3.2 Organizational Security Measures

Organizational security measures/controls are divided into:

- **Organization**—Danger: missing or unclear regulations, missing concepts, ...
- **Personnel**—Danger: human errors

Sensitization, awareness training of employees are also the means of choice here. Regulations for prevention and support in case of security incidents, email distribution lists for known weaknesses/vulnerabilities, patches and work around are appropriate examples.

2.3.3 Organization and Compliance

There are different types of contracts for securing with corresponding agreements:

- **Service-Level-Agreement (SLA):** Written agreement between a service provider and a customer to determine service objectives and responsibilities. An SLA can cover multiple services and/or customers.
- **Operational-Level-Agreement (OLA):** Written agreement between service provider and a part of the same organization.
- **Underpinning-Contract (UC):** Written agreement with external service providers to ensure the provision of services.
- **Data Processing Agreement (DPA):** Regulate the responsibility of processing personal data on behalf between the responsible party and the processor.

2.3.4 Gathering Information

One of the most important measures for risk reduction is the collection of information on the subject of security and determining whether it is relevant for own products and services. There are a number of relevant websites and newsletters that can be subscribed to, such as:

- www.heise.de, www.security-insider.de/: Daily, information on the topic of security is editorially prepared.
- www.cert.org, www.cert.dfn.de/ueberblick, www.hoax-info.de or www.sans.org contain many tips, advice, and information.

These are just a few examples. If you set up a page with information on the topic of security as your search engine's homepage, you will receive daily news without having to make any additional effort to read it on your screen.

2.3.5 Self-Assessment

Through a Self-Assessment it can be determined where there are gaps in technology and organization. Possible questions to be evaluated could be:

- Is there a **security officer**? Is he known?
- What is in the **information security policy**?
- Which information security policies are known? Where can they be viewed?

- What to do in an **emergency**? Is there emergency management?
- How **current** and **effective** are **existing measures** for information security?

This can result in various optimization measures:

- technical and infrastructural
- organizational and personnel
- Assessment according to effectiveness/prioritization/broad impact
- Necessity of constant adaptation of measures

Conclusion

Structured, organized, and systematic approach leads to security management.

2.3.6 Test Strategies

An essential component of information security is the specification of appropriate test strategiesfor validating security objectives. Compared to the development of non-security-critical systems, the planning and implementation of additional methods become necessary:

Testing

Functional Testing:	Fulfillment of functional security requirements (cryptography, authentication protocols, ...)
Interface Tests:	Verification if all inputs and outputs of a component meet the requirements
Penetration Testing:	Individual tests to exploit found weaknesses/Fault-Injection, to bypass routine checks
Vulnerability Scanning:	Detection of already known security gaps/weaknesses
Passive Scanning:	Search for coding errors that can be exploited
Active Scanning:	Access to processes, protocols, file systems, ...

Fuzz Testing

Systematic Fuzzing:	Systematic introduction/sending of data to find undocumented/unknown behavior/properties System or interface level

In addition to the verification of design activities carried out per development level, the implementation of further test methods is necessary.

Many standards distinguish between the terms **Verification** and **Validation**, but define them differently. Even though the same test methods can be applied to both terms, they can be distinguished as follows:

- **Timing** in the **Development Model:** Validation is usually carried out at the end, at the highest requirement level
- Validation determines whether the **right thing** is being developed, while verification determines whether it is being **developed correctly.**
- Validation determines whether (security) goals have been adequately achieved, verification determines whether specifications are being met.

Verification Confirmation of having done things correctly. Proof that security requirements are met.

Validation Confirmation of having done the right things. Proof that the security objectives are adequate and are being achieved.

Using a further taxonomy, test methods can be classified as follows.

Testing against the **"Known":**

- Functional testing (see above)
  - **Vulnerability Scanning** systematically tests whether known security vulnerabilities are present and exploitable in the developed system. Known, hardcoded passwords can also be checked, as can the presence of open ports, etc. The tests run largely automatically (unlike the pentest (see below)). Found security vulnerabilities can then be closed to thwart similar attacks. The general approach consists of the following parts:
    - Listing of values (assets) and capabilities (resources) of the system,
    - Creation of a ranking of the importance of values and resources,
    - Identification of vulnerabilities and potential threats to each value/resource,
    - Mitigation or elimination of serious vulnerabilities.

    For this purpose, known databases of vulnerabilities are used (e.g., [CVE]), as well as code and design are analyzed. Vulnerability scanning can be performed at all development levels (concept, system, hardware, software, …).

Testing against the **"Unknown":**

- With **Systematic Fuzzing,** the aim is to provoke undocumented and unknown behavior. Systematic input and sending of data is intended to reveal hidden properties. Successful attacks show that attack scenarios exploit design and specification gaps to achieve their goal.
- **Penetration Testing** uses (authorized, i.e., permission has been granted for execution) found weaknesses. With individual tests using means and methods that an attacker (hacker) would use, attempts are made to penetrate the system unauthorized (attack simulation). An essential part are the tools that replicate all attack patterns as far as possible and those resulting from known attack patterns. Penetration tests are usually carried out manually:
  - Inspection of the test object/pre-tests,
  - Planning of test procedures and goals/modeling of the attack,

- Weakness analysis,
- Selection of necessary tools and execution,
- Exploitation of the weakness,
- Test results are manually verified.

2.3.7 Turning Point after Stuxnet

The computer worm Stuxnet was discovered in June 2010. The malware was specifically designed to attack a Supervisory Control and Data Acquisition (SCADA) system from Siemens—the Siematic S7. It is believed that the control system of a uranium enrichment plant in Iran was the target of the attack. The extraordinary, and hitherto unsuspected, deployment of $50 million, 10 years of development time by 5-10 developers made it clear with what high motivation and high resource commitment attacks are attempted, which made the professional world sit up and take notice. Various experts took a year to determine how the attack was supposed to work using reverse engineering methods.

The result of the investigation shows how complex and complicated attacks can be. Various organizational and technical weaknesses, proprietary (and thus supposedly protected) knowledge were combined [Kus13]. The attack scenario consisted of several steps:

1. **Infection:** Occurred with a USB stick and infected the MS Windows system on computers and presented fake certificates.
2. **Search:** Stuxnet spied on computers running Siemens control systems.
3. **Update:** When the worm found appropriate attack targets, it updated itself via the internet.
4. **Compromise:** The worm exploited a security vulnerability unknown to experts.
5. **Takeover of control:** Stuxnet spied on the process on target computers and collected information to take control of centrifuges and cause them to fail.
6. **Deception** and **Destruction:** False information was sent externally, so the attack was not recognized from the outside until it was too late to do anything against the attack.

The level of motivation of attackers and the potential extent of malware had been completely underestimated until then. Misbehaviors are usually results of attacks over several (intermediate) stages and not independent.

2.4 NIS Directive

The **NIS Directive** [EU-NIS21] (Eng. NIS-Directive) is the first EU-wide legislation on cybersecurity. The directive provides for legal measures to raise the general level of cybersecurity in the EU. The following is to be ensured by it:

- Preparation of member states to be **adequately equipped,** e.g. with a Computer Security Incident Response Team (**CSIRT**) and a competent national NIS authority.
- Cooperation between all member states by setting up a cooperation group that supports and facilitates strategic cooperation and **information exchange** between member states.
- A **security culture** in all **sectors,** which are of **crucial importance to our economy and society** and also rely heavily on ICT (Information and Communication Technology), such as energy, transport, water, banking, financial market infrastructures, healthcare, and digital infrastructure.

Companies identified by member states as **operators of essential services** in relevant sectors must take appropriate security measures and inform the competent national authorities about serious incidents. Providers of important digital services, such as search engines, cloud computing services, and online marketplaces must comply with the security and reporting requirements of the new directive.

The directive is in line with the Commission's priorities to make Europe fit for the digital age and build a future-proof economy that works for people.

The communication, referred to as the ***"NIS Toolkit"*** referred, provides member states with practical information on the directive. For example, it presents best practices for implementing the directive from other member states, with explanations and interpretations of specific provisions to clarify how the NIS Directive is supposed to work in practice. The implementing regulation applies directly.

The European Union is working on various fronts to promote cyber resilience, protect communication and data, and keep the online society and economy safe. For Germany, the implementation law strengthens the cooperation between the federal states and the BSI (Federal Office for Information Security).

Two central requirements for Digital Service Providers (DSP) are:

1. **Identifying and implementing appropriate and proportionate** technical and organizational measures to control existing risks (Article 16 paragraph 1).
2. To inform the competent authority or the Cyber-Security-Incident-Response-Team (CSIRT) **immediately about any incident,** which has significant effects on the provision of a service (Article 16 paragraph 3).

For the DSPs, this involves:

- **Security** of **systems** and **facilities**
- **Incident handling:** DSPs are obliged to report incidents "without culpable delay" if they have a "significant impact" (Article 16 paragraph 3). The implementing regulation makes it clear that the DSPs must determine this themselves, and outlines in Article 3 corresponding metrics to determine whether an incident has a "significant" impact on the EU.

- Management of **business continuity**
- **Monitoring,** auditing and testing
- Compliance with **international standards.**

DSPs must maintain an **"appropriate documentation"** in order to be able to prove compliance with the regulations.

A good "start" is the establishment of an ISMS e.g. according to ISO/IEC 27001 [ISO27001] (Sect. 8.3). From the ENISA (European Union Agency for Network and Information Security), there is a list of 29 security objectives in a technical guide [EU-NIS20] that can be grouped into eight categories:

- **Governance** and **risk management:** Information security policy, corporate governance and risk management, security roles and responsibilities, security of third party assets
- Security in **human resources:** Background checks, security knowledge and training, personnel changes, dealing with violations
- Security of **systems** and **facilities:** Physical and environmental security, security of deliveries, access control to network and information systems, integrity of network and information systems, use of encryption, protection of security-critical data
- **Operations management:** Operational processes, change management, asset management
- **Incident Management:** Incident management procedures, ability to detect incidents, incident reporting and communication
- **Business Continuity Management:** Service continuity strategy and emergency plans, disaster recovery capabilities
- **Monitoring, auditing and testing:** Monitoring and logging policies, practicing emergency plans, testing of networks and information systems, security assessments, monitoring compliance with policies
- **Threat awareness:** Information about threats, informing users about threats

For all security objectives, corresponding security measures are divided into three levels:

- **Basis:** Measures that can be implemented and their evidence that they have been implemented.
- **Industry standard:** Security measures and their verification as well as evidence that the measures have been implemented and the verifications are taking place.
- **State-of-the-Art:** Advanced measures and their continuous verification. Proactive attention to changes, events, tests etc. Evidence that the measures have been implemented and structured reviews are taking place.

2.5 Summary

A security gap in IT security will—once known—most likely be exploited (at some point). Known gaps must therefore be closed quickly.

Basic thoughts on information security:

- **Investments in effective security measures/controls** can significantly reduce the number of successful attacks.
- The average **cost of a data breach** (determined in several studies) in Germany is several million euros. Main share: lost business opportunities, negative impact on reputation and hours spent on recovery.
- Possible **countermeasures:**
  - Holistic approach to cybersecurity, focusing on three key components: **people, processes** and **technology;**
  - Training and awareness campaigns in which employees learn to recognize attacks such as phishing attacks and take appropriate protective measures;
  - Availability of a competent security team that provides clear guidelines: **Efficiency in response** to security incidents;
  - Use of a **Threat Intelligence Network,** to recognize and block known attacks (e.g., ZETA attacks).
- **Attackers/Hackers:**
  - operate globally and exchange their information without regard for intellectual property;
  - have time, unlike the developers of a product;
  - only need to find and exploit one single weakness/vulnerability, while product developers need to know and keep all weaknesses/vulnerabilities closed;
  - Attacks only need to work once, while targets need to be protected at all times.
- Known vulnerabilities must be closed promptly (see also Zero-Day Exploit) and are statistically hardly detectable.
- Misbehavior is usually the result of attacks over several (intermediate) levels and is not independent. Therefore, they cannot be uncovered with conventional verification methods.

> Cybersecurity risks evolve over time as the motivations and capabilities of attackers change …

References

[be15] ***„Hacker der Hoffnung“***; brand eins 2015. Link: https://www.brandeins.de/magazine/brand-eins-wirtschaftsmagazin/2015/geschwindigkeit/hacker-der-hoffnung accessed: 10.04.2021

[Cap16] ***„Betrüger erbeuten 40 Mio. Euro von Leoni“***. Link: https://www.capital.de/karriere/betrueger-erbeuten-40-mio-euro-von-leoni accessed: 10.04.2021

[CAPEC] ***„Common Attack Pattern Enumeration and Classification“.*** Link: https://capec.mitre.org/ accessed: 18.04.2021

[CoT19] ***„Charter of Trust on Cybersecurity“.*** 2019; Link: https://csrc.nist.gov/CSRC/media/Projects/cyber-supply-chain-risk-management/documents/SSCA/Spring_2019/8MayAM1_190502_Charter_of_Trust.pdf accessed 10.04.2021

[CTS14] ***„Studie: Industriespionage 2014“,*** Corporate Trust Studie. Link: https://www.corporate-trust.de/wp-content/uploads/2016/06/CT-Studie-2014_DE.pdf accessed 10.04.2021

[CVE] ***„NIST Database for Vulnerabilities“***. Link: https://nvd.nist.gov/vuln accessed 10.04.2021

[EU-CA19] ***„Regulation (EU) 2019/881 of the European Parliament and of the Council of 17 April 2019*** **(EU-Cybersecurity-Act)“**. Link: https://eur-lex.europa.eu/eli/reg/2019/881/oj accessed: 10.04.2021

[EU-GDPR] General Data Protection Regulation; (EU) 2016/679; Link: https://eur-lex.europa.eu/legal-content/EN/TXT/?uri=CELEX%3A32016R0679; accessed: 10.04.2021

[EU-NIS20] ***„Guideline on Security Measures under the EECC“***; December 10, 2020. Link: https://www.enisa.europa.eu/publications/guideline-on-security-measures-under-the-eecc accessed: 13.04.2021

[EU-NIS21] ***„NIS-Richtlinie“***. Link: https://digital-strategy.ec.europa.eu/en/policies/nis-directive accessed: 10.04.2021

[Gen16] ***„The largest Cyber-Attack in Switzerland“;*** Link: https://www.gbnews.ch/discussing-the-largest-cyber-attack-in-switzerland/ accessed: 10.04.2021

[Gor20] ***„A Bug's Journey: Understanding the Software Vulnerability Lifecycle“,*** Brian Gorenc, escar 2020

[Hei15] ***„Betrüger erleichtern Ryanair um 4,6 Millionen“***; Link: https://www.heise.de/security/meldung/Betrueger-erleichtern-Ryanair-um-4-6-Millionen-Euro-2632181.html accessed: 10.04.2021

[Hei16] ***„Ransomware-Virus legt Krankenhaus lahm“***; 12. Februar 2016. Link: https://www.heise.de/newsticker/meldung/Ransomware-Virus-legt-Krankenhaus-lahm-3100418.html accessed: 10.04.2021

[Hei16a] ***„ÖPNV umsonst: Verschlüsselungstrojaner kapert Bezahlterminals der Straßenbahn in San Francisco“***; 28. November 2016. Link: https://www.heise.de/newsticker/meldung/OePNV-umsonst-Verschluesselungstrojaner-kapert-Bezahlterminals-der-Strassenbahn-in-San-Francisco-3506080.html accessed: 10.04.2021

[Hei17] ***„Was wir bisher über die Ransomware-Attacke wissen“***; 13. Mai 2017. Link: https://www.heise.de/newsticker/meldung/WannaCry-Was-wir-bisher-ueber-die-Ransomware-Attacke-wissen-3713502.html accessed 10.04.2021

[IM14] ***„EBay Under Fire After Cross Site Scripting Attack“***; 18. September 2014. Link: https://www.infosecurity-magazine.com/news/ebay-under-fire-after-cross-site/ accessed: 10.04.2021

[ISO27001] ***„Information security management systems – Requirements“***; ISO/IEC 27001

[Kas17] ***„Waschanlage gehackt, geht das tatsächlich?“***. Link: https://www.kaspersky.de/blog/hacking-a-carwash/14254/ accessed 10.04.2021

[KMC20] ***„Automotive Security. State of Practice 2020“***. Link: https://www.kuglermaag.de/automotive-security/state-of-practice/ accessed 10.04.2021

[KOR15] ***„Project HoneyTrain“;*** Koramis GmbH; 2015. Link: https://presselounge.tc-communications.de/media/files/Hontrain-WP_Sophos_Textfinal-layouted.pdf accessed 10.04.2021

[Kus13] ***„The Real Story of Stuxnet“***, David Kushner; 2013. Link: https://spectrum.ieee.org/telecom/security/the-real-story-of-stuxnet accessed 10.04.2021

[Law18] ***„Recent open source flaw highlights danger of social engineering hacks“***; TheServerSide Dezember 2018. Link: https://www.theserverside.com/feature/Recent-open-source-flaw-highlights-danger-of-social-engineering-hacks accessed 10.04.2021

[Mit18] ***„How a Hacker Convinced Motorola to Send Him Source Code“***. Link: https://www.youtube.com/watch?v=UBaVek2oTtc accessed 10.04.2021

[MV17] ***„Key Reinstallation Attacks: Breaking WPA2 by forcing nonce reuse“***; Mathy Vanhoef, KU Leuven 2017. Link: www.krackattacks.com accessed: 10.04.2021

[NHS16] ***„Appointments on hold as (computer) virus wreaks havoc with NHS trust system“***. Link: https://www.theregister.com/2016/10/31/virus_shuts_down_nhs_trust/ accessed: am 02.11.2016

[NHS17] ***„Wanna Decrypter 2.0 ransomware attack – what you need to know“***; 12.05.2017. Link: https://nakedsecurity.sophos.com/2017/05/12/wanna-decrypter-2-0-ransomware-attack-what-you-need-to-know/ accessed: 10.04.2021

[OÖ16] ***„Wie der FACC 50 Millionen abhanden kommen“***. 04. Februar 2016. Link: https://www.nachrichten.at/nachrichten/wirtschaft/wirtschaftsraumooe/Wie-der-FACC-50-Millionen-abhanden-kamen;art467,2109585 accessed: 10.04.2021

[PCW16] ***„San Francisco's Muni transit system slammed by ransomware“***; 28. November 2016. Link: https://www.pcworld.com/article/3144996/san-franciscos-muni-transit-system-reportedly-hit-by-ransomware.html accessed: 10.04.2021

[Pon18] ***„2018 Study on Global Megastrends in Cybersecurity - Ponemon Institute Research Report“***: Link: https://www.raytheon.com/sites/default/files/2018-02/2018_Global_Cyber_Megatrends.pdf accessed 10.04.2021

[Pon18a] ***„Securing the Modern Vehicle: A Study of Automotive Industry Cybersecurity Practices“***. Link: https://www.synopsys.com/content/dam/synopsys/sig-assets/reports/securing-the-modern-vehicle.pdf accessed 10.04.2021

[RF16] ***„This is how hackers hack you using simple social engineers“;*** 2016; Link: https://www.youtube.com/watch?v=lc7scxvKQOo accessed 10.04.2021

[Sch19] ***„Schutz gegen Social-Engineering“;*** Philipp Schaumann; 2019. Link: https://sicherheitskultur.at/social_engineering.htm accessed 10.04.2021

[SeIn17] ***“Gehackte Waschanlage demoliert mutwillig Fahrzeuge“***; 01. August 2017. Link: https://www.security-insider.de/gehackte-waschanlage-demoliert-mutwillig-fahrzeuge-a-630625/ accessed 10.04.2021

[SM08] ***„Chapter 6 LESSONS LEARNED FROM THE MAROOCHY WATER BREACH“;*** Jill Slay, Michael Mille, ifip, International Federation for Information Processing; Critical Infrastructure Protection. Link: http://www.ifip.org/wcc2008/site/IFIPSampleChapter.pdf accessed: 10.04.2021

[SO14] ***„Hacker legten deutschen Hochofen lahm“***; 18. Dezember 2014. Link: http://www.spiegel.de/netzwelt/web/bsi-bericht-hacker-legten-deutschen-hochofen-lahm-a-1009191.html accessed: 10.04.2021

[SOP13] ***„Doctors disabled wireless in Dick Cheney's pacemaker to thwart hacking“***, Link: https://nakedsecurity.sophos.com/2013/10/22/doctors-disabled-wireless-in-dick-cheneys-pacemaker-to-thwart-hacking/ accessed 10.04.2021

[Tal14] ***„Antifragilität: Anleitung für eine Welt, die wir nicht verstehen“;*** Nassim Nicholas Taleb; btb-Verlag, 2014

[Tre19] ***„Go Scooter, stop Scooter“;*** Moritz Tremmel; 2019. Link: https://www.golem.de/news/sicherheitsluecke-go-scooter-stop-scooter-1902-139365.html accessed 10.04.2021

[TT20] ***„IT Security Act (Germany) and EU General Data Protection Regulation: Guideline State of the artTechnical and orgainsational measures“***, TeleTrusT, Bundesverband IT-Sicherheit e.V., 2020. Link: https://www.teletrust.de/fileadmin/user_upload/2021-02_TeleTrusT-Guideline_State_of_the_art_in_IT_security_EN.pdf accessed 10.04.2021

[Ups20] ***„Upstream Security's global automotive cybersecurity report 2020“.*** Research into cyber-attack trends in the smart mobility ecosystem; Upstream Security Ltd.. Link: https://www.upstream.auto/ accessed 10.04.2021

[VM15] ***„Hackers Remotely Kill a Jeep on the Highway—With Me in It“;*** Chris Valasek, Charlie Miller. Link: https://www.wired.com/2015/07/hackers-remotely-kill-jeep-highway/ accessed: 10.04.2021

[ZDNet16] ***„Message-Bug ermöglichte Entschlüsselung von Fotos und Videos“.*** Link: https://www.zdnet.de/88263933/imessage-bug-ermoeglicht-entschluesselung-von-fotos-und-videos/ accessed: 10.04.2021

3 Data Protection (Privacy)

Today, it is very easy to collect, store and evaluate a large amount of personal data (see definition in Sect. 3.2.4). Neither the access and processing of large amounts of data nor the tools and techniques for storage and evaluation are a serious hurdle. Realistically, there can no longer be transparency about who owns which (personal) data from whom and for what purposes it is evaluated and used.

However, the protection of natural persons in the processing of personal data is a fundamental right and therefore deeply rooted in law:

- European Union: reference to the **EU Charter** according to Article 8 Paragraph 1 of the Charter of Fundamental Rights of the European Union
- Together, the **EU GDPR** [EU GDPR] and the **BDSG** [BDSG18] in Germany ensure the protection of the fundamental right to informational self-determination
- In the USA, corresponding **Bill of Rights** extend the **Constitution of the United States** to include the right to privacy (prevention of inappropriate searches, guarantee of freedom of speech and press, …)

> Data protection/Privacy is regulated by law. Unlike information security, the implementation for the processing of personal data/information is not solely at the discretion of a company. Also, risks in the processing of personal data are not so easily acceptable, as they always have to be in accordance with the law.

T. Liedtke, *Information Security*, https://doi.org/10.1007/978-3-658-45711-2_3

- Section 3.1 motivates the topic and presents the origin and goals of privacy.
- The basis in Europe is the EU GDPR, in Germany subsidiarily the BDSG. Both are presented in Sect. 3.2.
- Important articles of the EU GDPR are presented in Sect. 3.3.
- How the topic of privacy can be specifically applied in organizations and projects with regard to engineering is demonstrated in Sect. 3.4 with examples.
- Concrete methods and techniques (Privacy-Enhancing-Technologies) are used in Sect. 3.5.
- The privacy risk model is described in Sect. 3.6.
- Section 3.7 presents privacy frameworks and associated standards.
- A summary is given in Sect. 3.8 and a
- bibliography concludes the chapter.

3.1 Motivation/Origin

"Don't count us, count your days"
(Slogan on a poster at the May demonstration against the census 1987 in Berlin)

Since May 25, 2016, the European General Data Protection Regulation (EU GDPR, [EU GDPR]) has been adopted and has been effective since May 25, 2018. Against the background of potentially drastic high fines in the future (10 million euros or 2% of the worldwide previous year's turnover of a group (whichever is higher)), its introduction has caused a lot of uproar.

There are more and more services and applications that process personal data, so it is no wonder that the term data protection/Privacy is one of the trend terms of search engines.

Storing data no longer costs any money today, the complexity of data and their linking possibilities continue to increase steadily. A complete transparency about the purposes for which personal data are evaluated is impossible, sometimes even not desired.

3.1.1 Basic Principles of Privacy: Concepts

The basic principles **data economy**, **anonymization** and **pseudonymization** are no longer sufficient alone with currently available technologies. The responsibility of the data processor, who handles personal data and the associated duties, must be strictly defined,

▶ Basic principles/concepts of privacy (EU-GDPR [EU-GDPR]):

Data economy Personal data must be adequate and significant, and limited to what is necessary for the purposes of processing ("data minimization"). Data economy or data minimization are therefore closely related to the purpose limitation of data. The basic idea is that only as much personal data is collected in data processing as is absolutely necessary for the respective application.

Anonymization Process aimed at eliminating the personal reference of data. Sufficient anonymization results in the principles of data protection law—such as the principle of purpose limitation—no longer being applicable.

Pseudonymization Processing of personal data in such a way that the personal data can no longer be attributed to a specific data subject without the use of additional information. This additional information must be kept separately.

As with information security, the importance of data protection is usually only realized when it is violated. Some examples that became known:

- An **open email distribution list** in copy in connection with a large distribution list and thus the disclosure of foreign email addresses without the consent of the email owners in an authority was penalized [DSB13].
  - "Foreign" email addresses must not be visible to recipients. Email addresses are personal data within the meaning of the EU-GDPR. Consent of the data subject is generally required for the disclosure of email addresses.
- A serious data leak at a debt collection company exposed tens of thousands of debtor data. The precarious thing about it: The documents contained highly sensitive information, such as **medical records** or **credit card statements** [SZ17].
- **Cloud Services** repeatedly call for password renewals when they have been hacked or misappropriated.

3.1.2 Data Protection: History

The following provides a brief outline of selected milestones in the history of data protection:

Data protection Privacy originated in the USA. Edward Warren described it in **1890** as *"right to be alone"*. A state in which one is not observed or disturbed by others.

In Hessen (German federal state), the world's first law for privacy was passed on **07.10.1970**. The Hessian Data Protection Act (HDSG) secures the right to ***"informational self-determination"***. It determines how and in what way personal data may be processed in public administration.

As one of the first documents, a report on the "computerization" of government databases in the USA presents the rights of residents [USD73]. The principles and rights for those affected, established as early as **1973,** are still relevant today and can be found in articles of the current EU-GDPR (Sect. 3.4.2).

Based on the Basic Law Article 2: General personality right and right to free personality development, in Germany the ***"right to informational self-determination"*** was derived (**1983**).

Definition The **right to informational self-determination** refers to the right of the individual to generally decide for themselves about the disclosure and use of their personal data.

This right was recognized in Germany by the Federal Constitutional Court in 1983 in the **census judgment** as a basic right, which results from Articles 1 and 2 of the Basic Law (GG):

"***Free development of the personality*** under the modern conditions of data processing presupposes the protection of the individual against unlimited collection, storage, use and disclosure of his personal data. This protection is therefore covered by the basic right of Article 2 para. 1 in conjunction with Article 1 para. 1 GG. The basic right thus guarantees the individual's authority to generally decide for themselves about the disclosure and use of their personal data." (BVerfGE 65, 1, judgment of December 15, 1983).

The reason for this judgment was the development of electronic data processing.

While many were outraged about the planned data collection during the census in **1987,** this seems surprising and incomprehensible from today's perspective when looking at the questions asked at the time, as many people today voluntarily reveal much more—even intimate details—about themselves in both social and professional networks. Questions from the census questionnaire appear harmless, such as questions about the highest general school leaving certificate, workplace, activity, ...

1990: Federal Data Protection Act [BDSG90].

The EU Data Protection Directive 95/46/EC [EU-DSRiLi95] on the protection of individuals with regard to the processing of personal data and on the free movement of such data is a directive issued by the European Community in **1995** to protect the privacy of individuals in the processing of personal data.

In **2001,** the Federal Data Protection Act [BDSG01] (derived from the census judgment and the EU Data Protection Directive of 1995) enshrined the protection against misuse of personal data in data processing.

2003: revised BDSG [BDSG03] with changes:

- Data protection for employees; consumer credit limit; right of withdrawal; ...
- Principle of proportionality; purpose limitation; transparency; data protection audits

EU-GH Judgment **2011:** the countries may not establish any other principles regarding the permissibility of processing personal data than in Art. 7 of the RiLi.

2012: Treaty on the Functioning of the European Union (TFEU, 2012). Article 16 (1) provides that every person has the right to the protection of personal data concerning them.

Concurrently with the EU GDPR [EU-DSGVO], the revised version of the Federal Data Protection Act (BDSG) [BDSG18] came into force on **May 25, 2018.**

With the new data protection law in California, CCPA (California Consumer Privacy Act) [CCPA18], the strictest data protection law in the USA to date came into force on **January 1, 2020.** It applies in California. The USA does not have a uniform data protection law like the EU GDPR. However, the focus is not on data protection, but primarily on consumer protection. Nevertheless, the CCPA is a serious initiative because it brings the unpopular topic of data protection to the fore beyond the borders of California in the USA. The addressees are both the Californian consumer and companies that conduct business activities in California. However, the regulation falls short of the level of protection of the EU GDPR. In particular, it contains no control elements.

3.1.3 Privacy: Characteristics and Privacy Objectives

In the following section, the term privacy is described in terms of its characteristics, privacy objectives, and properties.

> **Privacy Characterization**
> **Privacy** is the protection of personal data, related to privacy objectives, such as: **Predictability**, **Manageability** and **Disassociability** (see below):

- Privacy can be seen as an **attribute of a trustworthy system.**
- A privacy **risk assessment** is based on the likelihood that an operation performed by a system poses a problem for individuals → **Problematic Data Action** (see Sect. 3.5)
- Privacy is partly **orthogonal** to information security. There are security issues that have nothing to do with privacy, and conversely, there are data protection issues that have nothing to do with information security.
- **Problems,** that can arise from **unauthorized access** to personal data are generally well known (e.g., Identity Theft)
- **Problems,** that can arise from **authorized processing** may be less visible or not as well understood (e.g., discriminatory/stigmatizing effects)
- Privacy **risk:** Loss of privacy objective → Loss of privacy → **Loss of trust,**

- Important terminologies related to privacy: ***"Privacy-by-Design"*** | ***"Privacy-by-Default"*** | Techniques to improve privacy
- Privacy is legally regulated and therefore also dependent on the country.

Many standards in the British language use ***personal data,*** in the US language the term ***PII*** (personal identifiable information) is used.

▶ Privacy objectives (see [NIST8062]):

Predictability	Affected individuals, owners, and operators can make reliable predictions about personal data and its processing by the system.
Manageability	Ability to administer personal data granularly (modify, delete, read, …).
Disassociability	Processing of personal data without association to affected individuals beyond the operational requirements of the system.

See also privacy objectives in the use of threat modeling (Sect. 3.6.2):

3.2 Basis of the EU-GDPR: Federal Data Protection Act n. F.

In the following subsections:

- Section 3.2.1, 3.2.2 and 3.2.3 present individual topics of the BDSG [BDSG18] and the EU GDPR [EU-GDPR], as well as the planned ePrivacy Regulation [EU-ePrV21].
- Section 3.2.4 defines personal data
- Section 3.2.5 presents the legality of processing.

3.2.1 Federal Data Protection Act n. F.

The areas of application of the BDSG n. F. [BDSG18] (Federal Data Protection Act new version) include:

- **Public bodies** of the federal and state governments
- **Non-public bodies** in
  - Collection, processing or use of personal data,
  - Automated processing (e.g. personnel data, address data, …),
  - Non-automated processing (e.g. personnel files, patient records, …)

Exceptions are federal priority norms (e.g. Telecommunications-Telemedia-Data Protection Act) or familial and personal purposes (e.g. a photo album with family pictures).

The BDSG n. F. is freely available on the internet [BDSG18]. It is part of the Article Act EU-DSAnpUG (EU Data Protection Adaptation and Implementation Act) [EU-DSAnpUG].

The BDSG n. F. applies:

- within the borders of Germany (existing exceptions are complicated)
- also for associations and organizations (innovation compared to the old BDSG)

Other legal provisions take precedence. A list with examples can be found in Table 3.1.

Obligations to maintain statutory secrecy or professional or official secrets that are not based on statutory provisions remain unaffected.

State Data Protection Acts: state law equivalents; regulate the data protection of the respective public bodies (e.g. legal status of the state commissioner for data protection).

3.2.2 EU General Data Protection Regulation

An EU GDPR [EU GDPR] does not need to be ratified into national laws unlike an EU directive and is valid with precedence over other national laws. This leads to the EU GDPR (**EU law**) having priority over national laws (such as the BDSG n.F. in Germany) (**constitutional law**). In case of contradictions between the EU GDPR and the BDSG n.F., the interpretation of the EU GDPR applies. These contradictions can crystallize piece by piece over time. The general assumption is that there are indeed such contradictions (e.g., in the area of video surveillance or penalties to be imposed).

Table 3.1 Legal provisions with precedence

Law	Content
TTDSG (Telecommunications-Telemedia-Data Protection Act)	Provisions on telecommunications secrecy and data protection in telecommunications and telemedia services
BetrVG (Works Constitution Act)	**Social secret;** data transmission; protection of social data; processing by third parties (Federal Employment Agency, health insurance, …)
StPO (Code of Criminal Procedure)	Monitoring and recording of telecommunications traffic (Code of Criminal Procedure)
UrhG (Copyright Act)	Act on **Copyright** and related rights
UWG (Act Against Unfair Competition)	Act against the **unfair competition** (e.g. §7 unreasonable harassment)

The EU GDPR is freely available on the internet. It comprises 88 pages, contains 173 recitals and 99 articles.

> The **EU GDPR** (General Data Protection Regulation) serves to protect natural persons in the processing of personal data, for the free movement of data and for the repeal of Directive 95/46/EC.

It leaves room in more than 70 so-called **opening clauses** to fill these with national content. This applies, for example, to the topics of employment data protection, appointment of data protection officers, contract processing, influence of works constitution laws, etc. Of course, national provisions must not contradict the recitals and articles of the EU GDPR.

For Germany, not much has changed with the introduction of the EU GDPR. 90% of the provisions of the Data Protection Directive [EU-DSDiLi95] and the old Federal Data Protection Act [BDSG03] were adopted. Essentially, privacy has not been modernized, but rather compliance has been enforced. The EU GDPR receives significant criticism for its misunderstood technology neutrality. It does not differentiate between low-risk (for example, a craftsman's customer list) and very risky data processing (for example, behavior tracking or personality profiles) in terms of privacy principles, the permissibility of data processing, and the rights of those affected. It is therefore risk-neutral towards threats to fundamental rights. It does not address new challenges of modern IT (such as artificial intelligence, self-learning systems, Internet of Things, Big Data or cloud computing, internet platforms or processing of biometric data). This means that smaller economic actors and associations are affected by the requirements of the EU GDPR in the same way as data-hungry corporations and social networks [SN20].

3.2.3 ePrivacy: Telecommunications-Telemedia-Data Protection Act

As long as the **ePrivacy Regulation** [EU-ePrV21] is pending and not effective, the **ePrivacy Directive** [EU-ePrRiLi] (Data Protection Directive for Electronic Communication) from the year 2002 (last amended on May 25, 2011) continues to apply.

The ePrivacy Regulation (formerly also Cookie Regulation) is intended to supplement the EU GDPR. It protects all electronic communication as inherently private and confidential and regulates the handling of personal data on the Internet and the associated protection of privacy. Various directives have been issued for this purpose, which are implemented into national law.

The protection of users is opposed by the profit interests of business associations. The ePrivacy Regulation primarily strengthens the **rights of users on the Internet:**

- Providers are required to encrypt data according to the **state of the art** and protect it from unauthorized access. The **trade in backdoors** is prohibited.
- The **spatial tracking** by programs that are not actively used is to become illegal. It should not be possible to unknowingly create movement profiles.
- Providers are required to disclose government requests, thus introducing detailed transparency and documentation obligations for law enforcement agencies.
- Processing should no longer be possible **without the user's consent.** What has been applicable to telephone providers for some time should be extended to providers of online communication, such as WhatsApp or Facebook Messenger.
- An effective **protection against tracking** should be established, which should include a comprehensive setting that disables tracking.
- All settings in software and devices must by default have the more privacy-friendly variant set up: **Privacy-by-Default**

The following are part of privacy **on the Internet:**

- simple measures, such as **secure passwords** and careful browser settings
- use of **encryption programs**
- The Telecommunications-Telemedia-Data Protection Act (TTDSG) and the Federal Data Protection Act set certain requirements for website operators, which are intended to ensure data protection for users

> ▶ There is no comprehensive protection. Data krakens and hackers always open up new possibilities.

To bridge the gap, the Telecommunications-Telemedia-Data Protection Act**Telecommunications-Telemedia-Data Protection Act (TTDSG)** (TTDSG) was initiated in Germany. With this law, the provisions on telecommunications secrecy and data protection previously contained in the **Telecommunications Act** (TKG) and the provisions contained in the **Telemedia Act (TMG)** are combined in a new parent law. In particular, **Over-the-Top services** (OTT services) such as Internet telephony, web-based email services and messengers are to be taken into account:

- The scope of application for employers as providers of telecommunications services with permitted private use is regulated. Companies that allow their employees to use email and the Internet privately at work fall under general data protection law (EU GDPR).
- Also regulated is the storage of information in the end user's terminal equipment or access to information already stored in the terminal equipment, such as cookies, browser fingerprinting, smartphone applications, etc.

▶ The **TTDSG** applies regardless of the personal reference of the information processed in this context.

3.2.4 Personal Data

Article 4 of the GDPR defines personal data as follows:

▶ **Personal Data**

- all information relating to an **identified** or **identifiable natural** person ("data subject");
- a natural person is considered **identifiable** if they can be identified, **directly** or **indirectly,** in particular by **association with an identifier** such as a name, an identification number, location data, an online identifier or **one or more special characteristics,** which are an expression of the physical, physiological, genetic, mental, economic, cultural or social identity of this natural person.

Examples of attributes for identifying natural persons are listed in the standard for privacy frameworks (ISO/IEC 29100) [ISO29100]: age and infirmities, allegations of criminal behavior, bank account, credit card number, date of birth, medical diagnoses, gender, GPS location, GPS trajectories, home address, IP address, name, personalized email address, ethnic origin, union membership, photo, telephone number, …

The second part of Article 4 of the GDPR also defines the term "processing":

▶ **Processing:** is any operation or set of operations which is performed on personal data or on sets of personal data, whether or not by automated means, such as collection, recording, organization, structuring, storage, adaptation or alteration, retrieval, consultation, use, disclosure by transmission, dissemination or otherwise making available, alignment or combination, restriction, erasure or destruction.

Further definitions follow: restriction of processing, **profiling**, **pseudonymization**, filing system, controller, processor, recipient, third party, consent, breach of personal data protection, genetic data, **biometric data,** health system and others.

In Article 9, the term ***special category of personal data*** is introduced. The BDSG n.F. (see §46 (14)) defines this in the same way:

▶ **Special categories of personal data:** Personal data revealing racial or ethnic origin, political opinions, religious or philosophical beliefs, or trade union membership, and the processing of genetic data, biometric data.

Both the GDPR and the BDSG require special legal templates for the permission to process these special categories. For this purpose, explicit consent, the necessity for the exercise of rights of the data subject or the controller, the protection of vital interests and others can be used. The BDSG (§48) also requires specific requirements for data security or data protection control, the sensitization of those involved in the processing operations, restriction of access etc.

▶ Special care must be taken when processing special categories of personal data.

3.2.5 Legality of Processing

Contrary to the general legal situation (*"What is not forbidden is allowed"*), it is the opposite with data protection. The **presumption of prohibition** applies. Before processing personal data, the legality of the processing must be ensured. Article 6 of the EU-GDPR accordingly provides possible **permission facts.** At least one of the following conditions must be met:

- The data subject has given their **consent** to the processing of their personal data for one or more specific **purposes;**
- the processing is necessary for the **performance of a contract,** of which the data subject is a party, or to carry out pre-contractual measures that are carried out at the request of the data subject;
- the processing is necessary to fulfill a legal **obligation** to which the controller is subject;
- the processing is necessary to protect the vital **interests** of the data subject or another natural person;
- the processing is necessary for the performance of a task carried out in the public **interest** or in the exercise of official authority vested in the controller;
- the processing is necessary for the protection of the legitimate **interests** of the controller or a third party, unless the interests or fundamental rights and freedoms of the data subject requiring the protection of personal data **prevail,** especially when the data subject is a child.

Further permission facts can be determined by national specific regulations. To a certain extent, the purpose determination can be seen as a certain softener. Thus, processing is also allowed if the purpose is compatible with the one for which the personal data were originally collected.

Example

An engineering service provider regularly informs via newsletter about engineering services in the field of functional safety. If new services, such as in the field of information security, are offered, they may be advertised in the same newsletter. However, the newsletter may not inform if the engineering service provider suddenly plans to sell washing machines. This (new) purpose cannot be reconciled with the previous one. ◀

What remains is the difficult balancing act in individual cases between the protection of legitimate interests of the controller and the interests or fundamental rights/freedoms of the data subject, which require the protection of personal data. Here, a judge may be the only one who can provide clarity with a corresponding judgment. This then gives an answer as to whether the processing is allowed or prohibited.

For processing to be legally permissible, at least one of the possible permission facts must apply. It also applies that a single applicable permission fact legitimizes the processing. This implies:

- If you are asked to sign a consent form, you can assume that it concerns purposes of processing personal data that are not already covered by other permission facts. So, you should check very carefully what it is about.
- If you have given a consent form and revoke it, this does not automatically mean that no personal data may be processed anymore. Only when no other permission fact applies anymore, the processing must be stopped.
- It makes no sense to always get additional consent for supposedly double security (see the first two notes).
- It makes no sense to offer a right of withdrawal while at the same time pointing out that the processing according to Article 6 is legal anyway. If the latter is true, a revocation automatically falls flat.

3.3 Important Articles of the EU-GDPR

The following subsections contain a selection of articles of the GDPR [GDPR]. The listings are not always complete or conclusive, but are intended to provide a basic understanding of the content.

- Processing: When may processing take place? Sect. 3.3.1
- Consent: What requirements apply to valid consents? Sect. 3.3.2
- Security: What security must be ensured? Sect. 3.3.3
- Rights of the data subjects: What rights must be granted to a data subject? Sect. 3.3.4
- Data protection impact assessment: How is it assessed whether procedures may be used? Sect. 3.3.5
- Fines: What parameters play a role in the amount of the fine? Sect. 3.3.6.

3.3.1 Principles for the processing of personal data

In Article 5 the **principles for processing of personal data** are stated:

- **Lawfulness, processing in good faith, transparency:** As described in Sect. 3.2.5, a permission fact must exist in order to be able to process personal data.
- **Purpose limitation:** There must be defined, clear and legitimate purposes. Personal data may not be further processed in a manner incompatible with this purpose (exceptions such as research/statistics see EU GDPR).
- **Data minimization:** Limit to measures appropriate and significant for the purposes of processing. Example: in an employee master data sheet of an engineering service provider, only personality traits that are relevant to the company may be processed. Hair and eye color are not, in a modeling agency, however, they are.
- **Accuracy:** Personal data must be factually correct and, if necessary, up to date. Incorrect personal data must be deleted or corrected immediately.
- **Storage limitation:** Personal data may be stored in a form that allows the identification of the data subjects only as long as necessary for the purposes for which they are processed. Beyond that, only a legal retention period can lead to data being stored. If the legal retention period expires, the data must be deleted.
- **Integrity and confidentiality:** Adequate security of personal data must be ensured including protection against unauthorized or unlawful processing. The same applies to accidental loss, destruction etc. This is achieved by appropriate technical and organizational measures.

A controller/processor has the accountability to demonstrate compliance with the principles.

In the BDSG n. F. §64, further principles are found (formerly §9 of the old BDSG [BDSG03] and the annex on technical and organizational measures (TOMs)):

- Denial of **access** to processing facilities, with which the processing is carried out for unauthorized persons (**access control**),
- Prevention of **unauthorized reading,** copying, modifying or deleting of data carriers (**data carrier control**),
- Prevention of **unauthorized input** of personal data as well as unauthorized knowledge, modification and deletion of stored personal data (**storage control**),
- Prevention of **use** of automated processing systems with the help of facilities for data transmission by unauthorized persons (**user control**),
- Ensuring that those authorized to use an automated processing system have permission to access only to the personal data covered by their **access authorization (permission to access control)**,

- Ensuring that it can be checked and determined to which places personal data have been transmitted or made available with the help of **data transmission** facilities or can be (**transmission control**),
- Ensuring that it can be checked and determined retrospectively which personal data have been **entered** into automated processing systems or modified by whom and when (**input control**),
- Ensuring that during the **transmission** of personal data and the transport of data carriers, the confidentiality and integrity of the data are protected (**transport control**),
- Ensuring that systems used can be restored in case of a malfunction (**recoverability**),
- Ensuring that all functions of the system are **available** and occurring malfunctions are reported (**reliability**),
- Ensuring that personal data being **processed on behalf** can only be processed according to the instructions of the client (**order control**),
- Ensuring that personal data are protected against **destruction** or loss (**availability control**),
- Ensuring that personal data collected for different purposes can be **separated** processed (**separability**)

Conclusion

When processing personal data (e.g., in a development project or organizational unit of a company), the above-mentioned principles for processing must be observed in detail.

3.3.2 Conditions for Consent

Consents must:

- **be verifiable** (the affected person has consented to the corresponding use)
- **be understandable** (easily accessible in a clear simple language; clearly separable from other matters)
- **be revocable at any time** (the affected person must be able to revoke as easily as they have consented)
- **be voluntary** (processing of the data must be necessary for the fulfillment of the contract)

3.3.3 Security of Processing

Article 32 sets requirements for the security. Accordingly, the following points must be considered by processors and controllers (see Sect. 2.3):

- **State of the art:** The EU-GDPR does not specify any specific techniques, one has to orient oneself to the state of the art.
- **Implementation costs:** They must be proportional and appropriate to the data to be protected—similar to the jeweler in the city who will install a more expensive alarm system, compared to the vegetable dealer next door.
- **Type and scope:** How many and which personal data are needed?
- **Circumstances and purposes:** Not every purpose must be secured with equally strong measures. Depending on the circumstance and purpose, milder means are allowed.
- **Likelihood of occurrence** and **severity of the risk** for the rights and freedoms of natural persons.

Based on the evaluation, technical and organizational measures are taken to ensure a appropriate **level of protection:**

- **Pseudonymization** and **Encryption**
- **Confidentiality, Integrity, Availability** and **Resilience** of the systems ensure in the long term
- **Availability** and **Access** quickly restore after physical or technical incident
- Regular **Review,** assessment and evaluation of the **Effectiveness** to ensure the security of processing

In assessing the appropriate level of protection, particular consideration should be given to risks associated with processing. Risks can be: accidental or unlawful destruction, loss, alteration, unauthorized disclosure, unauthorized access during their processing, such as transmission or storage.

▶ The processor and the client ensure that personal data are processed only on the instruction of the controller.

3.3.4 Rights of the Data Subject

An important aspect of data protection is the granting of specific rights to data subjects in the processing of their personal data. These are mentioned in various articles of the EU-GDPR. Examples include:

- **Compensation:** A person, who has suffered material or immaterial damage as a result of a violation of the EU-GDPR, has a claim for compensation against the controller or the processor.

- The controller must take appropriate measures to provide the affected person with all **information** relating to the processing in a precise, transparent, understandable and easily accessible form in clear and simple language.
- **Duty to Inform** when collecting personal data **from the** data subject. The controller must provide information (contact details, purpose of processing, possible legitimate interest, recipients or categories of recipients, duration of storage, existence of the right to information, …) at the time of collection.
- **Duty to Inform** when collecting personal data **not from the** data subject: Essentially the same as when collecting personal data from the data subject, plus the source of the personal data.
- **Right to Access** of the affected person regarding processing purposes, categories of personal data, recipients or categories of recipients, possible duration of storage etc.
- **Right to Rectification:** The affected person has the right to demand the immediate correction of incorrect personal data concerning them from the controller.
- **Right to Erasure** ("Right to be Forgotten"): The affected person has the right to demand that the controller immediately erase personal data concerning them. The controller is obliged to immediately erase personal data for corresponding reasons, e.g. if they are no longer necessary for the purpose, in case of withdrawal of consent (and no other legal basis for processing exists), in case of unlawful processing, …
- **Right to Data Portability:** The affected person has the right to receive the personal data concerning them, which they have provided to a controller, in a structured, commonly used and machine-readable format.
- …

The BDSG n. F. contains further supplementary additions (e.g. appeal to the Federal Commissioner, legal protection, …).

> In case of violation of the protection of personal data, there is a duty to inform the supervisory authority or the affected persons.

3.3.5 Data Protection Impact Assessment

Article 35 describes the so-called Data Protection Impact Assessment (formerly referred to in the BDSG as preliminary control). Controllers—especially when using new technologies—carry out an assessment of the consequences of the intended processing operations for the protection of personal data in advance, due to the nature, scope, circumstances and purposes of the processing, which are likely to pose a high risk to the rights and freedoms of natural persons.

The controller can seek advice from the data protection officer for this purpose. Furthermore, the article specifies special cases in which such a data protection impact assessment must be carried out. These include, among others:

- **systematic** and **comprehensive evaluation** of personal aspects of natural persons, based on automated processing
- extensive processing of **special categories** (see Sect. 3.2.4)
- systematic and extensive monitoring of **publicly accessible areas**

Impact assessments must be documented and are part of the procedures directory. They must contain the following—see also Privacy Risk Model (Sect. 3.5):

- a **systematic description** of the planned processing operations and the purposes of the processing (if applicable, legitimate interests)
- an **assessment** of the **necessity** and **proportionality** of the processing operations in relation to the purpose
- an **assessment** of the **risks** to the rights and freedoms of the affected persons
- the **remedial measures** planned to address the risks, including guarantees, security measures and procedures, through which the protection of personal data is ensured and evidence is provided that this regulation is complied with

3.3.6 General Conditions for the Imposition of Fines

A significant part of the concerns about the introduction of the EU GDPR has been contributed by the threat of potentially high to very high **fines** in case of violation. Article 83 requires the supervisory authorities to ensure that the imposition of fines for violations of the regulation is **effective, proportional** and **deterrent** in each individual case. The following parameters are included in the consideration of the amount:

- **Nature, severity** and **duration** of the violation, taking into account the nature, scope or purpose of the processing in question, as well as the number of people affected by the processing and the extent of the damage they have suffered;
- **Intentionality** or **negligence** of the violation;
- Any **measures taken** by the controller or processor to mitigate the damage suffered by the affected persons;
- **Degree of responsibility** of the controller or processor, taking into account the technical and organizational measures they have taken;
- Any relevant **previous violations** by the controller or processor;
- **Extent of cooperation** with the supervisory authority to remedy the violation and mitigate its possible adverse effects;
- **Categories of personal data** affected by the violation;
- **Manner** in which the violation became **known** to the supervisory authority, in particular whether and to what extent the controller or processor reported the violation;

- Compliance with the measures ordered under Article 58 paragraph 2 **previously** against the controller or processor concerned in relation to the same subject, if such measures were ordered;
- …

Depending on the type of violation (whether "only" obligations are violated or principles and rights of affected persons, unauthorized data transmission, …) fines between 10 and 20 million euros, or 2% and 4% of the total worldwide annual turnover (whichever is higher) are due.

Background Information
On the Internet, the GDPR Enforcement Tracker [GDPR-ET] publicly shows which violations by whom against which articles have so far been punished with what amount of fines.

3.4 Privacy Engineering—Privacy-by-Design

The following sections describe the treatment of the topic **Privacy/Data Protection** in the development of products—**"Privacy Engineering"**—, which process personal data.

Privacy Engineering is a special discipline of Systems Engineering, which focuses on achieving freedom from conditions that can create problems for individuals with unacceptable consequences resulting from the system when it processes personal data.

Systems Engineering and Data Protection are compatible disciplines! Privacy Engineering can help ensure that the relevant data protection principles are applied throughout the system lifecycle to achieve the stakeholders' objectives. Risk management is a key process that enables mission objectives to be achieved while minimizing adverse consequences.

- Section 3.4.1: Privacy Engineering:
- Section 3.4.2: Seven fundamental principles: Privacy-by-Design (PbD)
- Section 3.4.3: Privacy Strategies

3.4.1 Privacy Engineering

Privacy Engineering is addressed in NIST IR 8062 [NIST8062] and ISO/IEC 27550 [ISO27550] and is aimed at all those involved in the development of systems and the assessment of risks.

Privacy Engineering is understood as the discipline of how privacy as a **non-functional requirement in Systems Engineering** can be integrated.

▶ **Privacy Engineering** focuses on providing guidance that can be used to reduce privacy risks and enable organizations to make targeted decisions about resource allocation and the effective implementation of controls in information systems.

The goal:

- Provide an introduction on how Systems Engineering and Risk Management can be used to develop **more trustworthy systems** that include privacy as an integral attribute
- Guide to repeatable and measurable approaches to bridge the gap between privacy principles and their effective implementation in systems

With the development, the aim is to achieve **trustworthiness** by applying **High-Level Privacy Principles** [USD73] (e.g., the **Fair Information Practice Principles** (FIPP) see Chap. 3, as well as Sect. 3.5).

Privacy is seen as a property of a trustworthy System. A **trustworthy system** is a system that, in addition to meeting other critical requirements, meets **specific requirements** …

- for **privacy,**
- for **risks,** that go beyond **unauthorized access** to personal data, identify and address.

The ideal system optimizes benefits for those affected and society, while minimizing disadvantages. Systems Engineering and Risk Management processes integrate multidisciplinary approaches.

To characterize the different focus of privacy and security, here are a few thoughts on the differences:

▶ **Wichtig**

- For privacy and security, a **separate leadership** with unique skills is required.
- A **combined approach** does **not** necessarily mean an **identical** approach.
- **Security** is typically recognized as **one of the FIPPs** (Fair Information Practice Principle).
- There are security issues that have **nothing to do with privacy,** just as there are privacy issues that have **nothing to do with security**.
- The byproduct-**Risk model for Privacy** is conceptually different from the **Security risk model.**

In the security of personal data, security concerns are to be considered for both security and privacy.

Concerns

- **Security concerns** arise from **unauthorized system behavior** and lead to the loss of the classic security properties **Confidentiality, Integrity** and **Availability.**
- **Privacy concerns** arise **as a byproduct** through the authorized processing of personal data and lead to the loss of privacy properties **Predictability, Manageability** and **Disassociability.**

In relation to privacy, negative consequences can arise from the way a system processes personal data:

- Problems that can result from **unauthorized access** to personal data are generally well known (e.g., Identity theft)
- Problems arising from **authorized processing** may be less visible or not as well understood (e.g., discriminatory/stigmatizing effects)

Concerns about privacy and systems can lead to a loss of trust in services that could be beneficial (e.g., democratic institutions: E-Voting).

In information security, the achievement of security objectives/properties; ensuring that only authorized users (confidentiality) have access (availability) to accurate and complete information (integrity) is **threatened by threat scenarios.**

In data protection, data protection properties—developed to enable system designers and engineers to develop information systems that can achieve data protection objectives and support the management of data protection risks—are **threatened by problematic data actions.** (see Sect. 3.5).

3.4.2 Seven fundamental principles: Privacy-by-Design (PbD)

As early as 1973, the first paper on the issue of fair information practices (FIPs) was published [USD73]. It described concerns about the electronic processing of personal data on computers, which opened up a whole new dimension due to the technical progress at that time. Unwanted statistics, access for uninvolved parties, etc. were explained: The use of automated systems for processing personal data and the protection of potential harmful consequences for privacy. The paper was intended to provide initial answers.

> Questions when introducing electronic processing of personal data from a historical perspective:
>
> - What **harmful consequences** can arise from systems for automated processing of personal data?
> - What **security precautions** can work **against** potential **harmful consequences**?

- What **measures** provide **remedy against harmful consequences?**
- What influence do politics and practice have on the issuance and **use of social security numbers?**

The **main dangers** were already seen at that time as:

- **too much** data and
- **too easy** access

The paper can be considered the "cradle" of all subsequent data protection/privacy regulations.

In 2000, there was a letter in the USA to the heads of executive bodies: ***"Managing Information as a Strategic Resource"*** [A-130] which can be seen as a general guideline for planning, controlling and managing information systems, infrastructure and services. The **nine** known ***"Circular A-130-Fair Information Practice Principles (FIPPS)*** " were defined:

- **Access and Modification:** Individuals must be given reasonable access to their personal data, and a reasonable opportunity to correct or modify their data.
- **Accountability:** Someone must be responsible for complying with these principles and applicable data protection requirements, the roles and responsibilities regarding personal data must be clearly defined.
- **Authorization:** Personal data may only be created, collected, used, processed, stored, maintained, disseminated, or disclosed with appropriate authority.
- **Minimization:** Only directly relevant and necessary personal data for a legally authorized purpose may be created, collected, used, processed, stored, maintained, disseminated, or disclosed. The processing may only take place as long as it is necessary to fulfill the purpose.
- **Quality** and **Integrity:** Personal data must be created, collected, used, processed, stored, maintained, disseminated, or disclosed with such accuracy, relevance, timeliness, and completeness as is reasonably necessary to ensure fairness to the individual.
- **Individual Participation:** The affected individual should be involved in the process of using their personal data and, as far as practicable, their consent for the creation, collection, use, processing, storage, maintenance, dissemination, or disclosure should be obtained. Processes to handle complaints and requests from affected individuals must be established.
- **Purpose Specification** and **Use Limitation:** A notice must be given of the specific purpose for which personal data is to be collected, and it may only be used, processed, stored, maintained, disseminated, or disclosed for this purpose, which is explained in the notice.
- **Security:** Administrative, technical, and physical security measures must be introduced to protect personal data, commensurate with the risk and the extent of harm that would result from unauthorized access.

- **Transparency:** The information policy and practices regarding personal data must be made transparent, clear and accessible notices must be given.

These nine principles can be applied to the data protection/privacy objectives/data protection principles (see Fig. 3.1) [NIST8062].

The topic was taken up and further advanced by Ann Cavoukian (Canadian privacy advocate) with much commitment and corresponding publications and the foundational definition of the seven **"fundamental principles"** [Cav10]. The universal principles of the **Fair Information Practices** (**FIPs**) are affirmed by Privacy-by-Design, but these go beyond to strive for the highest possible global standard and set the bar significantly higher in the area of data protection:

1. **Proactive** instead of reactive; **preventive** instead of remedial
   - These measures anticipate and prevent privacy-infringing events before they occur. It does not wait for privacy risks to materialize—the goal is to prevent violations before they occur.
   - **FIPs:** Clear commitment and obligation to data protection at the highest level; Establishing methods to discover and anticipate poor data protection design and correct negative impacts before they occur.
2. Data protection as a **default setting**

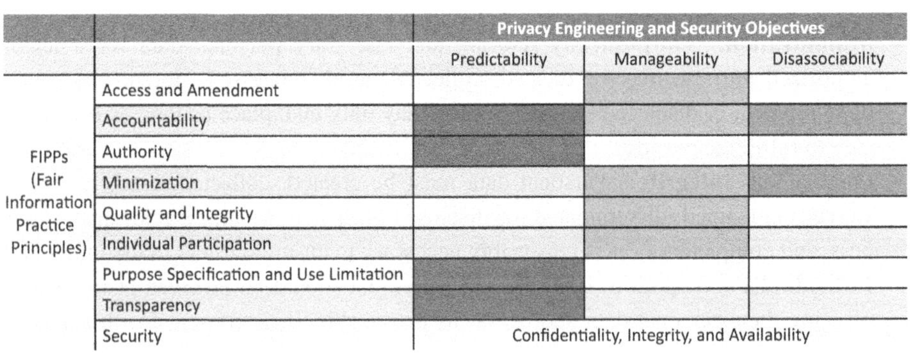

Fig. 3.1 Mapping of the FIPPs to data protection objectives and security objectives

  - These methods aim to ensure the highest level of data protection by ensuring that personal data in a specific IT system or business practice is automatically protected. The individual user should not have to do anything to protect their privacy—it should be automatically built into the system—by default.
  - **FIPs:** Purpose specification, collection limitation, data minimization (scope and linkability), use, storage and disclosure limitation
3. Data protection **embedded** in the design
  - These measures embed the data protection requirements into the design and architecture of IT systems and business practices. They are not added afterwards as add-ons. Data protection should be an integral part of the core functionality provided.
  - **FIPs:** Application of data protection standards and frameworks, strict application of Fair Information Practices, conducting risk and impact analyses, minimizing data protection consequences.
4. **Full functionality:** Positive-sum, not zero-sum
  - These measures attempt to accommodate legitimate interests and objectives in a positive-sum, "win-win" manner, not through a zero-sum approach (win/lose), where unnecessary compromises are made to protect privacy. The illusion of false dichotomies, such as privacy vs. security must be avoided—It must be shown that it is possible to have both.
  - **FIPs:** Clear documentation of all interests, embedding of data protection without impact on functions.
5. **End-to-end security:** Protection throughout the entire lifecycle
  - Security is key to data protection. These measures ensure comprehensive lifecycle management of information, so that at the end of the process all data is securely and timely destroyed.
  - **FIPs:** Taking responsibility and applying security standards for the entire lifecycle, ensuring confidentiality, integrity and availability, secure disposal, appropriate encryption, strict access controls and logging
6. **Visibility** and **Transparency :** Keep it Open
  - Stakeholders must be able to trust that all business practices and technologies are transparent to the user and operate according to the stated promises and objectives, which must be verified by an independent party. Trust is good, verification is better.
  - **FIPs:** Clear accountability and responsibility for data processing and data protection issues, openness and transparency, compliance, monitoring and review of regulations and policies.
7. **Respect** for the User's privacy: **User-centricity**
  - This method requires architects and operators to put the interests of the individual at the forefront by offering measures such as strong privacy defaults, appropriate notices, and user-friendly options. The implementation must be kept user-centric.
  - This principle goes beyond the FIPs. User interfaces to machines must be human-centric, user-centric, and user-friendly.

– **FIPs:** Consent is obtained, can be withdrawn, accuracy and completeness can be checked by data subjects, access for data subjects is provided.

Privacy-by-Design can be defined as a technical and strategic management approach that is committed to selectively and sustainably minimizing the privacy risks of information systems through technical and governance controls. A holistic approach is crucial for operationalization. The process challenges **programmers** and engineers to think creatively about all the requirements of a system. **Organizational leaders** are challenged to innovate, test, and find out what works best in their specific environment. As in information security, three levels can be distinguished here:

- Policies at the **corporate governance level,**
- **Business processes,** that have requirements and the
- **operational level,** which implements these requirements and functions.

Further publications followed with examples for implementation. For each of the seven fundamental principles, roles and responsibilities at the respective levels as well as implementation examples are described [Cav11].

Real case studies from various application areas are described in a publication on the operationalization of privacy practices [Cav12]. Example areas:

- **Video camera surveillance** in public transport,
- Use of **biometric data** in casinos,
- **Smart Meter/Smart Grid,**
- **Mobile devices** and communication,
- **NFCs** (Near Field Communications),
- **RFIDs,**
- **Geolocation data,**
- **Medical** remote care,
- **Big Data** and data analysis.

For the application examples, a corresponding implementation from a data protection perspective is described under the premise that functionality does not have to be restricted because of data protection. The examples are assigned to the principles used in an appendix, so that examples can be found easily for each principle.

3.4.3 Privacy Strategies

Based on the publications by Ann Cavoukian, the principles were explained in a scientific article on design strategies [Hoe14] and divided into three levels of abstraction:

1. Privacy-**strategies** (principles): abstract concepts without concrete realization (for the concept and analysis phases)
2. Privacy-**patterns:** generic solutions that can be applied directly (for the design phase)
3. Privacy-**Enhancing-Technologies:** Concrete technologies, which are not solution-oriented (for the implementation, see Sect. 3.5)

Example

Privacy-Design-**Strategy:** Personal data is hidden
Privacy-Design-**Pattern:** Confidential communication is applied
Privacy-**Enhancing-Technology:** Symmetric encryption (AES-256) is used ◀

In a publication by ENISA ***"Privacy and Data Protection by Design—from policy to engineering"*** [PDPbD14], the associations of the principles with the publications by Ann Cavoukian are established, as well as with the corresponding articles of the shortly thereafter released EU-GDPR EU-GDPR [EU-GDPR].

ENISA divides Privacy-Design-Strategies into non-disjoint **data-oriented** and **process-oriented** privacy strategies. The origins can be recognized in the partially much older publications described earlier in this section.

The given control examples are examples of Privacy-Enhancing-Technologies (see third level of abstraction defined above), which are classified and described in more detail in Sect. 3.5.

- **Data-oriented** privacy strategies:
  - **Minimize:** select before you collect; **Anonymization** and use of **Pseudonyms:**
    - the amount of personal data processed should be limited to the minimum possible extent.
    - Control example: Selection **before** collection, anonymization
  - **Hide** (Confidentiality): Encryption of data; mixing of networks; decoupling certain related events; **Anonymization; Pseudonyms**
    - all personal data and their relationships should be hidden from the public
    - Control example: Encryption, perturbation, pseudonymization, **Attribute-Based-Credentials**
  - **Separation:** Data processing in a separate manner
    - personal data should be processed distributed, if possible in separate departments
    - Control example: logical or physical separation, endpoint processing
  - **Abstraction:** Aggregation over time; dynamic location granularity; k-Anonymity; l-Diversity; differential privacy; …
    - Personal data should be processed at the highest level of aggregation and with the least possible degree of detail in which they are (still) useful
    - Control example: Aggregation over time, k-Anonymity

- **Process-oriented** privacy strategies:
  - **Inform:** Privacy Preferences Platform P3P; Data Breach Notifications, …
    - Affected individuals should be adequately informed when personal data is processed
    - Control example: Privacy Icons, policies at various levels
  - **Control:** User-centered identity management; End-to-end encryption supports control
    - The control strategy states that the affected individuals should gain control over the processing of their personal data
    - Control example: Privacy dashboard, consent
  - **Enforce:** Access control; (Privacy management); Digital rights management; Licenses
    - There should be a privacy policy in place that is compatible with legal requirements, and it should be enforced. This refers to the principle of accountability
    - Control example: Privacy management system, commitment of resources
  - **Demonstrate:** Privacy management systems; Logs; Audits
    - requires that a data controller is able to demonstrate compliance with the privacy policy and all applicable legal requirements
    - Control example: Logging and audits, privacy impact assessment

An important security value/protection goal for privacy (privacy goal) is the Confidentiality: unauthorized reading of data must be prevented. The confidentiality…

- must be sufficiently considered throughout the **entire development cycle** from the beginning;
- is to be determined both for **process definition** and for **process execution** (and process **end**);
- is usually an **unfamiliar** topic for system engineers;
- is **difficult** to guarantee in dynamic systems;
- is an increasingly **important topic** (even if not all measures (specifically) are legally required)
- is described in the EU General Data Protection Regulation (**GDPR**, (see Sect. 3.2.2)) (e.g., data protection impact assessment, EU data protection seal, technology design, …).

Both, ***"Privacy"*** and ***"Data-Protection"*** (the protection of (personal) data) are central issues for both individuals and social societies. The terms ***"Privacy-by-Design"*** (PbD) and ***"Data-Protection-by-Design"*** (DPbD) encompass the design activities and are seen as central topics.

Legal requirements are usually very general, nevertheless, the requirements for Privacy-by-Design are mostly derived from legal requirements. Privacy-by-Design is not a collection of mature methods and procedures and does not anticipate the implementation of PETs (see next section). Privacy-by-Design is not the same as Security-by-Design.

Conclusion

Privacy-by-Design is the process of several technological and organizational components for implementing confidentiality and data protection principles. Design includes conception, organization, transparency, intervenability, …

3.5 Privacy-Enhancing-Technologies (PET)

The best secret is the one that no one knows.

Privacy-Enhancing-Technologies (PETs) concretize Privacy-by-Design to embed it in the implementation of systems from the beginning. Well-known examples of PETs are encryption, protocols for anonymous communication, attribute-based credentials, …. Not all technologies are already standardized like e.g. encryption techniques. The technologies address both technical solutions and organizational processes.

Data protection-promoting (privacy-friendly) techniques are techniques that promote and enforce data protection in information and communication systems as far as possible, but at least support it.

These have been summarized in a document by ENISA [PDPbD14] (see Sect. 3.4.2). For all the methods mentioned in the following (not exhaustive) list, there are problem descriptions, solution approaches, and proven example techniques for practice, as well as the analysis of associated hazards. Here is a selection:

- **Authentication** (Data protection requirements for authentication protocols)
  - Requirements from a data protection perspective are client-server and end-to-end authentication, identity and access management.
  - Hazards are the recording of passwords, phishing, eavesdropping, …
- **Attribute-based Credentials** (ABC) (anonymous credentials)
  - The best secret is the one that no one knows.
  - Examples: Zero-Knowledge-Protocols, use of one-time credentials, secure container: the content is never shown to others.
- **Secure** private **Communication** (Cryptography between client and server)
  - Examples: Cryptographic methods between client and Server: Public Key Infrastructures (PKI), TLS, SSH, IPSec, VPN, …
  - Cryptographic methods for end-to-end Communication: PGP, S/MIME, OTR, …
  - Key rotation: Diffie Hellmann Key exchange for secure exchange in insecure networks.

- **Anonymity** and **Pseudonymity** in Communication (Metadata, sender and recipient anonymity)
  - Problem: Observation of metadata (sender, recipient, time, volume, duration, location, …) can indicate actual identity.
  - Examples: Contacts of journalists, browsing for sensitive terms, typical times for communications, …
  - Anonymity of sender (e.g., one wants to use a service anonymously) and recipient (service does not want to reveal its origin).
  - Threats:
    - Deletion or injection of messages must be excluded (e.g., election result falsifications)
    - Attackers control anonymous channels, alter, delete, delay messages (Tor?)
  - Countermeasures:
    - "Families", Proxies, VPN, Onion Routing (Tor), mixed networks, Broadcast, …
    - Steganography and Blocking Resistance (e.g., hidden encrypted messages).
- Privacy in **Databases** (Client, Controller, User, Owner)
  - Data protection of the individual regarding his data and the database as a whole: of the affected person, with more than one responsible party, of the user.
  - Threat: Linkage Attacks. Often, one can identify persons with high probability with just a few attributes.
- Technologies for the data protection **of respondents:** Statistical Disclosure Control (SDC)
  - Threats: Disclosure of an attribute (data suggest secret attribute values), Disclosure of an identity (attributes suggest identity).
  - Attack examples:
    - External (for average values there is only one affected person)
    - Internal (there are only two affected persons for one, thus the value of the other is known)
    - Dominance: Dominant (groups) can narrow down others
  - Countermeasures: **S**tatistical **D**isclosure **C**ontrol (**SDC**): Table data protection, database data protection in queries, query restrictions.
  - Danger: Tracker-Attack. Secret agreements to circumvent the past (e.g., several attackers join forces).
- Technologies for **owner** privacy: Privacy-preserving data mining (PPDM)
  - Threat: No potential conclusions at the individual level should be allowed from analysis results (various) databases/rights.
  - Cooperation while maintaining trade secrets (millionaire's problem).
  - Countermeasures: Data and knowledge are hidden.
- Technologies for the privacy of **users:** Private Information Retrieval (PIR)
  - User wants to query data about the i-th component (similar to search engine queries) without the database becoming aware of i.

- Problems:
  - Obfuscation costs O(n) time at maximum privacy
  - Unattractive for database operators, as no profiling is possible anymore
- Attempts at solutions: Standalone relaxations (e.g., masking, fake terms)/Multi-party relaxations (e.g., anonymous routing).

- **Storage** privacy (Access control, cryptography, security, …).
  - Only the responsible party (authorized) can read their data.
  - Solutions: Authentication, access control, encryption (FDE, FSE), format-preserving encryption (FPE, e.g., credit card numbers into other credit card numbers), steganographic storage, search in encrypted data, …
- Privacy-**preserving computations**
  - Homomorphic encryption: **P**rivacy **H**omomorphisms (**PH**), partially homomorphic (e.g., **RSA**); **F** ull **H**omomorphic **E**ncryption (**FHE**); **S** omewhat **H**omomorphic **E**ncryption (**SHE**), …
  - Secure Multi-Party Computation. Used in smart meters, cloud storage, …
  - Further solution approaches:
    - Oblivious transfer (concealing of metadata)
    - Secret Sharing & **V**erifiable **S**ecret **S**haring (**VSS**): The secret is distributed, can only be reconstructed when enough parties come together. Used in smart meter applications, online auctions, password safes, …
- **Transparency-enhancing** techniques/Transparency tools
  - Affected individuals should understand which data about them are stored and how they are used. Properties of Transparency-Enhancing-Techniques:
    - Provision of information about intended processing of data relevant to data protection and associated risks
    - Overview of which data relevant to data protection the affected person has published at which places under which policies
    - Supports the user in counter-profiling when evaluating his data; provides online access to data and to exercise data protection rights
  - Tools and processes necessary.
  - Seals and logos.
- **Intervenability**-improving Techniques
  - Possibilities to intervene by users; control of responsible bodies, preservation of the exercise of user rights.

3.6 Privacy Risk Model

Privacy-by-Design is conceived as a process (see Sect. 3.4.1). For risk analysis, for example, the so-called privacy risk analysis is suitable (**P**rivacy **I**mpact **A**nalysis (**PIA**)). ISO/IEC 29134 [ISO29134] contains corresponding evaluation tables for impacts and general threats. The standard also specifies which options are available for dealing with identified risks. The same four options as for information security (Chap. 7) are given.

3.6.1 Privacy Risk Analysis

A risk analysis for privacy can be carried out in the following steps.

1. **Identification of stakeholders**/environment
2. **Identification of risks/Expectation** of stakeholders
3. **Identification of solutions**/recommendations
4. **Implementation** of recommendations
5. **Reviews,** audits, measures

Privacy-by-Design is an iterative continuous process at various levels. **Specific privacy risk analyses** are **necessary.**

Damages to individuals (not to system owners) resulting from **problematic data actions** can be divided into four categories:

- **Economic loss:** The direct financial loss as a result of identity theft, or due to the failure to receive fair value in a transaction with personal information.
- **Discrimination:** The unfair or unequal treatment of individuals. This includes the damages of stigmatization and power imbalance.
- **Loss of trust:** The violation of implicit or explicit expectations or agreements about the handling of personal information.
- **Loss** of **self-determination:** The loss of personal sovereignty or the ability of a person to make free decisions. This includes the damages of loss of autonomy, exclusion, loss of freedom, and physical harm.

The NIST IR 8062 (2017) [NIST8062] picks up the **nine** known ***"Circular A-130-Fair Information Practice Principles"*** [A-130] (2000).

The standard introduces the **privacy risk model** and provides guidance on how privacy risk management can be conducted.

Risk Concepts:

- **Risk (Privacy Risk)** is a measure of the extent to which a company is threatened by a potential circumstance or event, and is typically a function of the following risk criteria:
  I. the **adverse effects,** that would arise if the circumstance or event occurs, and
  II. the **frequency of occurrence** (engl. likelihood) as **probability of occurrence** (engl. probability) that a data action becomes problematic.
- The process by which risks are identified is referred to as a **risk assessment**.
- Risk assessments require a **risk model** to define the risk factors to be assessed and the relationships between these factors.

The **security risk factors** include threats against the system and the vulnerabilities that can be exploited by these threats.

Problematic data actions occur when the data actions of an information system contradict the privacy objectives: the **predictability, manageability** and **disassociability:**

> **Problematic Data Actions**
> - **Unexpected Disclosure:** The non-contextual use of data reveals a person or facets of a person in an unexpected way.
> - **Distortion:** The use or dissemination of inaccurate or misleadingly incomplete personal data.
> - **Unauthorized Restriction:** The improper denial of access or loss of rights to personal information.
> - **Surveillance:** Tracking or monitoring of personal data that is disproportionate to the purpose or outcome of the service.
> - **Use:** Personal data is used in a way that exceeds a person's expectations or permissions.
> - **Induced Disclosure:** Pressure to disclose personal information.
> - **Insecurity:** Gaps in data security.

The **risk factors** for the privacy risk model are:

- **Problematic data actions** play the same role in the security risk model as threats to information security
- **Extent/Impact,** for which systems and processes are susceptible to problematic data actions
- **Frequency of occurrence** of a problematic data action

Key features that can facilitate the determination of the frequency of occurrence and the impacts of problematic data actions:

- **Data actions:** any system operation that processes personal data: collection, storage, logging, analysis, conversion, merging, disclosure, disposal, …
  - Identification of system discrete data actions and subsequent determination of which of these data actions could be problematic
- **Personal data:** Information that can be used to distinguish or trace a person's identity, either alone or in combination with other information that is linked or can be linked to a specific person
- **Context:** the circumstances surrounding the processing of personal data by the system
  - Basis for the interpretative analysis that is necessary to understand when a privacy boundary has been crossed

3.6.2 Privacy Threat Modeling: LINDDUN

In information security, a well-known threat modeling is the STRIDE model [STRIDE02] (see Sect. 7.7). Analogously, for data protection threat modeling, there is the LINDDUN model [LINDDUN]. As with STRIDE, the name is derived from the initial letters of the threats. It is a systematic threat analysis method. Inspired by the STRIDE model, it can be used for technical data protection impact assessment. It assists in identifying and mitigating data protection threats in software systems at an early stage in the development lifecycle.

From the data protection properties, one can derive the corresponding data protection threats (see Table 3.2).

Examples of data protection threats:

- **Identifiability, Linkability:** Being able to sufficiently identify the subject within a set of subjects (i.e., the anonymity set).

Table 3.2 Data protection properties—Data protection threats

Type	Data protection property	Description	Data protection threat
Hard Privacy	Disassociability	Hiding the connection between two or more actions	Linkability
	Anonymity	Hiding the connection between an identity and an action or identifiability	Identifiability
	Plausible Repudiation	Ability to deny having performed an action that other parties can neither confirm nor refute	Non-repudiation
	Undetectability and Unobservability	Hiding the user's activities	Detectability
Security	Confidentiality	Hiding the content of data or controlled release of data content	Disclosure of Information of Information)
Soft Privacy	Knowledge about the content	User's knowledge of his own data	Unawareness
	Compliance with policies and consents	The data controller must inform the affected person about the system's data protection policies or give the affected person the opportunity to give their consent in accordance with legal provisions	Non-compliance

  - Data elements/properties can be linked with a certain probability to the identity of the data subject.
- **Linkability:** Being able to sufficiently distinguish whether two IoI (Items of Interest) are linked or not, even without knowing the actual identity of the subject of the linkable IoI.
  - Data elements can be linked because they belong to the same data subject with a certain probability.
    - Data elements/subjects can be linked because they have the same property.
    - e.g., people living in the same neighborhood.
- **Non-repudiation:** An affected person cannot deny that they know, did, or said something:
  - There is evidence that can link the data subject to a specific action.
  - Threats of identifiability (and linkability) increase the risk of non-repudiation.
  - Security property vs. privacy threat
    - Important e.g., for a election system or a whistleblower platform
- **Detectability:** Being able to sufficiently distinguish whether an Item of Interest (IoI) exists or not.
  - Without having access to the data, the threat actor knows they exist. The presence of data is enough to infer further (sensitive) information (similar to a side-channel attack in information security).
- **Disclosure of Information:** Sharing information with people who are not authorized to see it.
  - The disclosure of information is actually a security category borrowed from STRIDE. Since privacy largely depends on security, a security evaluation of the system is necessary anyway.
  - Therefore, "Disclosure of Information" is often omitted.
- **Ignorance:** An affected person has no knowledge of the collection and further processing of their personal data or is not able to intervene.
  - Ignorance refers to the rights of the affected person and therefore focuses on the dangers of transparency (or predictability) and the possibility of intervention (or manageability).
- **Non-compliance:** The system is not compliant with data protection, the user's rights are unknown or principles are not implemented.

The LINDDUN data protection engineering framework proposes the following phases for risk management:

1. **System Modeling:** Creation of data flows, description of all data
2. **Identifying Threats:** Mapping threats to data flow diagrams
3. **Threat Identification** (e.g., using attack trees)
   - Support: Mapping tables, LINDDUN threat taxonomy
4. **Threat Treatment:** Prioritization in discussion with the data protection officer

Table 3.3 Mindsets for Security and Data Protection/Privacy

	Information Security (Security)	**Data Protection (Privacy)**
Protects …	Data	Personal data
Value to be protected …	Organization, Information	Affected person
Threatened by …	External attackers	External attackers and internal misconduct
Goal	Prevention of (unauthorized) access to data	Limiting the consequences of what can be done with personal data once access exists

5. **Identifying Avoidance Measures**
6. **Risk Reduction Measures** selection according to the taxonomy of Privacy-Enhancing-Technologies
   - Support: Taxonomy of risk reduction measures, classification of data protection solutions

As with STRIDE, various methods can be used for risk assessment. There is a mapping of data protection objectives and Privacy-Enhancing-Technologies [LINDDUN].

Threat modeling for security and data protection/privacy requires a different mindset (see Table 3.3).

The risk value determination (value or level) can be done with similar known models. For example, using a cross table with the dimensions severity of impact and attack feasibility e.g. **ISO/SAE 21434** [ISO21434].

3.7 Data Protection Framework

The ISO/IEC 29100 [ISO29100] describes principles for a Data Protection Framework/ Framework:

- **Consent** and **Choice:** Information of the affected persons, presentation of the available choices, and obtaining consent.
- **Purpose legitimacy** and **Specification:** Ensuring compliance with data protection laws and informing the affected persons.
- **Collection limitation:** Limiting the collection of personal data to what is within the scope of applicable law and absolutely necessary for the stated purpose(s).
- **Data minimization:** Amount of collected personal data, number of actors who have access, default options that do not infringe on privacy, deletion of data when no longer necessary.
- **Limitation** of use, retention, and disclosure: Limiting the use, retention, and disclosure of personal data to what is necessary for the purpose.

- **Accuracy** and **Quality:** Ensuring that the data is correct, current, appropriate, and relevant. Regular review and control.
- **Openness, Transparency** and **Notification:** Informing the affected persons about the data controller's policies, providing appropriate notices, …
- **Individual participation** and **Access:** Giving the affected persons a real opportunity to access and review their personal data.
- **Accountability:** Documentation of policies, procedures, and practices, The duty to implement data protection policies is assigned, …
- **Information security:** Achieving an appropriate level of security and implementing the right controls based on an appropriate risk assessment.
- Data protection-**Compliance:** Review and proof that the IT systems comply with legal requirements and have appropriate internal controls and monitoring …

These principles align with those already known from the previous sections and can be mapped onto the described Fundamental Principles and Fair Information Practices.

Examples of reference models for implementing a data protection framework are OASIS and PRIPARE:

- **OASIS** (Organization for the Advancement of Structured Information Standards)/Privacy Management Reference Model and Methodology (PMRM) [OASIS]
  - The reference model is intended to serve as a guide or template for the development of operational solutions for data protection issues, as an analysis tool for assessing the completeness of proposed solutions, and as a basis for defining categories and groupings of data protection management controls. For this, there is a step-by-step guide.
- **PRIPARE** (PReparing Industry to Privacy-by-design by supporting its Application in Research) [PRIPARE]
  - The PRIPARE methodology covers the entire lifecycle of both the system (before its introduction to its decommissioning) and the personal data (from planning its collection to its disposal). The structure of the PRIPARE methodology was designed to align with common technical practices and can be easily merged. 24 processes are divided into 8 meaningful and recognizable phases (from analysis, design, and implementation to disposal).

3.8 Summary

While Privacy-by-Design (see Sect. 3.5) describes the "what", Privacy Engineering explains the "how".

The essential touchpoints of privacy, in relation to information security (Security), are:

- **Divergent** (additional) **protection goals** (data protection/privacy objectives: predictability, manageability, and disassociability), which cannot be derived from the classic protection goals (confidentiality, integrity, and availability) alone.
- **Information security** can be seen as a **subset of data protection** (personal data must also be protected in terms of information). However, protecting personal data (and thus affected individuals) in the sense of information security is not sufficient from a data protection perspective.
- For privacy, it is not the storage of personal data as such that is problematic (this part of data security is covered by the protection goals of information security), but the processing (reading, merging, matching, transmitting, evaluating, …). See **problematic data actions** (see Sect. 3.5).
- **Different data sources**—with various attributes—can be linked to gain new information for purposes that were not previously specified (and possibly not even contemplated) were linked.
- Privacy—the processing of personal data—is **legally regulated.** It is not just about conformity to standards. High penalties are intended to deter and lead to higher compliance.
- Privacy is **very differently** pronounced country-specifically. Somewhere between the total control of the Communist Party in China and the data exploitation of Californian digital capitalism is Europe with its EU GDPR.
- Due to the **regionally** very different laws, the data protection legal assessment in individual cases becomes arbitrarily complicated.
  - Social plugins that are integrated into websites in such a way that when they are called up, data from website visitors is transmitted directly from the user's browser to social networks in third countries, can already be seen as a data transmission from the website owners to the social network. Using the data of website visitors for advertising purposes without their consent is viewed very critically from a legal perspective [Sch16]. Remember: IP addresses are personal data according to the corresponding court ruling.
- Complex situations with multiple stakeholders, **different roles** with opposing motivations must be analyzed very precisely. As an example, the complex data structure from the automotive sector is shown in Fig. 3.2 [SeDaFa18].
- Implemented **protection measures** must be **adequate** and **proportional.** This means that there are no milder means with the same effect. This assessment is particularly important when evaluating systematic surveillance.
  - Video surveillance may be allowed at a gas station because it is appropriate and proportional (no simple milder means with the same effectiveness known). Video surveillance in the refrigerator of a communal kitchen is much more difficult to justify.
  - Illegally obtained evidence (e.g., unlawfully created surveillance videos) can lead to a ban on the use of evidence. If the surveillance itself was allowed, but only the notice of video surveillance was missing, the ban only affects the collection of evidence, not the use of evidence.

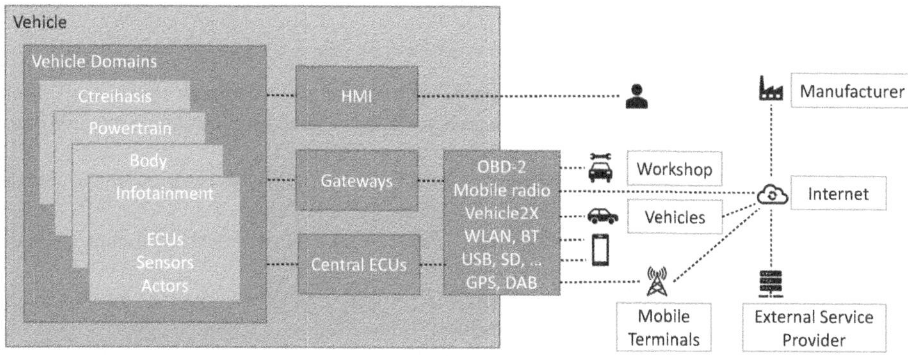

Fig. 3.2 Overview of various stakeholders and data categories

For all the principles of the **FIPPs** (Sect. 3.4.1), corresponding articles can be found in the currently valid EU GDPR [EU-GDPR], which shows their relevance and significance.

Two essential Fair Information Practices Principles (FIPPs), which accurately characterize the nature of data protection, are:

- **Purpose specification** (clear indications why an organization must collect personal data)
- **Usage restrictions** (use of the collected data only for the specified main purpose)

Privacy-by-Design (see Sect. 3.5)...

- is an approach to projects that promotes compliance with privacy and data protection from the outset,
- minimizes privacy risks, builds trust, and supports compliance with laws,
- may not cover all privacy risks,
- can be used in existing frameworks for operational implementation (also see PETs) (see Sect. 3.5).

Privacy Engineering is an emerging technical discipline for the operational implementation of Privacy-by-Design.

The **privacy risk** is the product of the frequency of problematic data actions and the associated damage to privacy (see Sect. 3.5). Both unauthorized and authorized accesses must be considered (see Sect. 3.4.1; keyword: linkability).

Privacy-Enhancing-Technologies (PETs) can be used as controls to address some of these risks.

References

[A-130] ***„Circular A-130 Managing Information as a Strategic Resource".*** Link: https://obamawhitehouse.archives.gov/sites/default/files/omb/assets/OMB/circulars/a130/a130revised.pdf accessed: 23.04.2021

[BDSG01] ***„Bundesdatenschutzgesetz 2001".*** Link: https://www.datenschutz-wiki.de/BDSG_2001 accessed: 14.04.2021

[BDSG03] ***„Bundesdatenschutzgesetz 2003".*** Link: https://www.datenschutz-wiki.de/BDSG_2003 accessed: 14.04.2021

[BDSG18] ***„Bundesdatenschutzgesetz (n.F.)".*** Link: https://www.gesetze-im-internet.de/bdsg_2018/BDSG.pdf accessed: 14.04.2021

[BDSG90] ***„Bundesdatenschutzgesetz 1990".*** Link: https://www.datenschutz-wiki.de/BDSG_1990 accessed: 14.04.2021

[Cav10] ***„Privacy-by-Design – The 7 Foundational Principles – Implementation and Mapping of Fair Information Practices";*** Ann Cavoukian. Published, May 2010. Link: https://www.ipc.on.ca/wp-content/uploads/resources/pbd-implement-7found-principles.pdf accessed: 10.04.2021

[Cav11] ***„Privacy-by-Design – The 7 Foundational Principles",*** Ann Cavoukian, published January 2011 by the Information and Privacy Commissioner of Ontario. Link: https://www.ipc.on.ca/wp-content/uploads/Resources/7foundationalprinciples.pdf accessed: 17.04.2021

[Cav12] ***„Operationalizing Privacy-by-Design: A Guide to Implementing Strong Privacy Practices"***; Ann Covukian, Information and Privacy Commissioner, Ontario, Canada. Published December 2012. Link: https://www.schwaab.ch/wp-content/uploads/2013/09/operationalizing-pbd-guide.pdf accessed: 17.04.2021

[CCPA18] ***„California Consumer Privacy Act of 2018".*** Link: https://oag.ca.gov/privacy/ccpa accessed: 14.04.2021

[DSB13] ***„Bußgeld für offenen E-Mail-Verteiler mit vielen Empfängern";*** Datenschutzbeauftragter INFO, 04. Juli 2013. Link: https://www.datenschutzbeauftragter-info.de/bussgeld-fuer-offenen-e-mail-verteiler-mit-vielen-empfaengern/ accessed: 14.04.2021

[EU-GDPR] General Data Protection Regulation; (EU) 2016/679; Link: https://eur-lex.europa.eu/legal-content/EN/TXT/?uri=CELEX%3A32016R0679; accessed: 10.04.2021

[EU-DSRiLi95] ***„EU-Datenschutzrichtlinie";*** Richtlinie 95/46EG. Link: https://eur-lex.europa.eu/legal-content/DE/TXT/PDF/?uri=CELEX:31995L0046&from=DE accessed: 14.04.2021

[EU-DSAnpUG] ***„Datenschutz-Anpassungs- und –Umsetzungsgesetz EU-DSAnpUG";*** Gesetzesentwurf Drucksache 110/17 02.02.2017. Link: http://www.bundesrat.de/SharedDocs/drucksachen/2017/0101-0200/110-17.pdf?__blob=publicationFile&v=5 accessed: 14.04.2021

[EU-ePrRiLi] ***„Datenschutzrichtlinie für elektronische Kommunikation"***; 2002/58/EG; 12. Juli 2002. Link: https://eur-lex.europa.eu/legal-content/de/ALL/?uri=CELEX%3A32002L0058 accessed: 25.04.2021

[EU-ePrV21] ***„Entwurf einer Verordnung über die Achtung des Privatlebens und den Schutz personenbezogener Daten in der elektronischen Kommunikation"***; 6087/21. Link: https://data.consilium.europa.eu/doc/document/ST-6087-2021-INIT/en/pdf accessed: 14.04.2021

[GDPR-ET] ***„GDPR Enforcement Tracker".*** Link: https://www.enforcementtracker.com/ accessed: 23.04.2021

[Hoe14] ***„Privacy Design Strategies";*** Jaap-Henk Hoepmann, 29th IFIP TC 11 International Conference, SEC 2014 Marrakech, Marocoo, June 2–4, 2014 Proceedings p446–459.

[ISO21434] ***„Road Vehicles – Cybersecurity Engineering",*** International Standard ISO/SAE 21434:2021

[ISO27550] ***„Information technology — Security techniques — Privacy engineering for system life cycle processes",*** ISO/IEC TR 27550

[ISO29100] ***„Information Technology – Security techniques – Privacy framework;*** ISO/IEC 29100:2011(E); First edition 2011–12–15.

[ISO29134] ***„Information technology — Security techniques — Guidelines for privacy impact assessment"***; ISO/IEC 29134

[LINDDUN] ***„LINDDUN: a privacy threat analysis framework"***; Link: https://people.cs.kuleuven.be/~kim.wuyts/LINDDUN/LINDDUN.pdf oder https://www.linddun.org/ accessed: 23.04.2021

[NIST8062] ***„An Introduction to Privacy Engineering and Risk Management in Federal Systems",*** Information Security U.S. Department of Commerce. Link: http://nvlpubs.nist.gov/nistpubs/ir/2017/NIST.IR.8062.pdf accessed: 10.04.2021

[OASIS] ***„OASIS".*** Link: https://www.oasis-open.org/committees/tc_home.php?wg_abbrev=pmrm accessed: 23.04.2021

[PDPbD14] ***„Privacy and Data Protection by Design – from policy to engineering"***, EINSA, December 2014 by European Union Agency for Network and Information Security. Link: https://www.enisa.europa.eu/publications/privacy-and-data-protection-by-design accessed: 23.04.2021

[PRIPARE] ***„PRIPARE".*** Link: http://pripareproject.eu/research/ accessed: 23.04.2021

[Sch16] ***„Like Button und Social-Plugins sind rechtswidrig".*** Link: https://allfacebook.de/policy/lg-duesseldorf-like-button-und-social-plugins-sind-rechtswidrig-faq-zum-urteil accessed: 23.04.2021

[SeDaFa18] ***„SeDaFa: Selbstdatenschutz im vernetzten Fahrzeug"***, Fraunhofer SIT; 2018

[SN20] ***„Vier Fragen der Redaktion zur Datenschutz-Grundverordnung an Alexander Roßnagel"***; Springer; 11.08.2020, Teil von Springer Nature 2020, Informatik Spektrum (2020) 43: 319–323

[STRIDE02] ***„The STRIDE Threat Model";*** 2002; https://msdn.microsoft.com/pt-br/windows/desktop/ee823878 accessed: 23.04.2021

[SZ17] ***"Schwerwiegendes Datenleck legt Zehntausende Schuldnerdaten offen"***; Süddeutsche Zeitung, 27.12.2017. Link: https://www.sueddeutsche.de/digital/it-sicherheit-schwerwiegendes-datenleck-legt-zehntausende-schuldnerdaten-offen-1.3805589 accessed: 14.04.2021

[USD73] ***„Records Computers and the rights of Citizens"***; Report of the Secretary's Advisory Committee on Automated Personal Data Systems. U.S. Department of Health, Education & Welfare. July 1973. Link: https://www.justice.gov/opcl/docs/rec-com-rights.pdf accessed: 14.04.2021

Functional Safety (Safety) 4

Ever since humans have introduced technical systems into circulation and accidents occur during their use, attempts have been made to learn from the experiences gained for the development of the next generation of technical systems in order to reduce/avoid accident numbers in the future. In this sense, many Safety standards (Safety hereafter used as **functional safety**) have been written in blood. Accidents and events lead to the improvement and revision of existing rules and standards. If one thinks, for example, of dealing with electricity, a lot of time and experience from past accidents are incorporated into current regulations. The same applies to the development of means of transportation. After accidents, regulations and requirements are regularly tightened. For example, after the Eschede railway accident [Esc98] when maintenance and inspection rules were tightened. Accident investigation and cause research are also a significant contribution to continuously improving safety in the aviation sector [Bäu19].

- The first section (see Sect. 4.1) motivates the concept of functional safety.
- Section 4.2 contains the characteristics of functional safety.
- Section 4.3 explains the interfaces between functional safety and information security.
- A summary is provided in Sect. 4.4 and
- finally, a bibliography.

4.1 Motivation

As an early example of how events, incidents, and accidents have influenced functional safety, here is the description of a spectacular train accident from 1895 at the Montparnasse terminus.

T. Liedtke, *Information Security*, https://doi.org/10.1007/978-3-658-45711-2_4

Background Information

On Tuesday, October 22, 1895, a train from Granville to Paris did not stop at the end of the track as planned, but instead overran the buffer stop, the platform, and broke through the wall of the station building (Fig. 4.1).

The train was a few minutes late when it arrived at the station. The experienced (!) driver drove at an increased speed to make up for the delay. However, the effect of the failing brakes was not enough to sufficiently slow down the heavy train. The stoker and the driver jumped out of the locomotive in time and were thus able to save themselves before the locomotive overran the buffer stop and cross-platform. The locomotive fell onto a square one floor below and narrowly missed a tram. There were five injured among the passengers and the train attendants. A newspaper woman died on the street. The railway company paid for the funeral and a pension for her two children. The driver and the train conductor were taken to court. The driver had to pay a fine and went to jail for two months.

Principles for functional safety that can be derived from this example:

The supreme **protection goal of functional safety** is to protect **the life and limb of people** and not to endanger them more than society accepts through the use of technical systems. The identification, determination, and handling of remaining risks/hazards to life and limb are the focus of applying functional safety/safety standards and regulations. The supposedly remaining residual risk must be **accepted by society** (if possible). Without this acceptance, technical facilities would not be used (although this acceptance can vary for different technical systems):

Fig. 4.1 Train accident at Gare Montparnasse 1895. *Source*: Wikipedia

- The **hazard** of technical systems not only affects their intended users (drivers, passengers, ...), but can also have effects on **uninvolved parties** (e.g., newspaper woman as above), who may not even need to be interested in using them. People living at a railway crossing want to be sure that it works as specified (safely), even if they never travel by train themselves.
- Even **before** the introduction/use of technical systems, one would like to be able to determine as accurately as possible the potential risks and the probability of accidents and their effects. In particular, to be able to determine the efficiency and effectiveness of risk-reducing measures **before** the introduction and use of technical systems, and thus to know the remaining residual risk.
- Not only technical measures (brakes, speed limit), but also organizational measures (e.g., what speed a driver may choose in which situation) and human behavior (stress of the driver) contribute to functional safety.
- How should human error in the use of safety-oriented systems be punished? How do you deal with misconduct that has led to an accident? From misconduct and accidents (e.g., those of a pilot), one can learn to make systems even safer. Automatically punishing them would probably lead to them being covered up and no longer known. In the long run, this would rather harm a society.
- Absolute statistics (e.g., number of accidents per year) reveal that the level of socially accepted residual risks (in the end the "product" of probability and impact of an accident) varies greatly in different domains. If as many deaths per year were counted in road traffic as in train or air traffic, no one would want to use these means of transport anymore. The acceptance of accident numbers is very different for each (technical) domain. Many people are afraid of using an elevator, although it is proven that very rarely (fatal) accidents happen with elevators, and it appears statistically much safer than driving a car.

4.2 Goals—Functional Safety—Characteristics

Better safe than sorry.

Unfortunately, possible measures to simultaneously achieve goals of functional safety and information security/security are not always in the same direction. In some cases, they are even mutually counterproductive.

Example

Open vs. closed doors are often an example of conflicts of objectives between functional safety and security. In the past, the door to an airplane's cockpit was always left open for reasons of functional safety (better possibility of pressure equalization), but a regulation after **Nine-Eleven** [91101] was issued that the cockpit door must be securely locked during flight and can only be opened by the cockpit crew (from the inside). Nearly 14 years later, after a **Germanwings flight disaster** [GW15], the issue of whether the door must remain locked and not be opened by the cabin crew in certain situations was controversially discussed again. Under certain circumstances, there may be situations where it can be sensible (safer) to provide a way for the door to be opened from the cabin. ◀

Further examples:

- Car doors lock automatically when driving off to better protect the car from simple theft at traffic light stops. However, in the event of an accident, car doors should by no means remain locked in order to enable quick, barrier-free rescue.
- Strong encryption of CAN bus messages for braking processes implemented in the vehicle protects against attacks on authenticity and integrity, but can lead to insufficient performance (response times). In a possible emergency braking situation, decryption may not be able to occur quickly enough, so that in this scenario strong encryption could potentially do more harm than good.
- The collection and transmission of unnecessarily many (helpful for rescue?) personal data in the event of an accident [Kau18] can contradict the data protection goal of data minimization (protection needs of those affected).
- Additional security mechanisms and degradation can increase the attack surface and represent attractive targets for hacker attacks (e.g., Denial-of-Service).

In case of doubt, it must be weighed and prioritized how much "Safety" and "Security" measures should be implemented so that the use is safe and necessarily equally "safe" and "secure" in the end. A technical system that has implemented security at the expense of safety would not be socially acceptable, so that safety must always remain the priority in the end.

An important aspect in considering functional safety is the intended use, the foreseeable misuse, and the deliberate abuse of technical products. The fact that one can deliberately drive a car into a crowd with terrible consequences cannot be prevented by functional safety. The difficulty lies in specifying what must still be considered foreseeable misuse (see also Product Safety Act), especially when the lifespan of products is long and the technology around the product is constantly evolving.

The boundaries of Safety and Security must always be re-evaluated event-driven, as the example of an accident of the Bonn tram [ntv19] shows:

Example

The driver of a tram became unconscious during the journey. The passengers noticed this when the tram did not stop at several stops and the driver was not responsive. Even pulling the emergency brake could not stop the tram. Due to regular misuse in the past, it had been adjusted differently. It no longer works in a tunnel and on open track. However, the tram driver receives a signal that it has been triggered. In this case, he could not react due to his unconsciousness. Ultimately, a passenger was able to forcibly open the door to the driver's cab and stop the vehicle under the guidance of the control center. In addition, many barriers at the level crossings remained open, as barriers that are behind stops only close with a delay of about half a minute. As long as the tram is stationary, cars can continue to cross the tracks, the barrier only closes when the tram leaves the stop. ◀

As the example shows, the definition of system boundaries, as well as the capture of all possible situations/scenarios is of utmost importance in order not to fall short with measures and the implementation of technical and organizational rules and not to overlook a later actually (rare, unusual) emerging scenario.

Functional Safety—Characterization

Protection against (unintentional) failure (during **intended use**) with **risk to life and limb** of **persons.**

- Focuses on analyzing the system for potential hazards so that safety mechanisms can be identified and integrated into the design to eliminate the causes of potential hazards and reduce the risk associated with these potential hazards
- Realized **actual functionality corresponds** to the **specified target functionality**
- Functionality is given under all (normal) operating conditions
- **Reliability** is also described with the abbreviation RAMS for Reliability, Availability, Maintainability, Safety
- Absence of (socially) unacceptable risks
- Application of (effective) safety mechanisms demonstrably leads to fewer accidents
- Many proven safety mechanisms are prescribed and required in various standards (top down)
- A system that has once been successfully assessed/certified must not be changed without having to renew the validity of the safety case

Errors must be **avoided, existing** ones must be **found, occurring** errors in operation must be safely **handled.**

In critical situations, a transition to a **safe state** or the **degradation of functionality** takes place.

- **Safety "needs Security".**
- Fragile systems must become robust.

The difficult question that arises is: how much "Security" is sufficiently "safe"? It was recognized early on that high integrity in terms of functional safety does not automatically go hand in hand with high integrity in terms of Security.

Due to a long history and many (painful) experiences, there are many proven approaches to get functional safety under control:

- Application of **rigid lifecycle models** (demand for V-model in standards)
- Implementation of **highly recommended Safety methods** of the applicable standards (e.g., redundancy, test coverage, traceability of requirements, execution of proven analyses, …)
- **Separation of roles and persons** (4-eyes, 6-eyes principle, independence, …)
- **Traceability/Linkability:** Requirement ↔ source code ↔ verification/ validation (bidirectional)
- **Rigid** vertical (**derivation**) and horizontal structure of the documentation (Plan → Specification → Report)
- Use of **semi-formal description languages** (requirements, specifications, …)
- (complete) **testing** at each (integration-) level
  - Automation of regression tests to ensure quality
  - (independent) **validation** at all levels: adaptation of the tests to the system and its basic requirements (functional and structural coverage)
  - Definition of end criteria based on a defined **coverage** (function, structure, calls, signals, …)
- Once **"certified" safety** change as little as possible (once developed the product is "safe")
- Application of risk analysis methods: "Risk management—Risk assessment techniques" [ISO31010].

> "Physical absence is safer than mental presence"
> (Spanish cave painting, Castellon)

This millennia-old motto of humanity still holds true today when it comes to functional safety. Evolution favors those who act, not those who think (see Fig. 4.2). If you are not in the danger zone, you are protected. This principle does not apply so generally to security in relation to security. Hackers and attackers operate most easily from a distance. Cause and effect can therefore be geographically far apart. As a rule, this is different with functional safety, the causes of an accident can be found in the immediate vicinity of the technical system (e.g. random hardware errors or systematic software errors). Security attacks with the potential impact on functional safety are not considered in this context.

An ever-increasing attack surface of technical systems and a consequent increasing number of attack vectors/attack paths opens up countless new opportunities for attackers to carry out successful attacks. In the automotive sector, almost three quarters of all attacks are already carried out remotely today [Ups20]. Back-end servers, with which

Fig. 4.2 Physical absence is better than mental presence (Spanish cave painting, Castellon)

vehicles are connected are, radio keys (Keyless-go) and mobile apps, with which the vehicle communicates, are currently the main entry points.

Another significant difference in achieving functional safety and information security is protection against implementation-, side channel- and re-engineering attacks. While these types of threats play little role in Safety, they form a significant portion of possible Security attack paths. A designed design/implementation is not deliberately bypassed during intended use.

▶ **Side channel attack** Exploitation of a property that has nothing to do with the actual functionality of a system, but which allows conclusions to be drawn about the functionality. Examples:

- betraying crack when turning the number wheel on a safe
- non-aggregated power consumption over time of a processor
- emitted electromagnetic waves of an electronic door lock
- Scanning/copying a fingerprint from a high-resolution photo of a shown finger in a social network (e.g. peace sign) to obtain corresponding credentials

▶ **Implementation attack** An implemented design is ignored and bypassed. Examples:

- Backdoors in software tools
- Bypassing barriers (see Fig. 4.3)

▶ **Re-engineering attack** By eavesdropping on communication channels, secrets (e.g. cryptographic keys) are recognized, which then allow security measures to be bypassed.

Fig. 4.3 Traces of an implementation attack

Side channel attacks use information that has nothing to do with the direct function, but from which a functionality or product feature can be inferred. For example, the information of the runtime of a piece of program is important information for an attacker (resolution of the example in Sect. 2.1). Any small gain in information can be enough for an attacker to find and exploit a vulnerability.

By electromagnetic irradiation of microprocessors, for example, they can be brought into inconsistent undefined states and/or knowledge about algorithms and program states can be read out by simultaneously observing their power consumption.

Securing against side-channel attacks is an extremely complex undertaking. As an example, the testing of hardware in cold chambers is mentioned [hei19].

4.3 Interface Functional Safety—Cybersecurity

Many companies "interweave" necessary development steps for cybersecurity directly into their existing/lived lifecycle models. This is most commonly observed for products that are safety-relevant in terms of functional safety. In existing product safety development models, safety work products are often "reused" 1:1 by replacing the word Safety in the title with Cybersecurity: x-plan, x-concept, x-proof, x-goals, x-analysis, x-requirements etc.. For this, the respective phases are extended by the creation of the corresponding cybersecurity artifacts: concept phase, design phase, test phase etc.

> The aspects of privacy, safety, and cybersecurity **do not always aim in the same direction.**

Goals and requirements must always be checked for prioritization, consistency, completeness, and non-contradiction. Example questions must be discussed and clarified:

- **"Data hunger"** of cybersecurity (availability: backups) and safety (reliability: redundancy) vs. which personal data may/must actually be stored where and for how long to fulfill the purposes?
- Which **log data** for intrusion detection and application of forensic methods are needed vs. need for protection against spying and profiling of those affected?
- What types of **camera movements** are necessary in the development of autonomous vehicles and who subsequently has access to captured and recorded personal characteristics, such as vehicle license plates?

A corresponding balancing of interests must be carried out in good time before development. Not to forget are legal regulations that must be strictly adhered to (see discussions about eCall systems [Kau18]).

4.3.1 Interfaces in the Automotive Safety Standard

In the Safety Standard ISO 26262:2018 [ISO26262] responsible for safety-oriented developments in the automotive sector, there are hints and information in several volumes about "expected/sensible" interfaces to cybersecurity (see Fig. 4.4); [Lie20].

In summary, the following primary touchpoints emerge:

- **Principles:**
  - Safety and cybersecurity activities must be synchronized.
  - Lifecycle models can be combined and similar methods used.
  - A cybersecurity culture must be established in accordance with the safety culture.

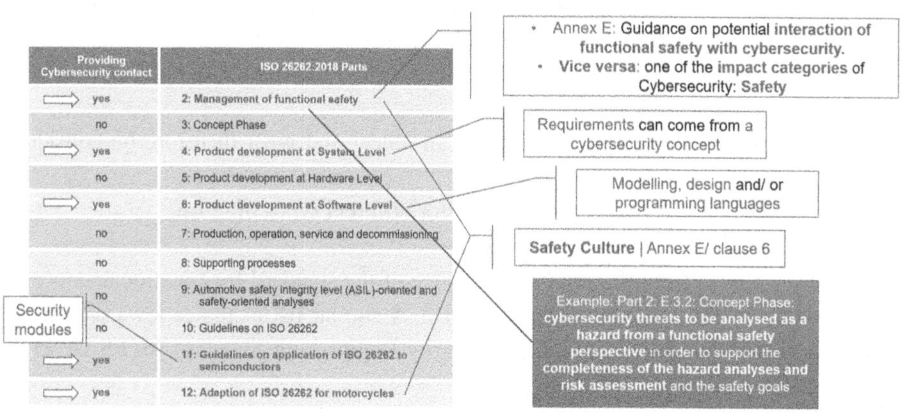

Fig. 4.4 "Touch-Points" Safety—Cybersecurity

- Project-**Initiation/Management:**
  - Interfaces for communication between safety and cybersecurity must be defined at the organizational and project management level. Interfaces to safety must be defined.
  - The cybersecurity plan and safety plan must be coordinated (milestones, activities, design guidelines, tool specifications, ...).
  - An item definition (subject of consideration) and the cybersecurity concept must be developed in accordance with the safety item, the functional and technical safety concept.
- **Risk Assessment**
  - Cybersecurity threats are analyzed as hazards from the perspective of functional safety to check the completeness of hazard analyses and risk assessment as well as the derivation of safety goals.
  - Hazard information, threat scenarios, cybersecurity goals, safety goals, cybersecurity requirements must be considered together and checked for contradictions.
  - HARA (Hazard Analysis and Risk Assessment) and TARA (Threat Analysis and Risk Assessment) must be checked for consistency (merged):
  - Safety impacts due to a cybersecurity attack should already have been identified during the HARA (due to a hazard).
  - Achievement of safety goals, safety measures, fail-safe states can be seen as an asset (value to be protected) (and thus input parameter) for the cybersecurity risk assessment (TARA).
- **Further Topics:**
  - During the concept phase and product development, assumptions, limitations, safety and cybersecurity goals must be regularly checked for consistency and contradiction.
  - The production control plan and the response plan to cybersecurity incidents must be reviewed with regard to potential safety impacts.
  - The response process to cybersecurity incidents must capture potential impacts on safety and provide updates/changes in response to a cybersecurity event.
  - Risk treatment in the context of vulnerability management must consider the potential impacts on safety.
  - **Tools** can affect the cybersecurity of an object and must therefore be considered accordingly.
  - The reuse analysis must be performed for different types of reuse.

This "ball"—played from the safety perspective of the standard for functional safety—is not picked up by the cybersecurity perspective. A similar list of topics towards safety is sought in vain in the Automotive Cybersecurity Engineering Standard **ISO/SAE 21434** [ISO21434].

4.3.2 Related Analysis Methods

Even the similarity of the names of analysis methods, such as **HARA** and **TARA** or **fault tree** and **attack tree,** suggest a related approach.

While a HARA aims to derive safety goals and requirements by identifying hazards and determining the severity of their effects, a TARA works in a very similar way. Instead of hazards, threats are identified and evaluated in terms of their effects.

For determining the risk value for safety, the probability (probability; or a. occurrence probability) is combined with the severity of effects (as well as controllability and exposure) in a risk matrix, this is not equally applicable for security. The occurrence of an attack cannot be calculated in advance with a probability. Only from observations can an occurrence frequency (engl.: likelihood) be assumed. Different standards use different evaluations for determination. Parameters can be (see Sect. 7.2.5: ISO/IEC 18045 [ISO18045]):

- potential attacker (Script-Kiddie, experts, intelligence services)
- Value of the asset to be estimated
- Simplicity of carrying out an attack
- monetary attractiveness of a target of an attack
- scalability of an attack
- …

Further, similar analysis methods are (see also [ISO31010]):

- **FMEA** (Failure Mode Effect Analysis) and Security FMEA:
  - Safety: Non-functionality as error input: Creation of error networks. Determination of causes and error impact analysis [VDA-4].
  - Security: Attack method as error input (security gaps as cause, attack as failure): Definition of security measures to reduce remaining risks.
- **Fault tree** (Top-level Event: Damage event) and **Attack tree** (Attack target)
  - Safety: Top-level Event: Assumed top hazardous event. Derivation of individual events that can lead to the occurrence of damage. Analysis of the shortest effect chains.
  - Security: Top-level Event: Successful attack on a value/asset. Derivation of combined attack paths. Analysis of combinations of individual steps that, when assembled, form an attack scenario [Sch99].
- **Verification methods:** Inspections, code analyses, …
- Requirement and structure covering dynamic **tests**
- …

4.3.3 SOTIF—Safety of the intended functionality

The planned automotive standard for **SOTIF** (Safety of the intended functionality) ISO PAS 21448 [ISO21448] is—in addition to the safety standard ISO 26262 [ISO26262]—applicable to the topics **autonomous driving** (currently covered are the entry levels) and the use of **AI algorithms** (Artificial Intelligence):

SOTIF provides guidance on avoiding system misbehavior in the absence of errors resulting from **deficiencies in system definition,** such as sensor misdetection, and due to foreseeable misuse. ISO 26262, on the other hand, deals exclusively with potential hazards caused by faulty behavior of E/E safety-relevant systems ("system errors").

The planned SOTIF standard is applicable as a guide for risk identification and assessment, function improvement, design, verification, and validation measures. Results of the application of SOTIF include, for example, improvements in function specification.

The scope of application refers to **ADAS** (Autonomous Driving Assistance Systems): Advanced driver assistance systems with automation levels 0-2. SOTIF is a supplement to ISO 26262 and should be applied early during the item definition and concept phase.

Safety standards generally do not demand system performance, but are aimed at monitoring and detecting occurring errors. How fast, for example, an autonomous car can drive on a snow-covered country road in a curve in winter is assessed using requirement analysis according to SOTIF, as no specifications can be derived from the safety standard in this regard.

The challenge for SOTIF lies in the complexity of the scenarios to be anticipated and considered. Weather conditions, road conditions, pedestrian behavior, etc. SOTIF therefore limits the scope of application for autonomous driving to **predefined design areas.** A significant difficulty is the deliberate disruption of autonomous systems. Children painted on the road, traffic signs projected onto a wall by drones with a beamer, overloaded vehicles, …

When thinking about networked autonomous vehicles, it quickly becomes clear that the safety of all individual vehicles at the expense of the operability of a vehicle fleet will not be equally seamless. If defensive driving is not the top priority, there will—as is the case today—continue to be accidents. In total (that is at least the goal) but fewer than today.

Another exciting topic is the interplay of Safety, Cybersecurity, and SOTIF.

Example

If you imagine an autonomously driving vehicle from A to B, the following error possibilities and scenarios are exemplary to consider:

- **Functional safety** ensures:
  - High reliability of the installed sensors and their error detection
  - Handling and safe reaction when detecting errors (e.g., by switching to a safe state; braking and pulling over to the right)
  - Absence of unacceptable risks due to hazards in case of malfunction of E/E systems

- **Cybersecurity** ensures:
  - Sufficient defense against attacks (Intrusion Prevention) and the intrusion of attackers (Intrusion Detection) into the car
  - Availability of a secure functionality even during an attack
  - Preservation of security objectives and protection objectives, such as integrity, confidentiality, and availability
- **SOTIF** ensures:
  - Appropriate response to different scenarios and environmental conditions, such as a puddle or ice on the road, low blinding sun, …
  - Absence of unacceptable risks due to hazards that can arise from inadequate specification of the intended functionality or from predictable misuse by individuals ◀

4.3.4 STPA—Systems Theoretic Process Analysis

Systems Theoretic Process Analysis (**STPA**) is a **proactive (hazard) analysis method,** which analyzes possible causes of accidents during development so that hazards can be eliminated or controlled. It is based on the Systems Theoretic Accident Model and Processes Method (**STAMP**).

It is carried out in the following steps (see [LT18, 16]):

1. **Define the purpose of the analysis**
   - Identify losses
   - Identify system-level hazards
   - Identify system-level constraints
2. **Model** the **control structure**
   - Identify control elements
   - Identify control actions
   - Identify feedback
3. **Identify Unsafe (in terms of Safety) Control Actions** (**UCA**)
   - Identify unsafe control actions
   - Identify safety constraints/requirements
4. **Define damage scenarios**
   - Identify control process models
   - Identify damage scenarios

With the STPA method, complex systems can be analyzed. It can be used early in the concept phase to determine further safety-relevant requirements and conditions.

STAMP [Lev12] is a system-theoretical modeling of accidents (accident causality model) that goes beyond the usual event chain simulation. It includes software, people, organizations, and the safety culture as a factor for accidents.

4.3.5 Artificial Intelligence

Algorithms for using artificial intelligence in safety-critical environments are currently under investigation and are increasingly being adopted. For example, automatic traffic sign recognition and an associated interface to the cruise control, which adjusts the speed of a vehicle accordingly, are now virtually standard.

4.4 Summary

There are many similarities between the aspect of functional safety and cybersecurity. In the until recently only cybersecurity guideline for automotive (the SAE J3061™) [SAE3061], these are very clearly brought to the point. In particular, there are analogies in the organization and the System Engineering of both disciplines. A few excerpts:

- **Integration** of **Safety** and **Cybersecurity** into the **design,** rather than trying to add them to an existing design.
- Cybersecurity Engineering is not just about the problem of compliance with best practices (e.g., authentication and cryptography).
- **Hazard vs. Threat:** Since potential threats include deliberate, malicious, and planned actions, they are more difficult to address than potential hazards.
- There is no way to determine probabilities when considering **risks** regarding Safety in cybersecurity.

Combination possibilities for Systems Engineering:

- Incorporation of suitable **control points** into the product lifecycle of both processes.
- Use of a **risk analysis method** to support the identification of threats with the highest risk.
- Incorporation of cybersecurity awareness and **interfaces** or communication points into existing processes.
- Identification, establishment, and dissemination of various **communication channels** between Safety and Cybersecurity.

When comparing the **principles** of both disciplines, the following are significant:

- To fully address potential threats, **analysts must think like attackers.**
- In system integrity (regarding safety), analysts can more easily identify potential dangers, identify potential causes, and take appropriate measures to mitigate potential consequences.
  - The causes of potential dangers can be determined based on experience and knowledge.

  - The potential causes are not unknown.
  - However, due to the large amount of unknown information that is likely part of a cybersecurity analysis, these techniques fundamentally differ from the empirical techniques that can be used based on experiences with safety-relevant systems.
- Regarding threats and the risks associated with threats, **additional factors** must be considered that do not have to be considered in relation to hazards and the risks associated with hazards. Additional factors must be considered for hazards and risks associated with threats.
  - None of these additional factors need to be considered when assessing the risks of potential hazards.
- Cybersecurity has a **broader focus:**
  - Example Automotive: Potential access to a safety-critical vehicle from non-safety-critical vehicle systems is not a hazard from a functional safety perspective.
- Valid or correct code from a safety perspective can still have weaknesses in cybersecurity.
- Some verification/validation methods for cybersecurity are different and more difficult than verification/validation methods used in system safety.
- Traditional structured tests of the **effectiveness** of cybersecurity controls (which can confirm that the design meets its requirements) are not sufficient to address Black-Hat-Out-of-the-Box attack types.
- Cybersecurity risks **evolve over time,** as the motivations and abilities of attackers change.
- Cybersecurity countermeasures can **collide with safety requirements** and vice versa.

In summary, a few observations when considering functional safety and cybersecurity together:

> - Functional safety deals with the universe (the sun randomly flips bits), cybersecurity deals with people (attackers flip bits intentionally).
> - Systems must function **continuously** and under all circumstances, attacks **only once** under one circumstance.
> - Functional safety has a **static character,** cybersecurity a **dynamic one.**
> - A (functionally) safe product **remains safe.**
> - The **longevity** of systems challenges the assumptions regarding cybersecurity.
> - Cybersecurity: Threats are not analyzed as a **cause of hazards** in functional safety.

References

[91101] ***„Terroranschläge am 11. September 2001“.*** Wikipedia-Link: https://de.wikipedia.org/wiki/Terroranschl%C3%A4ge_am_11._September_2001 accessed: 17.04.2021

[Bäu19] ***„Boeing-737-Absturz - Die vermeidbare Katastrophe“;*** Frank Bäumer, 2019. tagesschau.de-Link: https://www.tagesschau.de/wirtschaft/boeing-235.html accessed: 17.04.2021

[Esc98] ***„Eisenbahnunfall von Eschede“.*** Wikipedia-Link: https://de.wikipedia.org/wiki/Eisenbahnunfall_von_Eschede accessed: 17.04.2021

[GW15] ***„Germanwings-Flug 9525“;*** 2015. Wikipedia-Link: https://de.wikipedia.org/wiki/Germanwings-Flug_9525 accessed: 17.04.2021

[hei19] ***„Apple will mit Temperaturkammern seine Secure Encalve schützen“.*** heise.de-Link: https://www.heise.de/mac-and-i/meldung/Apple-will-mit-Temperaturkammern-seine-Secure-Enclave-schuetzen-4433594.html accessed: 17.04.2021

[ISO18045] **„Information technology — Security techniques — Methodology for IT securityevaluation“;** ISO/IEC 18045

[ISO21434] ***„Road Vehicles – Cybersecurity Engineering“;*** International Standard ISO/SAE 21434.

[ISO21448] ***„Road Vehicles – Safety of the intended functionality“;*** Public Available Standard ISO PAS 21448

[ISO26262] ***„Road Vehicles – Functional Safety“;*** International Standard; ISO 26262–2nd edition

[ISO31010] ***„Risk Management – Risk Assessment Techniques“;*** Internationaler Standard IEC 31010.

[Kau18] ***„eCall wird Pflicht in Neuwagen“.*** Leonie Kaufmann, 2018. Internet-Link: https://www.verti.de/blog/ecall-neuwagen-unfall-notruf.jsp accessed: 17.04.2021

[Lev12] ***„Engineering a Safer World“;*** Nancy G. Leveson, MIT Press (2012)

[LT18] ***„STPA Handbook“;*** Nancy G. Leveson, John P. Thomas, March 2018. Link: https://psas.scripts.mit.edu/home/get_file.php?name=STPA_handbook.pdf accessed: 17.04.2021

[Lie20] ***„Touch Points: Security and Safety Requirements regarding development projects“;*** Thomas Liedtke, Embedded Software Engineering Kongress, 2020

[ntv19] ***„Fahrer bewusstlos – Passagiere stoppen Bahn“;*** 2019. n-tv.de-Link: https://www.n-tv.de/panorama/Fahrer-bewusstlos-Passagiere-stoppen-Bahn-article21473654.html accessed: 17.04.2021

[SAE3061] ***„Cybersecurity Guidebook for Cyber-Physical Vehicle Systems“;*** SAE J3061$^{TM.}$ Issued 2016–01

[Sch99] ***„Attack Trees“;*** B. Schneier, Dr. Dobb's Journal, December 1999. Link: https://www.schneier.com/academic/archives/1999/12/attack_trees.html accessed: 17.04.2021

[Tho14] ***„Systems Theoretic Process Analysis (STPA)“;*** John Thomas, MIT. Link: https://psas.scripts.mit.edu/home/wp-content/uploads/2014/03/Systems-Theoretic-Process-Analysis-STPA-v9-v2-san.pdf accessed: 17.04.2021

[Ups21] ***„Upstream Security 's global automotive cybersecurity report 2021“;*** Research into cyber-attack trends in the smart mobility ecosystem, Upstream Security Ltd. https://www.upstream.auto/ accessed: 17.04.2021

[VDA-4] ***„Produkt- und Prozess-FMEA“;*** VDA-Band 4

Information/Cybersecurity Standards 5

Various studies have shown that the application of good processes in product development has a positive impact on the security of the product. Well-known examples include:

Example 1

Jeep Cherokee Hacking 2015 & 2016 [VM15, VM16] was thoroughly investigated and analyzed [VM15a, CMK+11]. In the attack path, various steps for exploiting security vulnerabilities were found, which could not have been exploited with careful implementation of appropriate cybersecurity measures, because they would have been closed and not present:

- The application of appropriate **Secure-Development practices** and an **Intrusion-Detection-System** would have prevented an open port from being sought and found.
- Restarting with malicious software could have been prevented by implementing a **Secure-Boot** mechanism.
- The execution of a script to change the update mode would have made a **Whitelisting** of scripts impossible. ◀

Example 2

An **Ethical Hack research project** of a **Security Assessment** of BMW vehicles [KSL18] uncovered 14 security vulnerabilities. Some of these have been published in the CVE database [CVE]. It was also shown that the success of the attack could have been detected and prevented by monitoring the integrity of the control flow. ◀

T. Liedtke, *Information Security*, https://doi.org/10.1007/978-3-658-45711-2_5

Example 3

KRACK (Key-Reinstallation-Attack) on **WPA2** [VP17]. It took fourteen years for cunning attackers to exploit a well-known encryption problem, which the designers of WPA2 actually wanted to avoid.

The XOR problem (a function often used in cryptography) is that as soon as you have encrypted different data with the same key, it becomes vulnerable. The WPA architects had planned that the keys used would be derived from a so-called **NONCE** (Number used once). The same NONCE should never be used twice.

The attack consists of intervening in the NONCE exchange of WLAN devices in the radio network in such a way that parts do not reach the recipient. The WLAN client still starts sending encrypted messages. The router resends the lost packet, the client receives it and after a reset performs a key reinstallation and encrypts data with the same NONCE as the first time.

WPA2 was considered very mature. There was a formal proof of the security of the procedure. In this example too, shortcomings in the development processes could be demonstrated:

- **Side-channel attacks** were not carried out and not documented.
- The formal proof was based on **false assumptions** (that the same NONCE is not used twice).
- The WPA2 standard was made very difficult to access, **independent tests were thus hindered.**
- A complete **state machine**—which precisely documents all allowed states and their transitions—**was missing.**
- Developers had to navigate along various **pseudo-code snippets,** which led to vulnerable implementations. ◀

▶ Good development processes can significantly hinder attacks and make attack paths impossible.

5.1 Security Development Lifecycle: Standards

What is common to life cycle models for cybersecurity is that they are all not entirely new and the underlying principles have been known for some time. However, the practical implementation often lags far behind the known possibilities. Here, there is obviously a lack of commercial pressure. Cybersecurity measures, the application of cybersecurity principles and methods are often—although theoretically known—not applied in favor of economic efficiency, adherence to deadlines. Cybersecurity does not seem to be a sufficiently good purchasing argument, and it is also the case that cybersecurity measures do not primarily agree with applicability, intuitiveness, and user-friendliness.

The following section will present some already longer known standards that deal with life cycle models for cybersecurity-relevant developments. These include those explained in the next sections.

- Section 5.1.1: Microsoft **Security-Development-Lifecycle** (SDL) [HL06]
- Section 5.1.2: IEEE Cyber Security ***"Avoiding the Top 10 Software Security Design Flaws"*** [IEEE15]
- Section 5.1.3: Automotive Spice® Process Reference Model, Process Assessment Model, Version 3.1 [ASPICE3.1]

Depending on the manufacturer, there are additional conditions to be considered in many companies for the development of security-oriented systems (in terms of security), which must be taken into account by suppliers, among others.

5.1.1 Microsoft Security-Development-Lifecycle (SDL)

"If you don't pay for it now, you'll pay an order of magnitude more if later"
(Jim Allchin, 2006, Computer Scientist, Microsoft Executive)

As early as 2006, Microsoft published the Security Development Lifecycle [HL06].

The principles for **Security** and **Privacy** are listed here as follows:

- Security by **Design:**
  - The security aspects of the software should be considered already in the planning phase. Security cannot be "injected" at the end of a development.
- Security by **Default/Standard:**
  - Despite the most careful planning, the existence of vulnerabilities must be assumed. For this reason, default settings (e.g., required permissions) should be as restrictive as possible and rarely used functions should be disabled by default.
- Security in **Use:**
  - The provided documentation and tools should help administrators to set up the software as optimally as possible.
- **Communication** (Software):
  - Developers should deal openly with potential vulnerabilities and quickly provide end users with patches or workarounds.
- Privacy by **Design:**
  - Privacy aspects of the software should be considered already in the planning phase.
- Privacy by **Default:**
  - The default settings of the software should be conservative.

- Privacy in **Deployment:**
  - Privacy mechanisms should be disclosed so that administrators can enforce the company's internal privacy policies.
- **Communication** (Privacy):
  - Privacy statements should be formulated transparently. A team for privacy incidents should be set up.

The security development lifecycle consists of six steps:

1. **Requirements phase:**
   - Identification of the security requirements and protection objectives of the software to be developed and its interfaces
2. **Design phase:**
   - Identification of the components essential for security; risk modeling
3. **Implementation:**
   - Use of tools and testing methods as well as code reviews
4. **Review** phase:
   - Beta test with users, systematic search for security flaws
5. **Release:**
   - Is the software really ready for delivery?
6. **Response:**
   - Creating the ability to quickly respond to identified errors and weaknesses

5.1.2 IEEE Cyber Security—Design Flaws

The **Center for Secure Design** (CSD) of the IEEE Computer Society collects software security expertise from industry, academia, and government. The CSD provides guidance on:

- Identifying software system designs that are likely to be vulnerable to compromise.
- Designing and creating software systems with strong, identifiable characteristics.

In the paper [IEEE15] the **Top 10 software security flaws** (flaws) and how to avoid them are presented.

In English, a distinction is made between bug and flaw.

▶ **Bug:** Program error, software error, or software anomaly. Generally refers to a malfunction of computer programs. A specific specification was not implemented or was implemented incorrectly. Incompleteness, inaccuracies, or ambiguities in the specification can also lead to bugs.

▶ **Flaw:** Deficiency; problem at a deeper level. Flaws are often much more subtle than a simple bug in an array reference or the use of a wrong system call. A flaw can be instantiated in the software code, but it is the result of a mistake or oversight at the design level.

Software always contains program errors (bugs) and deficiencies (flaws). Studies have found that the integrity (in terms of security) of many systems is broken due to design flaws. To reduce the number and impact of security breaches, flaws must be avoided in the design phase.

5.1.2.1 The Top 10 Design Flaws

1. Incorrect **trust assumptions**
2. Broken **authentication mechanisms,** that can be bypassed or manipulated
3. Neglect of **authorization** after authentication
4. Lack of strict **separation** between **data-** and **control instructions** and as a result, processing of control instructions originating from an untrusted source
5. Non-explicit **validation** of all data
6. Misuse of **cryptography**
7. Failure to identify **sensitive data** and how they should be handled
8. Failure to consider the **users**
9. Misunderstanding of how the integration of **external components** changes the attack surface
10. Inflexibility in the face of **future changes** to objects and actors

5.1.2.2 Countermeasures to Avoid the Top 10 Design Flaws

For the top 10 list of flaws presented in Sect. 5.1.2.1, corresponding countermeasures are described in the paper [IEEE15]:

1. **Inherit or give trust,** but **never assume it:**
   - Whether sensitive material needs to be stored on the client should be clarified.
   - If IP or sensitive material needs to be stored or sent to the client, the system should be designed to handle a possible compromise.
   - It must be ensured that all data received from an untrusted client are properly validated before proceeding.
2. **Use** an **authentication mechanism** that cannot be bypassed or spoofed:
   - The use of authentication procedures that do not fall into the category of "something you know" (e.g., password), "something you are" (e.g., biometric data), or "something you have" (e.g., smartphone) can allow users access to a system or service they should not be using.
   - A single authentication mechanism that uses one or more factors depending on the requirements of an application serves as a logical bottleneck.

  - Authentication data have a limited lifespan, are not forgeable, and are stored in such a way that they cannot be used by a thief in the event of theft to impersonate a legitimate user.
3. **Authorization after authentication:**
   - This order must be adhered to. One should not assume that authorization automatically follows authentication.
   - Use of a common infrastructure (e.g., a system library or a back-end) to authorize users.
4. **Strict separation** of **data** and **control instructions** and never processing control instructions originating from untrusted sources:
   - The integrity of the control flow and the separation of control data and potentially untrusted data are important design goals.
   - A design that relies on the ability to convert data into code should be cautious with:—*Eval functions*—Query languages—Disclosed reflection.
5. Definition of an approach that ensures all **data is explicitly validated**:
   - Design or use of a centralized validation mechanism.
   - Data transformation into a canonical form.
   - Use of common libraries for validation primitives.
   - Input validation requirements are often state-dependent.
   - Explicit re-validation of assumptions such as "local (nearby)" code that rely on them.
   - Use of types at the implementation language level to capture assumptions about data validity.
6. **Correct use** of **cryptography**:
   - Avoiding common pitfalls when using cryptography:
     - Developing your own cryptographic algorithms or implementations
     - Incorrect use of libraries and algorithms
     - Poor key management
     - Randomness that is not random
     - Lack of centralization of cryptography
     - No ability to adapt and evolve algorithms
     - Use of proven algorithms and libraries
7. **Identification of sensitive data** and how they should be handled:
   - Identification of sensitive data and determination of how they should be appropriately protected.
   - The sensitivity of data is context-dependent and depends on regulations, company policies, contractual obligations, and user expectations.
   - Identification of trust boundaries when data sets are transferred between systems and implementation of appropriate data protection policies.
8. Continuous **consideration of the user**:
   - Creating of designs that facilitate secure configuration and use by those who are interested in it.

   - Use of designs that motivate and incentivize secure use among those who are not particularly interested in software.
   - Use of designs that prevent or mitigate misuse by those who intend to weaken or compromise the system.
9. **Understanding** how the **integration** of **external components** changes the attack surface:
   - It is a common saying in software security that, whenever possible, functionality should be achieved by reusing proven parts of already tested and validated software, rather than developing from scratch each time.
   - Isolation of external components as far as your required functionality allows; use of containers, sandboxes, and reduction of privileges before uncontrolled code is entered.
   - Comprehensive documentation.
   - Design for flexibility.
10. Flexibility in considering **future changes** to objects and actors:
   - Software security must be designed for change, rather than being fragile, rigid, and static.
   - Design for secure updates.
   - Design for security properties that change over time, e.g., when code is updated.
   - Design with the ability to isolate or switch functionality.
   - Design for changes to objects that are to be kept secret.
   - Design for changes to the security properties of components that are beyond their control.
   - Design for changes to permissions.

5.1.3 Automotive SPICE®

Due to the importance of the topic of cybersecurity in the automotive domain, the **assessment model Automotive SPICE®** [ASPICE3.1] is expanded to include the topic of Cybersecurity [VDA21].

The Automotive SPICE® Process Assessment Model (PAM) is intended for use in conducting compliant assessments of process capability in the development of embedded automotive systems.

The (basic) model includes:

- **Development processes** (system and software) from requirement gathering to validation/qualification.
- **Management processes,** such as project management or risk management
- **Acquisition processes,** such as supplier monitoring.
- **Support processes** such as quality assurance, configuration management, problem-resolution management, and change management.

In order to specify and demonstrate the maturity of a integrity-oriented (in terms of security) development, additional processes, basic practices, and work results must be defined accordingly, and existing ones must be partially adapted.

This includes, in particular, additional processes for cybersecurity engineering such as requirement gathering for security, distributed development, threat analysis and risk assessment, as well as risk treatment.

Existing processes of the basic model must be partially adapted to address security-relevant topics (even if no basic practices are additionally defined in the standard for this):

- **Supplier qualification** and management. It must be ensured that suppliers have the ability to develop and deliver for security projects. The securing of delivery and delivery process must be ensured.
- **Quality assurance:** Security strategies must be supported and additional safeguarding measures defined.
- **Configuration management:** Artifacts must be secured unalterably and may only be changed by appropriately authorized persons.
- **Change management.** It must be ensured that changes do not introduce new vulnerabilities and security gaps into the project/product.

Other important points that need to be established in addition to processes and methods of good project development are:

- Definition of a **Security Policy.** The commitment of the management to the topic of security in the company. This has implications for all projects.
- Declaration of a **Security Culture.** Without an appropriate culture, security projects cannot be successfully carried out. Deadlines and the achievement of milestones must not be prioritized over security concerns.
- **Proof** of Security. The achieved security as well as open points must be proven at the end of the project (if possible).
- **Risk management:** Threat analysis, risk identification, and assessment must be carried out.
- The execution of **downstream processes** (especially production, operation and maintenance as well as decommissioning) must also be secured. It must be ensured that no further vulnerabilities enter the project, and that vulnerabilities discovered in downstream processes can be handled and managed accordingly.

The last point is not yet addressed by the Automotive SPICE® Process Assessment Model, as it only covers the project phases until the end of development.

5.2 Security Standards

This section provides an overview of various security standards from different domains:

- **Automotive:** Sect. 5.2.1: Engineering, Sect. 5.2.6: Requirements for an Information Security Management System, Sect. 5.2.7: Regulation for Homologation
- **General:** Sect. 5.2.2: Levels, Selection of Controls, Sect. 5.2.3: Risk Management, Sect. 5.2.5: Requirements for an Information Security Management System, Sect. 5.2.8: Certification of Security Products
- **Internet of Things, Industry 4.0, Transportation:** Sect. 5.2.4: System and Component Security, Project Management, Risk Management
- **Aviation:** Sect. 5.2.9
- **EU Regulations in General:** Sect. 5.2.10

5.2.1 SAE International J3061™ | ISO/SAE 21434

The first standard for cybersecurity in the automotive domain is the US-based standard SAE J3061™: ***"Cybersecurity Guidebook for Cyber-Physical Vehicle Systems"*** [SAE3061] This was published in January 2016 and is based on the Microsoft Security Design Lifecycle [HL06]. The principles presented in Sect. 5.1.2 [IEEE15] of the IEEE are also referenced in this.

The standard was mainly developed by safety experts, and so there is a lot of basic information for understanding the relationship between functional safety and security. Both lifecycle models are compared and similarities as well as differences are highlighted.

The content includes a complete cybersecurity process framework, to guide organizations in identifying and assessing cybersecurity threats. Furthermore, it helps design cybersecurity for cyber-physical vehicle systems for the entire product lifecycle.

The described cybersecurity process framework can be adapted (customized) to any organization's development process to consider cybersecurity throughout the lifecycle from the concept phase, production, operation, service, and decommissioning.

Although the standard is completely replaced by the new ISO/SAE 21434 standard [ISO21434], it contains many good hints that make it worthwhile to still know the contents.

The standard refers to many other valuable sources, so useful references for understanding and implementing cybersecurity topics can be found here.

Definitions for "integrity" as well as for integrity-oriented systems in terms of safety and security are established:

System safety vs. system cybersecurity:

- **System safety** (beyond regulatory requirements) is the state of a system that does not cause harm to life, property, or the environment.
- **System cybersecurity** is the state of a system that does not allow the exploitation of vulnerabilities to lead to losses, e.g., financial, operational, data protection, or safety-related losses.

Safety-critical system vs. cybersecurity-critical system:

- **Safety-critical system** is a system that can cause harm to life, property, or the environment if the system does not behave as intended or desired (specified).
- **Cybersecurity-critical system** is a system that can lead to financial, operational, data protection, or safety-related losses if the system is compromised by a vulnerability that may be present in the system.

Because integrity critical systems can have impacts on safety in case of attacks (directly or indirectly), all safety-critical systems are also cybersecurity-critical at the same time. The reverse is not true, not all cybersecurity-critical systems are automatically safety-critical.

Safety and cybersecurity development processes can be very well mapped onto each other (see also Sect. 4.3):

- **Concept phase:** Hazard analysis and risk assessment (HARA) and threat analysis and risk assessment (TARA)
  - Identification of functional safety objectives and identification of cybersecurity objectives.
  - Derivation of functional safety requirements and derivation of cybersecurity requirements.
- **Design phase:** Detailed hazard analysis of the greatest hazards and detailed security gap analysis of the greatest cybersecurity risks
  - Identification of measures and controls for safety and security.
  - Elimination of potential hazards to mitigate consequences and reduction of occurrence frequencies (likelihood) for successful attacks.

Examples of extended focus can be derived from the concept of safe states. Safe states may be an attractive target for attack. An attack on safe states can have effects on functional safety. In this case, the risk must be analyzed from a cybersecurity perspective. In the case without effects on functional safety, the attack can still have effects on the availability of other functions. This also needs to be analyzed from a cybersecurity perspective.

In Appendix D of the SAE J3061™, there are additional recommendations for applicable cybersecurity and privacy control families from the NIST SP 800-53 [NIST800-53R5, NIST800-53B]. This is a common procedure in other domains (see Sect. 5.2.3).

For automotive, relevant controls and measures are selected from a large number of controls. The list is a good starting point for the selection of cybersecurity controls that can be considered in the specification of requirements.

Annex G contains an overview of many cybersecurity standards and guidelines relevant to the automotive sector.

Background Information
In line with ISO/SAE 21434, there will be a corresponding standard for auditing the objectives of processes at the organizational level in the future (ISO PAS 5112, [ISO5112]). With this, the implementation of the engineering processes of an organization can be audited.

5.2.2 FIPS PUB 199/FIPS PUB 200/NIST SP 800-53

This section describes standards that provide guidelines for the categorization of information types, their classification and baselining, as well as the description of minimum requirements and for the selection of security controls. In particular, guidelines on which controls should be implemented at which security level (baseline) can be very useful to ensure transparency in the development of integrity systems.

- The two standards **FIPS PUB 199** [FIPS199] (see Sect. 5.2.2.1) and
- **FIPS PUB 200** [FIPS200] (see Sect. 5.2.2.2) help in the categorization of risks and thus form a basis for the selection of minimum controls to be selected.
- **NIST SP (Special Publication) 800-53** [NIST800-53R5] provides an overview of control families, security control measures, and sorts these for baselines into different levels.

5.2.2.1 FIPS PUB 199—Security Categorization

FIPS PUB 199 [FIPS199] divides the potential damage to organizations and individuals into three categories for damage amount: **low, moderate** and **high.** The "usual" security objectives are considered:

- **Confidentiality** including with reference to privacy (personal data) and company-owned information,
- **Integrity** including logging for achieving non-repudiation and authenticity,
- **Availability** especially access and use of information systems.

The severity of the damage, in the event of a breach of cybersecurity, such as loss of confidentiality, integrity or availability, can be classified into corresponding damage amounts:

- **Low**—limited effects:
  - temporary degradation of a functionality. An organization can perform its primary functions (perhaps with less effectiveness)
  - limited damage to organizational values
  - minor financial damage
  - minor harm to people
- **Moderate**—serious effects:
  - serious degradation, effectiveness is significantly impaired
  - serious damage to organizational values
  - serious financial damage
  - serious harm to people (not life-threatening)
- **High**—catastrophic effects:
  - Organization can no longer perform its primary functions
  - high damage to organizational values
  - high financial damage
  - life-threatening harm with possible fatal outcome

When security properties are breached, there are impacts for stakeholders. For each type of information, the damage can be determined, so that in the end a vector (confidentiality × damage level, integrity × damage level, availability × damage level) results.

If you know all types of information of your organization, you can, for example, determine such a summary vector for a SCADA system (as an envelope over all types of information).

The level concept can be applied to both types of information (personal, medical, financial, property, …) and information systems.

5.2.2.2 FIPS PUB 200—Minimum Security Requirements

FIPS PUB 200 [FIPS200] sets minimum security requirements.

Security-related areas correspond to the overview chapters of the security controls in the **NIST SP 800-53** [NIST800-53R5]. Policies and procedures are particularly important for an effective implementation of an information security program and the derived security measures.

Minimum requirements are set for all areas. For example, for the area of **access control:** "Organizations must restrict access to information systems to authorized users, processes acting on behalf of authorized users, or devices (including other information systems) and to the types of transactions and functions that authorized users may perform."

For the selection of security controls, reference is made to the **NIST SP 800-53** [NIST800-53R5] (see Chap. 9), which prescribes a corresponding classification (**low, moderate** or **high**) for all controls.

This provides a clear guideline for the determination of categories/risk values (see FIPS PUB 199, Sect. 5.2.2.1) and derived guidelines for mechanisms and controls to be implemented. The guidelines affect both management, organizational and technical aspects.

Background Information
For the automotive sector, the SAE J3061™ [SAE3061] (see Sect. 5.2.1) picks up the ball and specifies which control families of the NIST SP 800-53 [NIST800-53R5] are relevant for automotive.

5.2.3 NIST SP 800-Series

The publications of the **NIST** series **Special Publication (SP) 800** contain information of interest to the computer security community. The series includes guidelines, recommendations, technical specifications, and annual reports on the cybersecurity activities of the NIST.

SP 800 publications are developed to address and support the security and privacy requirements of US federal government information and information systems.

The series, launched in 1990, reports on the research, guidelines, and public relations of the Information Technology Laboratory in the field of computer security, as well as collaboration with industry, government, and academic organizations.

The **NIST SP 800-53** [NIST800-53R5] contains a catalog of **security** and **privacy controls**. The 492-page work (referenced by many security standards) provides an overview of mostly policy-, technology-, and domain-neutral controls. They focus on fundamental measures necessary to protect information and personal data throughout their entire lifecycle. This has decisive advantages for organizations:

- Focus on **security** and **privacy functions** and capabilities that are necessary for the success of the mission and business and for the protection of information and the privacy of individuals, regardless of the technologies used in organizational systems;
- **Analysis** of each security and privacy control in terms of its applicability to specific technologies, operating environments, mission and business functions, and stakeholders;
- **Specification** of security and privacy policies as part of the adaptation process for controls that have variable parameters.

NIST SP 800-53B [NIST800-53B] contains **baselines,** which include an indication for each control whether the control must be implemented at "low", "moderate" or "high".

An overview of the listed control families is presented in Chap. 9 (see Table 9.1).

NIST SP 160v1 [NIST800-160v1], NIST SP 160v2 [NIST800-160v2]: The two standards contain considerations and extensions for cyber resilience and trustworthiness for the development of trustworthy secure systems. This involves the extensions of the processes used in system engineering (see [ISO15288]). It can be considered a manual for achieving the identified trustworthiness and cyber-resiliency results, based on a systems engineering perspective of the system lifecycle processes, and it allows the organization's experience and expertise to determine what is right for their purpose. Examples of cyber resilience design principles are:

- **Elimination of the need for trust**
- **Planning and maintenance of diversity**
- **Focusing on critical values**
- **Reduction of attack vectors**
- ...

NIST SP 800-115 [NIST800-115]: This standard describes different information security test and assessment techniques to determine the effectiveness of specific security objectives. The following methods are described:

- **Security testing** and examination
- **Review** techniques
- **Analysis** techniques
- **Validation** of security gaps (Penetration testing, Social Engineering, ...)
- Security **assessments**

5.2.4 ISA/IEC 62443—IT Security for Networks and Systems

ISA/IEC 62443 [IEC62443] is an international series of standards for cybersecurity in industrial automation. The beginnings are about 20 years old and go back to the International Society for Automation (ISA). The associated standards, technical reports, and related information define procedures for implementing secure industrial automation and control systems (IACS). The term IACS describes all components necessary for the reliable and secure operation of an automated production plant. This includes both hardware and software components. Furthermore, IACS includes the organizational processes for the establishment and operation. Originally, the documents were published as ISA99 **standards**. Meanwhile, the standard and technical reports are also used in the areas of automation, medical devices, and transportation.

5.2.4.1 ISA/IEC 62443—Objectives

The goal of the ISA/IEC 62443 series is to improve the security, reliability, integrity, and protection of **industrial automation and control systems (IACS)** through a risk-based, methodical, and comprehensive process over the entire lifecycle. It covers all industrial sectors and critical infrastructures (**KRITIS**). It aims to reduce the risk of compromised information or production failures.

Observable **trends** in **IACS technologies:**

- Migration from manufacturer proprietary systems to commercial off-the-shelf technologies such as Microsoft Windows™ and TCP/IP networks.
- The value of data contained in the IACS systems is increasing.
- Both the internal and external connectivity of organizations is increasing.
- The means, resources, capabilities, and motivation of attackers have significantly increased.

Initially, IT standards and practices were applied to IACS. It was quickly realized that this was not sufficient to ensure functional safety, integrity, reliability, and security. The consequences of a successful cyber attack on an IACS are fundamentally different:

▶ While the primary consequences of an attack on **IT systems are financial**, pertain to **data protection**, or unauthorized **disclosure of information**, possible additional consequences for an **IACS** are the **loss of life or health,** damage to the **environment** or the loss of **product integrity.**

These documents describe a methodical, technical approach to address the cybersecurity of IACS. The Security Triad includes:

- People
- Processes
- Technology

Without adequately trained staff, risk-appropriate technologies and countermeasures, and work processes throughout the entire security lifecycle, an IACS could be more vulnerable to cyber attacks.

Examples of consequences of a successful cyber attack can include:

Examples

- Endangering the safety or health of the public or employees
- Damage to the environment
- Damage to the controlled equipment
- Loss of product integrity
- Loss of public trust or company reputation
- Violation of legal or regulatory requirements
- Loss of copyrighted or confidential information
- Financial loss
- Impact on corporate, local, state, or national security ◀

In **contrast to IT systems**, IACS have the following characteristics:

- more predictable types of errors
- stricter time criticality and determinism
- higher availability
- more consistent management of changes
- longer periods between maintenance
- significantly longer component lifetimes
- **functional safety, integrity, availability** and **confidentiality** (SIAC) instead of CIA

The **UNECE** organization (Sect. 5.2.7) plans to incorporate the standard series into the regulatory framework **CRF** (Common Regulatory Framework on Cybersecurity).

5.2.4.2 ISA/IEC 62443—Structure of the Standard Series

The standard series is divided into four groups:

1. **General:** includes topics that are **universally valid** for the entire series.
2. **Guidelines and Procedures:** The documents in this group focus on the guidelines and procedures related to **IACS security.**
3. **System Requirements:** The documents of the third group address requirements at the **system level.**
4. **Component Requirements:** The fourth and final group includes documents that provide information about the more specific and detailed requirements related to the development of **InVeKoS products** (Integrated Administration and Control System).

The **first group General** comprises four volumes:

Part 1-1: **Terminology, Concepts** and **Models** introduces the concepts and models used throughout the series. The target audience includes anyone who wants to familiarize themselves with the basic concepts that form the basis for the series.

Part 1-2: **Master Glossary** of **Terms** and **Definitions** is a list of terms and abbreviations used throughout the series.

Part 1-3: **Metrics** for **System Security Compliance** describes a methodology for developing quantitative metrics derived from the process and technical requirements of the standards.

Part 1-4: IACS **Security Lifecycle** and **Use-cases** (Lifecycle of IACS security and use cases) provides a more detailed description of the underlying lifecycle for IACS security as well as several use cases illustrating various applications.

The **second group Guidelines** and Procedures comprises five volumes:

Part 2-1: **Establishment** of an IACS **Security Program** describes what is required to define and implement an effective IACS cybersecurity management system. The target audience includes plant owners who are responsible for designing and implementing such a program.

Part 2-2: **Assessments** of IACS **Security Programs** provides a methodology for assessing the level of protection that an operational InVeKoS offers in relation to the requirements of the ISA/IEC 62443 standard series.

Part 2-3: **Patch Management** in the IACS environment provides guidance on patch management for IACS. The intended audience includes anyone responsible for designing and implementing a patch management program.

Part 2-4: Requirements for **Security Programs** for IACS service providers specify requirements for IACS service providers such as system integrators or maintenance providers.

Part 2-5: **Implementation Guide** provides guidance on what is required to operate an effective IACS cybersecurity program. The intended audience are plant owners who are responsible for operating such a program.

The third group System Requirements form three volumes:

Part 3-1: **Security Technologies** for IACS describes the application of various security technologies in an IACS environment. The target audience includes anyone who wants to learn more about the applicability of certain technologies in a control system environment.

Part 3-2: **Security Risk Assessment** for System Design deals with the assessment of cybersecurity risks and system design for IACS. The result of this standard is a **Zone and Conduit** model and the associated risk assessments and target security levels. These are documented in the specification of cybersecurity requirements. This standard is primarily aimed at plant owners and system integrators.

Part 3-3: **System Security Requirements** and Security Levels describes the requirements for an InVeKoS system based on the security level. The main addressees are suppliers of control systems, system integrators, and plant owners.

Finally, two volumes in the fourth group Component Requirements:

Part 4-1: Requirements for the **Lifecycle** of Product Security Development describes the requirements for the security development lifecycle of a product developer. The main target group includes suppliers of control systems and component products.

Part 4-2: **Technical Security Requirement** for IACS-**Components** describes the requirements for IACS components based on the security level. Components include embedded devices, host devices, network devices, and software applications. The main target group includes suppliers of component products used in control systems.

5.2.4.3 ISA/IEC 62443—Foundational Concepts (Foundational Requirements)

The foundational concepts of the **ISA/IEC 62443** include:

Security Program

Part 2-1 specifies the requirements for the plant owner's security program for the IACS. A security program consists of the implementation and maintenance of personnel, policy and procedure-related, as well as technology-based capabilities that reduce the cybersecurity risk of an IACS. The asset owner is also the operator of the IACS and the devices to be controlled. The security program covers the entire lifecycle of the IACS and must be coordinated with the organization's **Information Security Management System** (ISMS). Because an **IACS differs significantly from IT systems**, additional requirements must be implemented and considered for the security program.

Risk Management

- **Risk Assessment:** Part 3-2 describes the requirements for dealing with cybersecurity risks in an IACS, including the use of zones and conduits as well as security levels. Although Part 3-2 contains the requirements for the risk assessment process, it does not specify the exact methodology to be used. The methodology used must be determined by the asset owner and should be consistent with the organization's general risk assessment methodology.
- **Zones and Conduits:**
  - A **zone is defined** as a grouping of logical or physical assets, based on risk or other criteria such as the criticality of the assets, operational function, physical or logical location, required access, or the responsible organization.
  - A **conduit is defined** as a logical grouping of communication channels that share common security requirements and connect two or more zones. An important step in the risk assessment process is the **partitioning** of the system under consideration into separate zones and conduits. The intention is to identify assets with common security characteristics to establish a set of common security requirements that reduce the cybersecurity risk. The following criteria can be used for the partitioning:
    - should separate business and control system assets
    - should separate security-relevant assets
    - should separate temporarily connected devices
    - should separate wireless devices
    - should separate devices connected via external networks
- **Specification of Cybersecurity Requirements:** Part 3-2 also requires that the necessary security measures from the risk assessment as well as the **security requirements,** which are based on company- or facility-specific policies, standards, and relevant regulations, be documented in a Cybersecurity Requirements Specification (CRS). The CRS does not have to be a standalone document; it can be included as a section in other relevant IACS documents.
- **Threat Modeling** Part 4-1 describes the requirements for the **Security Development Lifecycle** (SDL) of control system and component products. One of the key processes in the product SDL is threat modeling, a systematic process for identifying data flows,

trust boundaries, attack vectors, and potential threats to the control system. The security issues identified in the threat model must be considered in the final version of the product, and the threat model itself must be regularly updated during the product lifecycle.

Foundational Requirements:

Foundational Requirements (FRs) form the basis for technical requirements throughout the entire ISA/IEC 62443 series. All aspects required to achieve a desired IACS security level (people, processes, and technology) are derived by fulfilling the requirements, which follow from the seven following foundational requirements. They are comparable to the terms protection objectives or cybersecurity properties defined in other standards.

> FR 1—**Identification and Authentication Control** (IAC)
> FR 2—**Use Control** (UC)
> FR 3—**System Integrity** (SI)
> FR 4—**Data Confidentiality** (DC)
> FR 5—**Restricted Data Flow** (RDF)
> FR 6—**Timely Response to Events** (TRE)
> FR 7—**Resource Availability** (RA)

The protection objectives defined in ISA/IEC 62443 can be mapped to the classic CIA protection objectives accordingly (see Table 5.1). A cross in the table indicates a corresponding assignment.

The Foundational Requirements are used to establish the requirements for IACS systems (Part 3-3) and components (Part 4-2).

Security Levels (Security Level):

The security level is defined as the measure of confidence that the system under consideration, the zone, or the channel is free from weaknesses and functions as intended. Part 3-3 further defines the security level in terms of the means, resources, capabilities, and motivation of the threat actor. It is used as a means of distinguishing between requirement extensions for systems (Part 3-3) and components (Part 4-2).

> This is where cybersecurity standards differ: The meaning and definition of a **security level** as well as the **risk criteria,** which ultimately lead to the **risk assessment.**

Table 5.1 Foundational Requirements—Classic Cybersecurity Protection Objectives

CIA I FRs	IAC	UC	SI	DC	RDF	TRE	RA
Confidentiality	X	X		X			
Integrity	X	X	X			X	
Availability					X	X	X

The ISA/IEC 62443 introduces equal three types of security levels (Table 5.2):

- The **Capability** Security Levels (**SL-C**) are the security levels that systems (Part 3-3) or components (Part 4-2) can provide when they are properly integrated and configured. These levels state that a particular system or component is capable of meeting the SL-T natively without additional compensating countermeasures.
- **Target** Security Levels (**SL-T**) are the desired security levels for a specific automation solution. They are determined as a result of the risk assessment process (Part 3-2) and are documented in the specification of the cybersecurity requirements. SL-T are used to select products and design additional countermeasures during the integration phase of the IACS lifecycle.
- **Achieved** Security Levels (**SL-A**) are the actual security levels for a specific automation solution. These are measured after the automation solution has been commissioned and is in operation. Part 2-2 combines SL-A with operational and maintenance policies and procedures to form the security program rating for a specific automation solution.

Maturity Model

While the security levels are a measure of the strength of the technical requirements, the maturity levels are a **measure of the processes** (people, policies, and procedures). Parts 2-1, 2-2, 2-4, and 4-1 use maturity levels to measure how thoroughly the requirements are met. The maturity model is based on the **Capability Maturity Model Integration** (CMMI) [CMMI], with levels 4 and 5 being combined into level 4.

Table 5.2 Security level definition according to ISA/IEC 62443

Security Level	Definition	Means	Resources	Skill	Motivation
1	Protection against unintentional or accidental misuse	Simple	Low	Generic	Low
2	Protection against intentional misuse by simple means with few resources, general skills and low motivation	Simple	Low	Generic	Low
3	Protection against intentional misuse by sophisticated means with moderate resources, IACS-specific knowledge, and moderate motivation	Sophisticated	Moderate	IACS-specific	Moderate
4	Protection against intentional misuse using sophisticated means with extensive resources, IACS-specific knowledge, and high motivation	Sophisticated	Extended	IACS-specific	High

The higher the level, the more formal the product development maturity:

- Level 1 (**initial**):
  - Product development is typically ad-hoc and often undocumented
  - Consistency and repeatability may not be possible
- Level 2 (**managed**):
  - Product development is guided by written policies
  - Staff have expertise and are trained to follow procedures
  - Processes are defined, but some may not be established in practice
- Level 3 (**defined/practiced**):
  - All processes are repeatable throughout the organization
  - All processes are established in practice with documented evidence
- Level 4: (**improve**):
  - CMMI levels 4 and 5 are combined
  - Process metrics are used to control effectiveness and performance
  - Continuous improvement

Design Principles

- **Security-by-Design:** Design principle, in which Security Control measures early in the Lifecycle of the IACS implemented are. Robust Security policies, security architectures and secure practices should be established early in development established and during the entire lifecycle are implemented
- **Reduction of the attack surface:** Design principle in which the physical and functional interfaces of an IACS, which can be accessed and are exposed to potential attacks, are minimized, making it more difficult for an attack to be successful. The reduction of the attack surface includes design principles such as:
  - **Access control**—Restriction of physical and logical access to IACS systems and networks.
  - **Network segmentation**—Segmentation of IACS networks and control of data traffic between them.
  - **Least Function**—Hardening of IACS systems and networks by removing unnecessary functions.
  - **Least Privilege**—Limiting privileges to the minimum necessary for the role or function.
- **Defense-in-Depth:** Provision of multiple security protections, especially in layers, with the intention of delaying or preventing an attack. Defense in depth implies layers of security and detection, even on individual systems, and requires attackers to break through or bypass multiple layers without being detected. The IACS is still protected even if a weakness in one layer is exploited. Special attention must be paid to a single vulnerability that allows the potential compromise of multiple layers.
- **Essential Functions:** Functions or capabilities that serve to maintain health, safety, the environment, and the availability of equipment. Essential functions include:

- the Safety Instrumented Function (SIF).
- the control function.
- the operator's ability to see and get the device under control.

This results in corresponding requirements for the design:

- Access control must not prevent the operation of essential functions.
- Essential functions must be maintained when the zone boundary protection (firewall) switches to a Fail-Close/Island mode.
- A Denial-of-Service event in the control system network or the safety-oriented system must not prevent the safety-oriented functions from working.

Various views can be defined on the ISA/IEC 62443 and the corresponding parts assigned to roles/phases become:

- **Hierarchical** according to involved roles:
  - Asset owner (2-1, 2-2, 2-3, 2-4, 3-2, 3-3),
  - Operator (Integration) (2-1, 2-3, 2-4, 3-2, 3-3),
  - Operator (Maintenance) (2-3, 2-2, 2-4),
  - Product manufacturer (4-1, 3-3, 4-2, 3-2).
- **Lifecycle:**
  - Product development (1-1, 3-3, 4-1, 4-2) –
  - Integration (1-1, 2-1, 2-2, 2-3, 2-4, 3-2, 3-3) –
  - Operation and maintenance (1-1, 2-1, 2-2, 2-3, 2-4, 3-2).

5.2.5 27k-Family—Information Security

The **ISO/IEC 27000** series (also known as ISO/IEC 27000 family, briefly referred to as ISO 27k) is a series of standards for information security. As part of the standardization, ISO and IEC decided to consolidate various standards for information security under the number range 27k Information Technology—Security Techniques.

The standard **ISO/IEC 27001** [ISO27001], which sets requirements for an information security system and against which one can be certified, as well as **ISO/IEC 27005** [ISO27005] which describes the corresponding Security Risk Management, are essential.

The following subsections will examine the standards

- ISO/IEC 27001 [ISO27001]: Information Security Management Sect. 5.2.5.1
- ISO/IEC 27005 [ISO27005]: Risk Management Sect. 5.2.5.2
- ISO/IEC 27701 [ISO27701]: Privacy Engineering Sect. 5.2.5.3

in more detail.

5.2.5.1 ISO/IEC 27001—Information Security Management

The **ISO/IEC 27001** [ISO27001] sets requirements for the establishment, implementation, maintenance, and continuous improvement of an **Information Security Management** in the context of an organization. It is domain-independent and follows the Deming cycle/ PDCA cycle. An organizational unit can be certified for conformity to the standard. The Annex A, the so-called SoA (**Statement of Applicability**) which tailors the application of the standard according to the business processes of the organization, plays a crucial role. It is divided into 14 groups of control objectives and controls which, together with parts 4 (Context of the Organization) to 10 (Continuous Improvement), represent the management for information security of a company (High-Level-Structure). This is in addition to/ integrated with other management systems such as quality, risk, environment, etc.

The goal of the standard is to ensure the survival of an organization (company) against **information security risks.** This applies both internally and externally. In addition to an appropriate policy, the application consists of a series of organizational and technical measures and guidelines. These include, among others, regulations for the use of home offices, application of password rules, installation of firewalls, hardening of laptops, etc.

The core is a properly set up **Asset Management.** The identification of assets worth protecting from the respective perspective of relevant stakeholders. These can be laptops, server room access, access rights, licenses, …

Also, the definition of emergency plans in case of a (successful) attack and documentation of a successful execution of emergency scenarios is part of the scope of certification.

The ISO/IEC 27002 [ISO27002] is informative and serves to better understand the requirements defined in ISO/IEC 27001 (especially from Annex A).

5.2.5.2 ISO/IEC 27005 Security Risk Management

The **ISO/IEC 27005** [ISO27005] defines, very similar to the **BSI 200-3** [BSI200-3], an information security risk management process. This is based on the overarching **ISO 31000** [ISO31000], which is to be referenced and considered for all ISO standards that include risk management.

Section 7.4 will go into more detail on this.

5.2.5.3 ISO/IEC 27701—Data Protection Management System

The standard **ISO/IEC 27701** [ISO27701] extends the ISO/IEC 27001 [ISO27001] and **ISO/IEC 27002** [ISO27002] to a **Data Protection Management System (PIMS** (Privacy Information Management System)). The additional requirements for each volume are described in relation to ISO/IEC 27001.

Additional requirements are "only" necessary for parts 4 (Context of the Organization) and 6 (Planning). For the **SoA**, however, additional requirements must be met for almost all controls.

Example

- The policy must be expanded accordingly: Support and conformity must also be achieved with regard to applicable data protection and its rules/laws in the organization, partners, and third parties (customers, suppliers).
- The use of mobile devices must not compromise affected individuals. ◀

The appendix contains various mapping tables:

- **Extension of the SoA** (Statement of Applicability) of ISO/IEC 27001 from the perspective of the two roles of controller and processor
- **ISO/IEC 27701** [ISO27701] clauses to articles of the EU-GDPR [EU-GDPR]
- **ISO/IEC 29100** [ISO29100] principles to the controls

5.2.6 TISAX—Automotive ISMS

TISAX [TISAX] (**T**rusted **I**nformation **S**ecurity **A**ssessment E**X**change) is a standard defined by the automotive industry for information security. Since 2017, many business partners have been requesting car manufacturers and suppliers in the German automotive industry to have an existing TISAX certification. The VDA questionnaire "**I**nformation **S**ecurity **A**ssessment" **(ISA)** is publicly available and free of charge.

The ENX (formerly **E**uropean **N**etwork **Ex**change Association) network is a joint solution of the European automotive industry for the secure exchange of critical development, purchasing, and production control data and acts as a governance organization.

In terms of content, TISAX is similar to ISO/IEC 27001 [ISO27001] (reference to **SoA** (**S**tatement **o**f **A**pplicability)) + extensions. Approximately 80% of the questions are very similar in meaning, especially the catalog for information security.

Up to TISAX version 5, the numbering of parts 5-18 was identical to ISO/IEC 27001. Some questions were dropped, some questions were added. The structure has since been changed, the similarities with ISO/IEC 27001 are no longer quite as obvious. TISAX is divided into the following requirement catalogs:

- 1–7: **Information security** (based on ISO/IEC 27001). **Supplier management** (separated in earlier TISAX versions, is now covered in the information security part)
- 8: **Prototype protection** (still separate in addition)
- 9: **Data protection** (Privacy)

The traceability to ISO/IEC 27001 is given informatively within the TISAX Excel template by means of a corresponding information column.

The main difference to ISO is in the additional chapters such as protection of prototypes, which is extremely important in the automotive industry, as well as a defined maturity model. TISAX does not follow the ISO high-level structure for management systems. The model is not binary in the sense of certificate is issued or not (e.g., despite (minor) deviations), but each group of requirements is individually evaluated against a corresponding maturity level (from 0 incomplete to 5 optimizing) according to predefined criteria. In the end, the capability of an organization is visually represented using a spider diagram.

5.2.7 UNECE/NHTSA—Automotive Regulations

The **UNECE** (**U**nited **N**ations **E**conomic **C**ommission for **E**urope, www.unece.org) harmonizes vehicle regulations worldwide (see Fig. 5.1) [UNECE]. In the responsible **W**orking **P**arty 29 (WP.29), about 58 countries have joined together and contractually assured mutual acceptance for the homologation of road vehicles. Thus, a vehicle type does not have to undergo the same homologation again in another country after successful homologation in one country. About one third of all vehicles worldwide are produced in the 58 countries. Some countries like the USA, Canada, and China have a veto right, but usually follow with a delay of 2-3 years to optimize their own production and reduce the number of different platforms to be developed or their differences.

On June 24, 2020, two regulations were initiated [UNECE20]: UN Regulation No. [155] for Cybersecurity (Management System) [UNECE-155] (Interpretation document and connection to ISO/SAE 21434: [UNECE-155a]) and UN Regulation No. [156] for Software Updates (Management System) [UNECE-156] (Interpretation document: [UNECE-156a]). For Europe, UNECE regulations are made effective by the European Parliament and Council through the General Safety Regulations [GSR19]. This also stip-

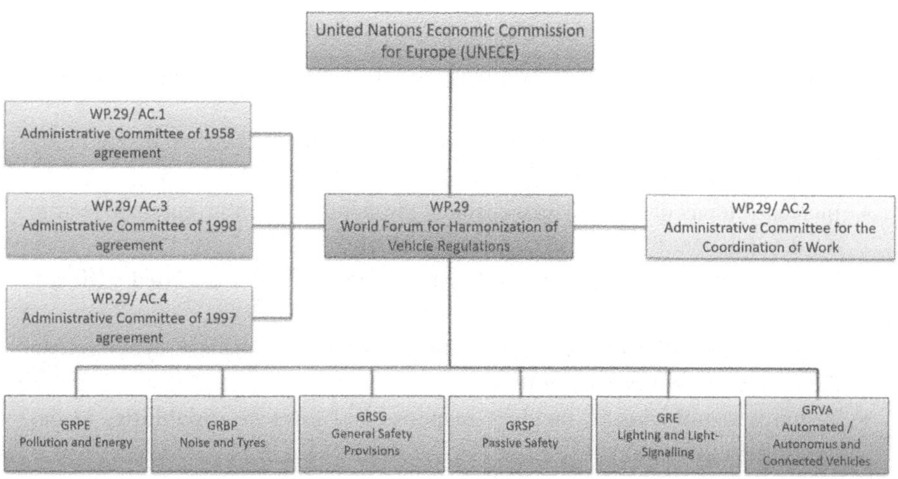

Fig. 5.1 UNECE Organization (www.unece.org)

ulates the deadlines by which the UNECE regulations must be implemented for Europe. In this case, mid-2022 and 2024 are relevant dates by which new and then also updated type approvals according to UNECE must be implemented. Prior to this, vehicle manufacturers must have their management systems, which are to be established by mid-2022, successfully certified by independent national authorities.

The two regulations are each divided into several sections. On the one hand, they contain requirements for the reviewing authorities for the certification process, homologations (type approval) and marking, and on the other hand, a whole bundle for the vehicle manufacturers. These are divided into two groups of requirements:

1. **Procedural requirements** for the management system to be established
2. Requirements for the homologating **vehicle types**.

> The two new UN regulations, adopted by the UNECE World Forum for Harmonization of Vehicle Regulations, require the implementation of measures in four different areas:
>
> - **Management** of **vehicle cyber risks,**
> - **Securing** vehicles by design to minimize **risks along the value chain,**
> - **Detecting** and **responding to security incidents** across the entire vehicle fleet,
> - **Providing secure software updates** and ensuring that vehicle safety is not compromised, introducing a **legal basis for so-called "Over-the-Air Updates"** (**OTA**) of vehicle software.

The regulation for cybersecurity can be summarized as follows:

- **Separation of technical** (requirements for type approval) and **procedural requirements** (requirements for the management system)
- Increased focus on conducting and maintaining a **comprehensive threat analysis** and **risk assessment**
- Increased **focus** on security management throughout the entire automotive product development lifecycle and the **supply chain**
- Need for proper **identification** and management of **risks associated with suppliers**
- Requires specific **processes** and **technical controls,** to manage **cybersecurity** throughout the **entire company**
- Requires **monitoring** of **incident response** and **forensic capabilities** of data during post-processing
- High **focus** on the **securing** and **control** of **Data-at-Rest** and **Data-in-Transit**, especially when it comes to personal data

To conduct a threat analysis and risk assessment, Annex 5 of the UNECE Regulation No. [155] prescribes mandatory threats and countermeasures to be considered (Sect. 7.2).

Very similar requirements for processes and controls can be found at the NHTSA (**N**ational **H**ighway **T**raffic **S**afety **A**dministration), the US federal agency for road and vehicle safety. In ***"Cybersecurity Best Practices for the Safety of Modern Vehicles"*** [NHTSA20], process requirements, vehicle requirements, and threats to be considered are specified very similarly to the UNECE regulations [UNECE-155], [UNECE-156] and can be easily mapped to each other. Here too, a distinction is made between process and technical requirements and vehicle security:

- **General process requirements/Best Practices:** (e.g., reported at Auto-ISAC [Auto-ISAC])
  - Leadership, priority on product safety,
  - Requirements for the development process regarding cybersecurity: risk assessment, security gaps in sensors, risk minimization in design, penetration testing, monitoring, data, industry best practices, …
  - Information sharing: membership in relevant organizations,
  - Security gap reporting process,
  - Organization: incident management process,
  - Self-audit: documentation process management, review, and audit.
- **Training,**
- **After-Market,**
- **Service,** …
- **Technical vehicle security/Best Practices** based on long-term experience:
  - Development access possibilities in production,
  - Cryptographic credentials,
  - Vehicle diagnostic functionality and tools,
  - In-vehicle communication,
  - Event logging,
  - Wireless communication paths into the vehicle,
  - Software updates and specifically,
  - Over-the-air software updates.

5.2.8 IEC 15480—Common Criteria

Common Criteria (**CC**) (ISO15408) [**IEC 15408**] offers a rigorous, standardized, and repeatable process for the specification, implementation, and evaluation of a computer security product. The process usually starts with a protection profile, which defines the threats, values, and objectives. This was already started in 1993.

Common Criteria is a framework in which users of computer systems can specify their functional security and reliability requirements (SFRs or SARs) through the use of protection profiles (PPs), manufacturers can then implement the security attributes of their products and/or make claims about them, and testing laboratories can evaluate the products to determine whether they actually meet the claims. In other words: Common Criteria provides assurance that the process of specification, implementation, and evaluation of a computer security product was conducted in a rigorous, standardized, and repeatable manner at a level appropriate to the target environment for use.

Common Criteria is used as the basis for a government-operated certification scheme and typically evaluations are conducted for use by federal agencies and critical infrastructures.

Evaluation and Certification:

- **Main focus** of CC is the support of the evaluation and certification of IT products with security functionality
- CC **enables the comparability of the results** of independent security evaluations. CC does this by providing a common set of requirements for the security functionality of IT products and for the trustworthiness measures that are applied to these IT products during a security evaluation. These IT products can be implemented in hardware, firmware, or software.
- CC is useful as a **guide for the development, evaluation, and/or procurement** of IT products with security functionality.
- CC **addresses the protection of assets** from unauthorized disclosure (**confidentiality**), alteration (**integrity**), or loss of use (**availability**).
- CC is applicable to risks arising from **human activities** (malicious or otherwise) and to risks arising from **non-human activities**.
- CC does not contain security evaluation criteria that relate to administrative security measures that are not directly related to IT security functionality

> The protection objectives in the Common Criteria standard are **confidentiality, integrity** and **availability.**

The standard is public and comprises 3 volumes:

1. **Introduction and general model:** Introduction to the core concept "Target-of-Evaluation" (evaluation object). These can be, for example: a software application, an operating system, cryptographic co-processor, a LAN, a database, etc.
   - CC Volume 1 defines general concepts and principles of IT security evaluation and presents a general model of evaluation.
2. **Functional security components:** Establishes a set of functional components that serve as standard templates on which the functional requirements for evaluation objects are based.
   - CC Volume 2 catalogs the set of functional components and divides them into families and classes.

3. **Security components:** Establishes a set of security components that serve as standard templates on which the security requirements for evaluation objects can be based.
   – CC Volume 3 catalogs the set of security components and divides them into families and classes. CC Part 3 also defines evaluation criteria for protection profiles and protection objectives and introduces seven predefined assurance packages, referred to as **E**valuation **A**ssurance **L**evels (**EAL**s).

To support the three volumes of the CC listed above, additional documents have been published. The Common Methodology for Information Technology Security Evaluation (CEM) provides the methodology for IT security evaluation that CC uses as a basis. It is expected that further documents will be published, including technical justifications and guides:

- CC is flexible in what is to be evaluated and is therefore **not bound to the boundaries of IT products in the usual sense.** Therefore, CC uses the term "ToE" (Target of Evaluation) in the context of evaluation. An EVG (evaluation object) is defined as a set of software, firmware, and/or hardware.
- Customers or user groups specify Protection Profiles. These are defined and consistent subsets of the requirements specified in the CC. Protection profiles are evaluated.
- In the context of CC, manufacturers implement security specifications in their ToEs. A ToE is evaluated against defined security specifications.
- Target audience for the CC: Consumers, developers, and evaluators

In the end, Common Criteria represent internationally harmonized **criteria** for the security evaluation of IT technology. They form a catalog for the **specification** of security requirements. Comparability of the results of evaluations should be given. In this context, levels of trustworthiness (**EAL E**valuation **A**ssurance **L**evel) are defined. The higher the level, the more stringent the verification methods applied.

Verification Methods

EAL 7 = **Formally verified design** and **tested**
EAL 6 = **Semi-formally verified design** and **tested**
EAL 5 = **Semi-formally designed** and **tested**
EAL 4 = **Methodically developed, tested** and **reviewed**
EAL 3 = **Methodically tested** and **checked**
EAL 2 = **Structurally tested**
EAL 1 = **Functionally tested**

Considered risk factors:

- **Force majeure** (lightning strike, fire, flood, …)
- **Negligence** (error, misuse, improper operation, …)
- **Intentional** (manipulation, burglary, hacking, espionage, sabotage, …)
- **Technical failure** (power outage, HW failure, …)
- **Organizational deficiencies** (unauthorized access, piracy, untrained staff, …)

In contrast to other risk assessment models, the Common Criteria approach is attack potential-oriented.

5.2.9 RTCA DO 326-A—Aviation Security

The standard **RTCA DO 326**-A [DO-326] (2014, 88 pages) supplements the current guide for the certification of aircraft, to address the threat to aircraft security from deliberate unauthorized electronic interaction. It adds data requirements and compliance objectives, which are structured according to general activities for the development and certification of aircraft, to handle the threat to aircraft security from unauthorized interaction, and is intended to be used in conjunction with other applicable guidance, including SAE ARP 4754A/ED-79A, DO-178C/ED-12C (Software) and DO-254/ED-80 (Hardware), and with advisory material in conjunction with FAA AC 25.1309-1A and EASA AMC 25.1309 in relation to Part 25 for transport category aircraft that include an approved passenger seat configuration with more than 19 passenger seats. This guidance is not intended for CFR Parts 23, 27, 29, 33.28 and 35.15, normal, utility, aerobatic and commuter category aircraft, normal category rotorcraft, transport category rotorcraft, engines and propellers.

This document **does not address:**

- **Physical security** or physical attacks on the aircraft (or the ground element),
- **Security of airports, airlines** or **air traffic service providers** (e.g., access to aircraft, ground control facilities, data centers),
- **Communication**, **navigation** and **surveillance services,** managed by national authorities or their international equivalents (e.g., GPS, SBAS, GBAS, ATC communication, ADS-B).

This guide is aimed at equipment manufacturers, aircraft manufacturers and all others, for a type certification (TC) and thereafter.

When applying this guide to existing developments or operations, special caution is recommended. The guide is designed to be applied throughout the entire lifecycle of an aircraft from development through operation to disposal. As such, it should first be applied to the design phase before being used in subsequent phases of the lifecycle.

When objectives are applied to aircraft that have not previously been subject to these objectives in all phases of their lifecycle, it should be considered that some aspects of the objectives will not be applicable. These aspects should be described and addressed separately. For existing or in-development aircraft, alternative processes are acceptable that may utilize some or all processes of this document.

Intended, unauthorized electronic interaction (also referred to as "unauthorized interaction" within the document) is defined as human-initiated actions with the potential to impair the aircraft through unauthorized access, use, disclosure, denial, disruption, modification, or destruction of electronic information or electronic aircraft system interfaces. This definition includes the effects of malware on infected devices and the logical effects of external systems on aircraft systems, but does not include physical attacks or electromagnetic interference.

The FAA (Federal Aviation Administration) publishes additional guidance that can be used in conjunction with this document. As the requirements and regulations for electronic security of aircraft change, it is strongly recommended that applicants contact the relevant certification authorities (FAA or international civil aviation authorities) to obtain the latest guidance for using this document for certification projects.

5.2.10 EU Cybersecurity Act

In the future, there should be EU-wide Cybersecurity certifications. They are intended to strengthen security and competitiveness within the Union of States.

With the **EU Cybersecurity Act** ([EU-CA19], April 17, 2019), the EU Cybersecurity Agency (Agency of the European Union for Network and Information Security, **ENISA**) is revised and strengthened, and an EU-wide cybersecurity certification framework for digital products, services, and processes is created. It is part of a comprehensive package of measures to increase cybersecurity and to **strengthen resilience against cyberattacks** of the European Union.

The Cybersecurity Act grants the agency a permanent mandate, more resources, and new tasks. It is supposed to promote the readiness for defense. The ENISA prepares the technical basis for specific certification systems and informs the public about the certification systems and the certificates issued via its own website.

With the EU Cybersecurity Act, an EU-wide **cybersecurity certification framework** for ICT products, services, and processes is introduced for the first time. Companies operating in the EU will benefit from having to certify their ICT products, processes, and services only once and having to recognize their certificates throughout the European Union. Similar to the EU General Data Protection Regulation [EU-GDPR], the principles of ***"Security-by-Design"*** and ***"Security-by-Default"*** are written down for the first time as regulatory principles for security-relevant products. Other basic principles are **authorization management**, **non-repudiation** and **availability** of data.

Depending on the intended risk of use, different requirement levels are determined. A certification according to the security level

- "**high**" includes a test of the defense **against state-of-the-art cyberattacks** with extensive resources, the presence of IT security features at the latest technical level, and the corresponding proof by **penetration testing**
- "**medium**" must provide a defense capability with regard to **known cyber risks** by actors with limited resources, a review of publicly known vulnerabilities, and the correct function of the security measures must be proven by **tests**
- "**low**" must at least minimize **basic risks** and the technical documentation of the product or service must be reviewed. For this level, a manufacturer can carry out a **self-assessment** for conformity.

5.3 Summary

In the standards, norms, and best practices, the topics addressed in the following sections run through in different shades and are particularly relevant for solving the challenges in the field of cybersecurity.

- **Secure Software Engineering (see Sect.** 5.3.1)
- Software Lifecycle **(Security-by-Design)**
- Challenges and **measures (see Sect.** 5.3.2)

5.3.1 Secure Software Engineering

The different "building blocks" of Secure Software Engineering, which need to be considered and addressed individually, are summarized here in corresponding questions:

- **Analysis:** Threat analyses—What threat analyses need to be conducted to provide guidance on the development of secure systems?
- **Design phase:** Secure architecture—What must an architecture contain to be considered "secure" in terms of cybersecurity?
- **Implementation:** Code reviews—Which software components are security-critical?
- **Implementation/Commissioning:** Penetration test: Which components must have undergone a penetration test?
- **Commissioning:** Hardening—Which components need to be hardened and how?
- **Usage:** Incident response—What security vulnerabilities are known? How are they addressed?
- **Further development and maintenance:** Update management—Maintaining security requires updates. How can the update procedure itself be secured?

5.3.2 Challenges and Measures

Challenges can be focused on the following topics:

- **Protection** of **security attributes/protection objectives:**
  - **Authenticity,** e.g. data comes from known sensors
  - **Availability,** e.g. door lock opens within a certain timeframe
  - **Confidentiality,** e.g. personal data is only visible to the user
  - **Integrity,** e.g. firmware is unchanged
- **Defense** against **threat scenarios:**
  - **Spoofing,** e.g. pretending to be a user's smartphone
  - **Tampering,** e.g. manipulating sensor data
  - **Repudiation,** e.g. denial of use of vehicle functions
  - **Disclosure** of **information,** e.g. reading of driver profiles
  - **Denial-of-Service,** e.g. disruption of the keyless remote control
  - **Privilege elevation,** e.g. changing the control unit configuration as a user
- **Mitigation** of possible **damage categories:**
  - **Functional safety,** e.g. endangering the lives of drivers
  - **Finances,** e.g. freeloading on billable functions
  - **Operation,** e.g. failures
  - **Laws,** e.g. disclosure of driver profiles

In the automotive sector, the biggest challenges can be specified, but they can also be transferred to other industries/domains:

- **Product complexity:**
  - diverse, increasing number of attack points
  - mainly software-based
- **Back-end systems:**
  - IT and operation connections
  - Back-end systems are connected to many IT systems
  - The network of services is increasing
- **Supply chain**
  - Complexity of the supply chain
  - Threat scenarios at all levels
  - Long lifetime of components
- **Threat landscape**
  - Constant change of threat landscapes
  - Function updates over the air change products over time

The challenges must be approached holistically, both procedurally and role-based. People, processes, technology, and data must be taken into account.

References

[ASPICE3.1] ***„Process Reference Model Process Assessment Model Version 3.1"*;** VDA Automotive SPICE®

[Auto-ISAC] ***„Automotive Information Sharing and Analysis Center"*;** Link: https://automotiveisac.com/ accessed: 18.04.2021

[BSI200-3] ***„Risikoanalyse auf Basis von IT-Grundschutz"*;** BSI-Standard 200–3. Link: https://www.bsi.bund.de/SharedDocs/Downloads/DE/BSI/Grundschutz/BSI_Standards/standard_200_3.pdf?__blob=publicationFile&v=2 accessed: 18.04.2021

[CMK+11] ***„Comprehensive Experimental Analyses of Automotive Attack Surfaces"*;** Stephen Checkoway, Damon McCoy, Brian Kantor, Danny Anderson, Hovav Shacham, and Stefan Savage University of California, San Diego; Karl Koscher, Alexei Czeskis, Franziska Roesner, and Tadayoshi Kohno University of Washington. Link: http://www.autosec.org/pubs/cars-usenixsec2011.pdf accessed: 18.04.2021

[CMMI] ***„Capability Maturity Model Integration (CMMI)"*;** Link: https://cmmiinstitute.com/ accessed: 18.04.2021

[CVE] ***„NIST Database for Vulnerabilities"***. Link: https://nvd.nist.gov/vuln accessed 10.04.2021

[DO-326] ***„Airworthiness Security Process Specification"*;** RTCA DO-326

[EU-CA19] ***„Regulation (EU) 2019/881 of the European Parliament and of the Council of 17 April 2019* (EU-Cybersecurity-Act)"**. Link: https://eur-lex.europa.eu/eli/reg/2019/881/oj accessed: 10.04.2021

[EU-GDPR] General Data Protection Regulation; (EU) 2016/679; Link: https://eur-lex.europa.eu/legal-content/EN/TXT/?uri=CELEX%3A32016R0679; accessed: 10.04.2021

[FIPS199] ***„Standards for Security Categorization of Federal Information and Information Systems"*;** Federal Information Processing Standards Publication 199; February 2004. Link: https://nvlpubs.nist.gov/nistpubs/FIPS/NIST.FIPS.199.pdf accessed: 18.04.2021

[FIPS200] ***„Minimum Security Requirements for Federal Information and Information Systems"*;** Federal Information Processing Standards Publication 200; March 2006. Link: https://nvlpubs.nist.gov/nistpubs/FIPS/NIST.FIPS.200.pdf accessed: 18.04.2021

[GSR19] ***„Regulation (EU) 2019/2144 of the European Parliament and of the Council of 27 November 2019"*.** Link: https://eur-lex.europa.eu/eli/reg/2019/2144/oj accessed: 18.04.2021

[HL06] ***„SDL: A Process for Developing Demonstrably More Secure Software"*;** Michael Howard; Steve Lipner; Microsoft, 2006;

[IEC62443] ***„New ISA/IEC 62443 standard specifies security capabilities for control system components"*;** ISA.org home page: https://www.isa.org/intech-home/2018/september-october/departments/new-standard-specifies-security-capabilities-for-c accessed: 18.04.2021

[IEEE15] ***„Avoiding the Top 10 Software Security Design Flaws"***; IEEE Cyber Security, November 2015. Link https://ieeecs-media.computer.org/media/technical-activities/CYBSI/docs/Top-10-Flaws.pdf accessed: 18.04.2021

[ISO5112] ***„Road vehicles – Guidelines for auditing cybersecurity engineering“,*** ISO PAS 5112

[ISO15288] ***„Systems and software engineering — System life cycle processes“;*** ISO/IEC/IEEE15288

[ISO15408] ***„Information technology – Security techniques – Evaluation criteria for IT security –“,*** Common Criteria, ISO/IEC 15408 Band 1 – 3

[ISO21434] ***„Road Vehicles – Cybersecurity Engineering”,*** International Standard ISO/SAE 21434.

[ISO27001] ***„Information security management systems – Requirements“;*** ISO/IEC 27001

[ISO27002] ***„Information technology — Security techniques — Code of practice for information security controls“;*** ISO/IEC 27002

[ISO27005] ***„Information technology – Security techniques - Information security risk management“;*** ISO/IEC 27005

[ISO27701] ***„Security techniques — Extension to ISO/IEC 27001 and ISO/IEC 27002 for privacy information management — Requirements and guidelines“;*** ISO/IEC 27701

[ISO29100] ***„Information Technology – Security techniques – Privacy framework“;*** ISO/IEC 29100:2011(E); First edition 2011–12–15.

[ISO31000] ***„Risk management – Guidelines“;*** DIN ISO 31000

[KSL18] ***„New Vehicle Security Research by KeenLab: Experimental Security Assessment of BMW Cars“***; Keen Security Lab Blog. Link: https://keenlab.tencent.com/en/2018/05/22/New-CarHacking-Research-by-KeenLab-Experimental-Security-Assessment-of-BMW-Cars/ accessed: 18.04.2021

[NHTSA20] ***„Cybersecurity Best Practices for the Safety of Modern Vehicles“;*** Draft 2020 Updates. Link: https://www.nhtsa.gov/sites/nhtsa.dot.gov/files/documents/vehicle_cybersecurity_best_practices_01072021.pdf accessed: 18.04.2021

[NIST800-53B] ***„Control Baselines for Information Systems and Organizations“;*** NIST SP 800-53B https://csrc.nist.gov/publications/detail/sp/800-53b/final accessed: 18.04.2021

[NIST800-53R5] ***„Security and Privacy Controls for Federal Information Systems and Organizations“***; NIST SP 800-53 Revision 5. Link: https://csrc.nist.gov/publications/detail/sp/800-53/rev-5/final accessed: 18.04.2021

[NIST800-115] ***„Technical Guide to Information Security Testing and Assessment“;*** NIST SP 800–115

[NIST800-160v1] ***„Systems Security Engineering: Considerations for a Multidisciplinary Approach in the Engineering of Trustworthy Secure Systems“,*** NIST SP 800–160 volume 1 (2016)

[NIST800-160v2] ***„Developing Cyber Resilien Systems: A Systems Security Engineering Approach“;*** NIST SP 800-160v2 (2019)

[SAE3061] ***„Cybersecurity Guidebook for Cyber-Physical Vehicle Systems“;*** SAE J3061™, Issued 2016–01

[TISAX] ***„Trusted Information Security Assessment Exchange“;*** Link: https://www.vda.de/en/services/Publications/vda-isa-catalogue-version-5.0.html accessed: 18.04.2021

[UNECE] ***„Common Regulatory Framework on Cybersecurity“;*** Link: https://unece.org/trade/wp6/groups/cybersecurity accessed: 18.04.2021

[UNECE-155] ***„Addendum 154 – UN Regulation No. 155";*** Link: https://unece.org/sites/default/files/2021-03/R155e.pdf accessed: 18.04.2021

[UNECE-155a] ***„Proposal for the Interpretation Document for UN Regulation No. [155] on uniform provisions concerning the approval of vehicles with regards to cyber security and cyber security management system";*** Link: https://unece.org/fileadmin/DAM/trans/doc/2020/wp29/WP29-182-05e.pdf accessed: 18.04.2021

[UNECE-156] ***„Addendum 155 – UN Regulation No. 156";*** Link: https://unece.org/sites/default/files/2021-03/R156e.pdf accessed: 18.04.2021

[UNECE-156a] ***„Proposals for Interpretation Documents for UN Regulation No. [156] on software update and software update management system";*** Link: https://unece.org/sites/default/files/2020-12/ECE-TRANS-WP29-2021-060e.pdf accessed: 18.04.2021

[UNECE20] ***„UN Regulations on Cybersecurity and Software Updates to pave the way for mass roll out of connected vehicles"; Link:*** https://unece.org/press/un-regulations-cybersecurity-and-software-updates-pave-way-mass-roll-out-connected-vehicles accessed: 18.04.2021

[VM15] ***„Hackers Remotely Kill a Jeep on the Highway—With Me in It";*** Chris Valasek, Charlie Miller. Link: https://www.wired.com/2015/07/hackers-remotely-kill-jeep-highway/ accessed: 10.04.2021

[VM15a] ***„Remote Exploitation of an Unaltered Passenger Vehicle";*** Chris Valasek, Charlie Miller. Link: https://ioactive.com/pdfs/IOActive_Remote_Car_Hacking.pdf accessed: 18.04.2021

[VM16] ***„The Jeep Hackers are back to prove car hacking can get get much worse";*** Chris Valasek, Charlie Miller. Link: https://www.wired.com/2016/08/jeep-hackers-return-high-speed-steering-acceleration-hacks/ accessed: 18.04.2021

[VP17] ***„Key Reinstallation Attacks: Forcing Nonce Reuse in WPA2";*** Mathy Vanhoef, Frank Piessens. Link: https://papers.mathyvanhoef.com/ccs2017.pdf accessed: 18.04.2021

[VDA21] ***„Automotive SPICE® for Cybersecurity",*** VDA Yellow Book, February 2021

6 Hacking

"It doesn't take more to get more. That's what emergence means"
(Murray Gell-Mann)

To successfully prepare and defend against cyberattacks, one must understand how attackers think and act. Security measures and controls must be able to anticipate threats in order to fend them off. One can never be completely sure that sufficient security has been achieved.

Specifying and implementing security measures is like setting up pillars to protect a fort. In the end, one must hope that enough sufficiently stable pillars have been placed closely enough together so that attackers will run into one of the erected pillars during their attacks and can no longer pass between the pillars.

If one looks more closely at carried out (successful) attacks, they often are based on the exploitation of **emergent properties** of a complex (potentially also confusing) system. These emergent properties are usually not known beforehand and (of course) have not been consciously implemented. They emerge from the interaction of elements of the system. In this context, emergent properties of the system cannot be obviously traced back to properties of the elements that exhibit them in isolation [Tal14].

It cannot be prevented that complex systems possess not only explicitly specified properties, but also additional, initially unknown ones as a "by-product", which can be used by attackers for an attack.

Attackers are often not destructive, but exploit inadequacies and gaps in a specification and emergent properties of a system.

In practically all domains, there have already been events and incidents that reveal where security is not given (see, for example, Sect. 2.1 and 2.3.7).

Known attacks (increasingly emerging in the automotive sector) make it clear that on the one hand complex attack paths and specialized knowledge are necessary, but on the other hand even simple tools and "easily found" knowledge from the internet are sufficient to carry out successful attacks.

T. Liedtke, *Information Security*, https://doi.org/10.1007/978-3-658-45711-2_6

6.1 Mindset

Hackers are usually creative minds with highly specialized know-how. The first hackers to become known were students at MIT who reconfigured a telecommunications system in the late 1950s to control a model railway system [KS]. From this environment, the term ***"hack"***, which stands for the creative solution of a technical problem, was born. For example, the technicians had managed to control the model trains by pressing the dial buttons of old telephones. If one of the technicians had managed to make a calculator more efficient by building a new type of circuit, this innovation was called a successful ***"hack"***. The members called themselves ***"hackers"*** for the first time. To them, a hacker was simply a clever tinkerer. A vocabulary of its own developed there, which later became known as ***"hacker jargon"***.

Facets of the mindset of hackers and their classification can be characterized as follows:

- **Hackers are motivated** to find extraordinary and non-obvious solutions.
- Hackers have the talent to (accidentally) find **alternative,** hidden **applications** for others.
- **Developers need criminal energy** to develop secure products (to be able to withstand hackers/attackers).
- **Security engineering processes are not sufficient** to identify all possible attack paths.
- The **application of standards,** using generally known methods, is the **opposite of the behavior of attackers.**

Hackers are not crackers (term e.g., for pirates). They do not want to destroy things, but to exploit them for other purposes.

One of the most well-known early representatives of a hacker is John T. Draper, known as Cap'n Crunch [Dra]. He gave himself this nickname after a breakfast cereal brand known in the USA as Cap'n Crunch. During a promotional campaign, the packages included a toy whistle that could produce two tones. One of them had the frequency of 2600 Hz. If you whistled this tone into the telephone receiver, you were—with two additional codes—able to make free telephone calls worldwide in the analog telephone world of the 1970s. Draper received his tips for Phreaking from a student in California, with whom he came into contact while testing a pirate radio station.

Hacker A person who illegally attempts to gain access to a system or gains access to a system with the intention of obtaining something or causing losses from the perspective of the parties involved, e.g., fame, finances, terrorist attack.

Attack/Assault Attempted deliberate action or interaction with the object or component or its environment that can lead to an adverse consequence.

Cracker People who enjoy breaking into computers to cause destruction.

Hackers can be divided into different groups from different perspectives. For example, by their motivation:

- **Researchers:** publish vulnerabilities and weaknesses. Motivation: raising awareness, gaining knowledge, alerting, warning, …
- **Security companies:** also publish vulnerabilities and weaknesses for marketing purposes
- **Attackers:** who pursue commercial illegal purposes

Working method:

- **White-Hats:** use their knowledge to work within the laws e.g., as security analysts
  - **White-Hat Ethical-Hacking:** Terms that describe hacking performed by a company or individual to identify potential threats on a computer or network
- **Grey-Hats:** Individuals (within the White-Hat category) who work both offensively and defensively for their personal use at different times (e.g., access to services without payment)
- **Blue-Hat** is a term referring to external computer security consulting firms that are commissioned to test a system for errors before its market launch, to look for weaknesses so that they can be closed (term is mainly used by Microsoft)
- **Black-Hats:** work with criminal energy (e.g., also as crackers)

Further grouping possibilities:

- **Red-Team:** Independent group that is supposed to help an organization improve its effectiveness by acting as an opponent. The goal is always to discover security weaknesses before an external third party can exploit them (e.g., via bug-bounty parties; see Sect. 2.2.5)
- **Scriptkiddies:** Individuals with limited computer knowledge who only know how to get crack programs and how to run them. (e.g., also as crackers)
- **Suicide-Hackers:** Individuals who want to bring down critical infrastructures for a "purpose" and don't care that they could go to jail for 30 years for their actions
- **Nation-State-Hackers:** Government officials who steal secrets from opponents, disrupt or damage the opponent's infrastructure; spread propaganda; distract an opponent during a real attack

While there were more white-hat than black-hat motivated attacks a few years ago, the latter are catching up. More and more attacks are happening today in secret for the financial advantage of the attackers.

For an attacker, there are now many different "lucrative" opportunities to capitalize on an identified security weaknesses to strike [Gor20].

- Security vulnerabilities that are found (e.g., by researchers or participants in a bug bounty program) can be sold to **manufacturers** of the corresponding (hacked) products. For many manufacturers, this is an effective means to harden their products (e.g., through appropriate updates) and is more efficient for them than laboriously searching for previously unknown security vulnerabilities.
- Discovered security vulnerabilities can be sold on the **Darknet**, so that others can plan and carry out further attacks based on them. Security vulnerabilities sold in this way can help botnet creators to carry out Denial-of-Service attacks, spy on credentials to enable even more extensive attacks, etc.
- **Governments** may be interested in using security vulnerabilities unknown to outsiders for their own intelligence services, as long as they are not closed.
- **Security vulnerability brokers** can be used as additional intermediaries.

In the field of using social engineering methods (see Sect. 2.2.4), Kevin Mitnick became known as early as 1992 [Mit18]. Social Engineering is widely a successful method for hackers to "manipulate" others to get confidential information.

Background Information
In the 2000s, Excel security vulnerabilities were sold and auctioned on eBay [KZ07].

The mindset of hackers is fundamentally different from that of developers different. The hacker mentality includes:

- Strategy to make money from security vulnerabilities.
- Focus on lucrative **scalable attacks:** Once an attack path is recognized, it should be repeated as often as possible (odometer fraud, chip tuning, repeated use of ransomware, …).
- Functional goals: To disable, degrade or falsify functions, such as stopping wind turbines, making vehicles pull over, …
- Hacks can often be realized with little money, necessary knowledge is often easily accessible.

Information and attack targets for the Internet of Things area can be easily found via corresponding search engines (like Shodan [sho]). With Shodan, all devices registered on the Internet can be found. In addition, other websites with standard passwords are helpful for directly dialing into (e.g., devices found with Shodan). Under the premise that manufacturers still deliver devices with (known) standard passwords (or use hard-coded non-changeable passwords), the probability is high to easily connect unauthorized to many devices (e.g., private webcams, printers, servers, …) with simple means.

There are also easy-to-use tools on the Internet for homepages (like Observatory [obs]) that provide "useful" information for attackers to find vulnerabilities and get information, such as

- used software versions,
- open ports,
- used protocols,
- …

without much effort.

The possibility of deception on the internet has also become very easy:

- Systems for **imitating speech** and **faces** are almost perfect.
- **Facial recognition software,** for example, to find existing Facebook profiles to self-photographed faces, works reliably to a high percentage.
- **Speech analysis tools** can be used in job interviews to infer characteristics of the applicant.
- Image recognition systems are used to monitor examinees and automatically detect attempts at fraud (Online-Proctoring).

Conclusion

Eyes and ears can be almost perfectly deceived over the internet.

6.2 Hacking Examples

6.2.1 Google Hacking

Google Hacking is a method for undetected collection of information. The targeted use of corresponding search operators helps. Even with a small number of operators, complex searches can be started to find vulnerable pages and devices. A targeted chaining of search terms and operators greatly increases the effectiveness.

Google Hacking is not about attacking Google or one of their servers. It's also not about finding hacking tutorials. Nor is it about increasing your own page rank or lowering others.

Google Hacking means that a potential attacker can search very effectively for vulnerabilities and weaknesses using appropriate Google queries.

While many use Google by entering appropriate search words to find corresponding pages, there are operators with which searches can be effectively controlled, optimized and results pre-filtered. There are operators to search for corresponding terms on pages, exclude pages with terms from the result, preset file types, search for terms in URLs, etc.

For example, you can search for pages with admin logins with the search for "inurl:login inurl:admin". Directories can also be searched: intitle: "index of". A separate Google Hacking Data Base is freely accessible [GHD] and provides corresponding examples.

In more offensive approaches, for example, private cryptographic keys, web consoles, errors in databases, etc. can be searched for in order to get hints about vulnerabilities and weaknesses.

Conclusion

Google Hacking is simple, fast, of good quality, and offers many possibilities.

6.2.2 Password Hacking

The use of passwords is a crucial means to enhance security. However, they (no matter how complex they are) are also always crackable (a matter of time). For this, there exist various methods:

- **Brute-Force Attack** (raw force): All allowed character combinations are tried in sequence until the correct one (the password) is found. The average time required for this attack depends on the complexity of the password. The method has high applicability. Any small additional information (e.g., someone uses words from the dictionary) helps to drastically shorten the time needed to guess the password.
- **Shoulder Surfing:** When entering a password, one is observed. This can happen directly (someone stands behind the person entering the password) or indirectly (a surveillance camera records the password entry, WPA-2 passwords can be read from a device, …). The applicability is rather low with a strong password policy, but it is easy to apply, e.g., when entering a PIN code. Countermeasure: Password policy; Lockout policy; Time locks; Notification to administrator; Log files; …
- **Credential Stuffing:** A type of cyber attack, in which stolen access data, typically consisting of lists of usernames and/or email addresses and the corresponding passwords (often from a previous data breach), are used to gain unauthorized access to user accounts through large-scale automated login requests.
- **Hash Cracking:** Entered plaintext passwords are encrypted before sending with a hash encrypted. On the recipient side, this hash value is compared with the hash of the password stored there. If someone gets to read the hash value, one can try to guess the corresponding plaintext. For a number of passwords (e.g., words from the dictionary or simply composed passwords), these have already been calculated and can be found directly in corresponding databases without trying and recalculating. A suitable countermeasure here could be, for example, adding a salt value to the password before calculating the hash value to increase the entropy, so that it cannot be obtained by combining simple words.

- **Rainbow Table Attack:** Correspondingly prepared tables with already calculated hash values have been optimized for quick finding so that not all combinations have to be tried.
- **Memory Dumping:** If possible access to the computer memory, passwords in plaintext or their hash values can be read out.
- **Pass The Hash (PtH):** The hash value of a password is used for authentication against a system. Due to vulnerabilities in the system or in the authentication protocols, the hash value can be read out with tools and used for authentication. The attack method is usable in various operating system environments.

6.3 Automotive Hacking Example

As a ***"wake-up call"*** for the automotive industry and the turning point for automotive cybersecurity, the Jeep Cherokee hack in July 2015 [VM15] can be considered. In this case, two attackers managed to remotely hijack a Jeep driving on a highway near St. Louis via the internet and control vehicle functions remotely. The specially invited journalist who was driving the Jeep only had partial control over the vehicle. From a distance, for example, the engine could be switched off. Without touching the dashboard, ventilation, radio volume, windshield wipers, washer fluid, and other functions were switched. The digital display showed—to demonstrate what is possible—the image of the two attackers …

The hacking technique—referred to in the security industry as a Zero-Day Exploit—targets Jeep Cherokees: The attacker is given wireless control over thousands of vehicles via the internet. Their source code is every car manufacturer's nightmare: Software that allows hackers to send commands via the Jeep's entertainment system to the dashboard functions, steering, brakes, and transmission—all from a laptop that may be located at the other end of a country.

As with many attacks, a complex preparation scenario is carried out until the actual damage can be inflicted. One must gain access to the vehicle, manipulate firmware to install malicious software, restart the system, etc. Security measures such as an intrusion detection system, whitelisting and secure boot could have made the attack unfeasible.

Even after the software was updated and wireless access from the outside was made impossible, driving functions could still be manipulated. Another hack by the same two attackers half a year later proved how easy manipulation still is [VM15a]. The Jeep could be directed into the ditch from the back seat while driving.

Bus messages can be read and also sent via the standardized diagnostic interface. A correspondingly attached inconspicuous hardware plug can send any vehicle data directly to the cloud and forms the bridge between the attacker and the bus. Attack tools to support are now easily and cheaply available. Neither necessary know-how nor necessary financial means are a hurdle to carry out attacks. Known, existing attack tools are increasingly turning to the automotive domain, making it easier for attackers to use existing tools to attack vehicles.

Since this ***"wake-up call"***, further attacks in the automotive environment could be reported every month. Not all attacks are directly on vehicles. They are equally against leasing companies, fleet management systems, fleets, etc. By now, there are examples for all theoretically conceivable attacks of how they were successfully applied in practice. Vehicle functions could already be compromised via all interfaces: diagnostic interface, smartphone apps, mobile interfaces, physical access to the bus, side channels, malicious software, Wi-Fi, … Types of attacks are known and publicly (e.g., internet) accessible to everyone. There is also now sufficient "jump start" in the literature [Smi15].

With the introduction of automatic or even autonomous driving, the attack surface becomes even larger and attacks on e.g. algorithms of artificial intelligence are easily possible (see e.g. MobilEye hack [MEye]).

6.3.1 Connectivity makes it Possible

For functional safety in the vehicle, cybersecurity is an essential prerequisite. The **attack surface** of safety-relevant (in terms of functional safety) systems is constantly growing, not least due to the **increasing automation** of vehicles. The increased **use of Ethernet** (well known in the IT world but also among attackers) and further **digitization** in the vehicle reinforce the trend further.

The five primary vehicle connectivities are:

- Vehicle to **Infrastructure:** e.g., wireless data exchange between the vehicle and road infrastructure to receive information about accidents, construction sites, parking lots, and more.
- Vehicle to **Vehicle** (Vehicle to Vehicle): Data exchange between vehicles, typically including location, to avoid traffic jams and accidents.
- Vehicle to **Cloud:** Communication between a vehicle and cloud-based back-end systems, enabling the vehicle to process information and commands sent between services and applications.
- Vehicle to **Pedestrian:** Communication between vehicles, infrastructure, and personal mobile devices to receive information about the pedestrian environment, thus enabling safety, mobility, and environmental improvements.
- Vehicle to **Everything:** Any data exchange or communication between a vehicle and other objects or road users, such as traffic lights, road markings, traffic signs, etc.

Countermeasures/Security Controls that can be used:

- **Separation and Isolation:**
  - Definition of different zones/segments/domains.
  - Definition of the valid communication flow between zones.
  - Complication of Denial-of-Service attacks.

- **Access Control:**
  - Minimization of external interfaces.
  - Control of access to the vehicle network.
  - Ensuring the authenticity and authorization of access requests.
- **Secure Communication:**
  - Ensuring transport protection.
  - Consideration of additional E2E protection.
- **Continuous Protection:**
  - Ensuring and validity of the communication flow.
  - Detection of abnormal behavior.
  - Prevention of known attacks.

Another important principle is the **Defense-in-Depth principle** for architectures. Different attacks are necessary to overcome each defense ring. As with medieval castles, one defense ring alone is not enough today. Translated to vehicles, this means the implementation of different security controls: Whitelisting, Authentication, Firewalling, protection of Integrity, Isolation, secure Communication, secure Diagnosis, Key Management, protection of Software, … It must be ensured that an attacker who penetrates a vehicle from the outside has to work his way through an onion model to get to the "crown jewels" and is not undetected by Intrusion-Detection Systems at all levels or is repelled by an Intrusion-Prevention.

Statistics prove that the number of successful attacks has been increasing exponentially for years [Ups20]. The vast majority of these attacks take place remotely (radio or internet).

Trends in current architectural developments for vehicles are increasingly facilitating attackers. The possibilities of an attack are increasing, on the one hand by providing new functionalities, on the other hand by an increasing number of non-functional requirements.

Functional Influences:

- **Autonomous Driving** (ADAS, AI, …): Higher data rates and a larger data volume are required. Disruptions due to attacks are easy to implement.
- **Increasing number of interfaces:** Number and complexity increase the attack surface.
- **System of Systems** (Car2X): Vehicles are networked and dependent on information outside the vehicle.
- **Increasing number of assistance systems/sensors** (see ADAS).
- **Increasing functionality** leads to an increase in the software scope: It is expected that the software scope will increase by another order of magnitude in the coming years.

- **OTA** (over-the-air) **Software Updates.** ([UNECE-156], Sect. 5.2.7) creates another possible attack vector.
- Use of a **Back-end infrastructure** allows a multitude of attacks from afar regardless of distance and time. Software must be able to be updated at any time in the future (new functions, bug fixing, ...), the **update process** itself is another target for attack.
- **Service as a Product** (new functions, access to user data, e-mobility, infotainment, ...) can be manipulated.
- **Algorithms** (e.g., for the use of artificial intelligence) can be manipulated.
- **Connectivity:** With their integration of external services (Facebook, Spotify, Android Auto, Whatsapp, ...) a large attack surface is offered.

Non-functional Influences:

- **Privacy/Data Protection** (see Chap. 3). The enlargement of the attack surface increases the demand for separation and necessary isolation: Hypervisor, Defense-in-Depth approach, ... The use of personal data for more and more services allows more and more people to spy.
- The **Reuse of established IT solutions:** Firewall, Gateway, Ethernet, ... allows attackers to reuse known attack possibilities.
- **Standardization and adaptability** demand new architectures.
- **Possible reconfigurability** during runtime. It should be possible to change product characteristics later (e.g., via software update) after product release.
- **Reliability:** Ensuring performance and security **over the entire lifecycle** for possibly long lifetimes. This is extremely difficult to ensure for digital products.
- **Performance and scalability** should remain **adjustable in real time**.
- The **Networking and availability of products around the clock** allows attackers to carry out attacks around the clock.

6.3.2 Example: Roll-Jam Technique (Replay Attack)

The attack introduced by Samy Kamkar in 2015 Attack [SK15], allows an attacker to easily persuade vehicles to open their doors. For a small amount of money, the attacker acquires a jammer. Now, if the driver/owner of a car wants to open it with his radio key, the corresponding command is intercepted and stored by the jammer at the first button press. At the same time, the jammer sends a jamming signal to the car, so the car does not notice the first opening command. The car does not open, the driver/owner, who may be briefly confused, presses a second time. The jammer also intercepts this signal and stores it as well. At the same time, it sends the previously first stored command to the car. The car opens, the driver/owner can get in and drive off. The jammer now has another valid command (the second stored command) to open the car in its memory. With this, the attacker can subsequently also open the car.

Background Information
Technical security measures that can make roll-jam attacks impossible can easily be specified here. Nevertheless, these are not implemented in many vehicle models, as investigations on various car models over the past years repeatedly reveal.

If no requirements related to the security objective Non-repudiation are implemented, the owner/driver has no way of proving that the second command, which may have been used for theft, was not sent with his radio key (but, for example, by an attacker).

An implementation of the security objective Authentication alone is insufficient at this point, as the first (later repeatable) command must have been authorized. The car would have accepted it and opened, the command was sent by an authorized radio key.

The security objective Freshness remains to be implemented, which recognizes the replayed message of a Replay Attack as such, since an additional timestamp in the commands would reveal that the command is "outdated" in terms of time.

6.3.3 Example: (Key-) Relay-Station Attack

As early as 2010, an article on so-called Relay-Station Attacks [FDC10] was published at ETH Zurich. Using this attack method, passive Keyless-Entry and start systems can be broken.

Modern cars can be unlocked by passively using the key when opening. The key only needs to be in sufficiently close proximity to the car to be unlocked (Keyless-Entry). While the reception range on the car's side is very small (<30 cm), the key can send responses from a greater distance (up to 10–100 m).

The attack consists of capturing the reception signal near a vehicle and sending it over a suitable frequency over a greater distance to a more distant receiver (e.g., the original vehicle key). This more distant receiver receives on one side the forwarded reception signal of the vehicle and on the other side the key (which can be recognized from a further distance (e.g., 8 m)). Now the communication to open can be started via this "bridge". The key reacts and responds to the forwarded vehicle signal. Conversely, the vehicle does not notice that the benign response signals for opening and starting come from the (valid) key outside the usual distance (within which it must react).

The attack can be carried out by two people, with one attacker staying at the vehicle with a receiver for forwarding, while the second attacker tries to get close to the key with his receiver, e.g., by walking along the house wall of the key owner, behind which he suspects the vehicle key.

Technical countermeasures can also be easily implemented here. For example, the runtime of the signals can be measured and the message in the car for opening or starting can be rejected if the runtime is correspondingly long. Another possibility is to install an additional (secure) wireless communication between the vehicle and keychain (additional receiver), which calculates the distance using runtime measurements and switches off the receiver for opening on the vehicle receiver side as long as no key can be detected close enough to the vehicle.

In 2019, it was demonstrated for seven vehicle models from different manufacturers that security gaps in their keyless entry systems can be exploited in this way [Ups19]. All hacked models could be broken into in a matter of seconds.

6.4 Cyber Kill Chain

The Cyber-Kill-Chain describes cyber attacks/scenarios of an attack. The attacker's ever-increasing penetration is described in several stages/steps. Experience shows that in many cases, information gathering is possible within a year, i.e., the attacker can position himself to successfully carry out the attack. Different phase models exist. An example is described below.

Phase 1: **Reconnaissance:** An organization, a target is determined. Information about the attack target is spied from public sources: structure, data networks, contacts, suppliers. Through targeted spying, it is possible, for example, to get remote access to certain systems.

Phase 2: **Find suitable attack method.** The goal is to get information about the software used. Popular methods for this are, for example, Spear-Phishing (Sect. 2.1) or Water-Holing (attack on an organization's infrastructure via manipulated high-traffic websites outside an organization).

Phase 3: **Targeted Attack:** If enough information about the target has been collected, more targeted attacks can be carried out to obtain further information, e.g., victims can be persuaded to reveal more detailed information such as usernames, passwords, etc.

Phase 4: **Bridgehead:** A program is deposited in a recognized weak point that allows access from the outside (e.g., by installing a backdoor).

Phase 5: **Takeover:** After the successful installation of a backdoor, it can now be used to take over the target. From now on, the attacker is firmly established. He can, for example, proceed to create further accesses and thus completely take over the target.

Depending on the domain and target object, the Kill-Chain can be adapted and customized accordingly. For completely unnoticed/invisible attacks, the term **Silent-Kill-Chain** is often found in the literature.

Example

Example of a Kill-Chain for automotive control units:

1. **Hardware Teardown:** In the primary phase of the attack, a list of control units and a circuit diagram are created.

2. **Footprinting:** The target area is defined, resulting in a list of access points for further analysis.
3. **Protocol Scan:** It is now determined which of the access points identified during the footprinting offer protocols that are supported for hacks. Various methods are used. Whenever possible, this is done secretly.
4. **Enumeration:** An attempt is made to find out which software is behind open ports. Helpful information is obtained, for example, by reverse engineering the control unit software.
5. **Vulnerability Scan:** The collected information is evaluated and matched against vulnerabilities/security gaps using a tool. This often takes the form of plug-ins in frameworks designed for attacks.
6. **Exploitation/Penetration:** The application software is attacked. These attacks are made possible by vulnerabilities in programming, configuration, or implementation.
7. **Covering Tracks:** Finally, all entries that could indicate an attack or successful intrusion are deleted. ◀

Individual steps of analyzed attack scenarios are often divided into different phases for description. The nature of successful attacks is revealed in the fact that the attack scenarios used often consist of a sequence and combination of quite complex individual actions.

Example

Kill-Chain for Relay-Station Attacks:

1. **Visual inspection** (Identification of electronic components)
2. Radio signal **localization**
3. Radio signal **analysis**
4. Examine common **radio attacks** (Replay/Relay, Crafting, Brute Force, Jamming, …) ◀

Once a security vulnerability has been discovered (e.g., by attackers), the clock starts ticking for all . The period between discovery and the announcement of a solution (e.g., in the form of a **software patch**) is referred to as During the time until a solution is found, attackers have the opportunity to exploit the security vulnerability and cause damage. In between is the point at which the manufacturer becomes aware of the security vulnerability. After the patch is made available, it takes time for all products to adopt it. At some point thereafter, the security vulnerability is finally closed in one of the next software versions.

6.5 Summary

The following observations can be made and summarized regarding the topic of hacking:

- **Networking** and the drive for **higher performance** in devices and the cloud automatically lead to an **even larger attack surface.**
- **Connections to cloud services** offer corresponding additional (and sometimes simpler) attack possibilities.
- Individual devices are increasingly becoming **systems of systems** and thus more susceptible to attacks.
- Always **new** and **additional functions** (which have less and less to do with the original product goals) offer corresponding attack possibilities (e.g., Denial-of-Service).
- There is a need for **further standards** to embed information security even deeper into product developments and to set the bar for attackers as high as possible.
- **Classic IT methods are spreading more and more** in all possible control devices. However, this also enables the execution of already known attacks.
- The **number of external interfaces of products continues to increase rapidly** and thus also enlarges the attack surface.

> **Derivable Countermeasures**
> - **Collect information:** Attackers exchange information worldwide, product manufacturers must ensure to keep up with the state of the art. This can only be achieved by "reading" corresponding information sources.
> - **Secure-Programming, Secure-Design** must be applied as standard to achieve a minimum level of security.
> - Hacking is a global business. Keeping up with it can only be achieved through corresponding **international information exchange** in appropriate committees,
> - The **mindset of attackers** must be taken into account during development. It is different from the mindset in usual development teams.
> - **Costs are no longer a hurdle for attackers.** Systems can no longer be considered secure because they are proprietary or can only be broken using appropriate tools.
> - **Defense-in-Depth** architectures must become the standard so that attackers who break one hurdle do not immediately gain access to the "crown jewels".

References

[Dra] ***„John T. Draper“.*** Wikipedia-Link: https://de.wikipedia.org/wiki/John_T._Draper accessed: 20.04.2021

[FDC10] ***„Relay Attacks on Passive Keyless Entry and Start Systems in Modern Cars";*** Aurélien Francillon, Boris Danev, Srdjan Capkun. Department of Computer Science ETH Zurich, 2010. Link: https://www.researchgate.net/profile/Srdjan_Capkun/publication/220333841_Relay_Attacks_on_Passive_Keyless_Entry_and_Start_Systems_in_Modern_Cars/links/541d6d520cf241a65a17df2d/Relay-Attacks-on-Passive-Keyless-Entry-and-Start-Systems-in-Modern-Cars.pdf accessed: 20.04.2021

[GHD] ***„Google Hacking Database".*** Link: https://www.exploit-db.com/google-hacking-database/ accessed: 10.04.2021

[Gor20] ***„A Bug's Journey: Understanding the Software Vulnerability Lifecycle"***, Brian Gorenc, escar 2020

[KS] ***„Die ersten Hacker (ab 1955)"***; Jan Krömer, William Sen. Link: https://www.digitalwelt.org/hackerkultur/inhalt/die-ersten-hacker accessed: 20.04.2021

[KZ07] ***„Excel-Sicherheitslücke wird auf eBay versteigert"***; 21.08.2007. Link: https://www.krone.at/39521 accessed: 18.04.2021

[MEye] ***„MobilEye-Hack".*** Link: https://www.youtube.com/watch?v=C-JxNHKqgtk&feature=youtu.be accessed: 20.04.2021

[Mit18] ***„How a Hacker Convinced Motorola to Send Him Source Code"***. Link: https://www.youtube.com/watch?v=UBaVek2oTtc accessed 10.04.2021

[obs] ***„How to configure sites safely and securely".*** Link: https://observatory.mozilla.org/ accessed: 20.04.2021

[sho] ***„Suchmaschine für das Internet der Dinge".*** Link: https://www.shodan.io/

[SK15] ***„This Hacker's tiny device unlocks cars and opens garages";*** Samy Kamkar. Link: https://www.wired.com/2015/08/hackers-tiny-device-unlocks-cars-opens-garages/ accessed: 20.04.2021

[Smi15] ***„The Car Hacker's Handbook – A Guide for the Penetration Tester";*** Craig Smith, 2016. Link: https://docs.alexomar.com/biblioteca/thecarhackershandbook.pdf accessed: 20.04.2021

[Tal14] ***„Antifragilität: Anleitung für eine Welt, die wir nicht verstehen";*** Nassim Nicholas Taleb; btb-Verlag, 2014

[UNECE-156] ***"Addendum 155 – UN Regulation No. 156";*** https://unece.org/sites/default/files/2021-03/R156e.pdf accessed: 18.04.2021

[Ups20] ***„Upstream Security's global automotive cybersecurity report 2020",*** Research into cyber-attack trends in the smart mobility ecosystem, Upstream Security Ltd. Link: https://www.upstream.auto/ accessed: 20.04.2021

[Ups21] ***„Upstream Security's global automotive cybersecurity report 2021";*** Research into cyber-attack trends in the smart mobility ecosystem, Upstream Security Ltd. https://www.upstream.auto/ accessed: 17.04.2021

[VM15] ***„Hackers Remotely Kill a Jeep on the Highway—With Me in It";*** Chris Valasek, Charlie Miller. Link: https://www.wired.com/2015/07/hackers-remotely-kill-jeep-highway/ accessed: 10.04.2021

[VM15a] ***„Remote Exploitation of an Unaltered Passenger Vehicle";*** Chris Valasek, Charlie Miller. Link: https://ioactive.com/pdfs/IOActive_Remote_Car_Hacking.pdf accessed: 18.04.2021

Risk Assessment 7

The identification of risks and the determination of a **risk level/risk value** in information security is not trivial. Attackers are unpredictable, attacks are complex, exploit hitherto unknown emergent properties, and cannot be precisely predicted in terms of time or location.

> **Risk** is defined by the impact/effect of uncertainty on objectives.

An impact/**effect** is a deviation from the expected. It can be **positive, negative** or both, and can result in **opportunities** and **threats.** Objectives can have various aspects and categories and can be applied at different levels. Risks are usually expressed in terms of risk sources, potential events, their consequences, and their frequency of occurrence.

Regardless of the specific method, when conducting a **risk assessment** one generally encounters the following challenges (depending on the method used, possibly in a different order).

> **Challenges:**
>
> 1. Sufficiently "good" **definition** of the **subject of consideration,** including its internal and external interfaces.
> 2. As **complete identification** as possible of all **values to be protected** and their associated **protection objectives/goals.** Experience, catalogs, and adaptable checklists are most helpful here. Various organizations have published different guidelines on this, such as **ENISA** [GPoSC19, GPfSoIOT19] the **UNECE** [UNECE-155] or the **NIST SP 800-30** [NIST800-30].
> 3. Identification of all **potential threats.** Here, experience and attacker know-how are required.
> 4. Identification and analysis of **attack scenarios,** evaluation of their **feasibility** and estimation of a **"likelihood".**

T. Liedtke, *Information Security*, https://doi.org/10.1007/978-3-658-45711-2_7

5. **Determination** of a **risk level** or risk value (different terms depending on the underlying standard) is usually systematically possible via a corresponding cross-table. The decision on risk treatment can usually also be made very intuitively.
6. **Selection** of (**security**-) **controls** or measures, taking into account their effectiveness in achieving security objectives and reducing residual risks. There are also various standards for this, such as in the NIST SP 800 series (see Sect. 5.2.3).

7.1 Overview

The core of every security standard/policy is risk assessment/risk analysis/risk management. The approach to dealing with the topic of security is (as with functional safety, for example) risk-oriented. Since there are different types of risks, these are logically addressed appropriately in different standards. For development organizations, these can be divided into different levels (see Table 7.1).

Table 7.1 Types of risk and their relation to associated standards

Standard/Guideline	Type of Risk	Organizational Roles
ISMS (e.g. ISO/IEC 27001/27005)/TISAX	Company Risks: • Fire in the server room • Clean desk violations • Faulty backups • Gaps in access rights management	Chief Security Officer, IT Security Officer
ISMS/CSMS (e.g. ISO/IEC 27005, BSI, NIST SP-800, HEAVENS, …)	Secure Project Environment: • Manipulated HW deliveries in shipping • Incomplete securing of cryptographic keys in development and production	Security Manager in the project/organization
Domain-specific standards organization-related (e.g. ISO/SAE 21434, ISA/IEC 62443, CC, …)	Project-independent Risks: • Handling of security gaps after discovery/awareness • Information monitoring (internal, external)	Security Manager (Organization)
Domain-specific standards development-related (e.g. ISO/SAE 21434, ISA/IEC 62443, CC, …)	Product Safety Risks: • Invasive HW attacks • Unauthorized access in the field • Back-end attacks on networked products	Security Manager (Project)

Risk management essentially consists of three parts (see ISO 31000 [ISO31000]):

- Section 7.1.1: **Principles:** Integration, adaptation to corresponding needs, …
- Section 7.1.2: **Framework:** Design, implementation, …
- Section 7.1.3: **Process** for risk assessment

In the following subsections, these basic components, which can be found derived and adapted accordingly in all other risk management systems, are explained.

7.1.1 Principles

Every risk management system consists of corresponding principles it follows:

- Risk management must become an **integral** part of all organizational activities.
- A **structured** and **comprehensive approach** to risk management contributes to consistent and comparable results.
- The framework and process of risk management are appropriately **tailored** to the external and internal context of an organization in relation to its objectives.
- The appropriate and timely **inclusion of stakeholders** allows for the consideration of their knowledge, views, and perceptions. This leads to improved awareness and informed risk management.
- Risks can arise, **change** or disappear as the external and internal context of an organization changes. Risk management anticipates, recognizes, appreciates, and responds to these **changes** and events in an appropriate and timely manner.
- The inputs for risk management are based on **historical** and **current information** as well as future expectations. Risk management takes into account all limitations and uncertainties associated with this information and expectations. The information should be timely, clear, and available to the relevant stakeholders.
- **Human behavior** and **culture** significantly influence all aspects of risk management at every level and stage.
- Risk management is continuously improved through **learning** and **experience.**

7.1.2 Framework

The purpose of the risk management framework is to assist the organization in integrating risk management into essential activities and functions. The effectiveness of risk management depends on its integration into the organization's leadership, including decision-making. This requires the support of stakeholders, especially the top management level. The components are:

- **Leadership and commitment:** The top management should ensure that risk management is integrated into all organizational activities, and should show leadership strength and commitment, e.g., by implementing the components for the framework, establishing a policy, providing necessary resources, …
- **Integration:** The structures vary depending on the purpose, objectives, and complexity of the organization. Risks are managed in every part of the organizational structure. Everyone in an organization is responsible for risk management.
- **Design:** To successfully design the framework, …
  - the organization must understand the internal (vision, governance, strategy, organizational culture, standards, capabilities, …) and external (social, political, cultural, laws, finances, contractual relationships) context.
  - the commitment to risk management must be articulated.
  - roles, responsibilities, authorities, and resources in the organization must be defined, assigned, and provided.
- **Implementation:** Designing a plan including time and resources as well as identifying where when and how decisions are made by whom.
- **Evaluation:** the effectiveness of a risk management process must be periodically measured by comparing performance, execution, and implementation.
- **Improvement:**
  - Adjustment: An organization must continuously monitor and adjust the process framework.
  - Continuous improvement: An organization must continuously improve the suitability, adequacy, and effectiveness of the risk management framework.

Successful implementation depends very much on the commitment and awareness of stakeholders. The correct design of a risk management process is part of all activities of an organization, including decision-making and adjustment when internal and external contexts change.

7.1.3 Process

The risk management process includes the systematic application of policies, procedures, and practices for communication and consultation activities, context determination, and the assessment, treatment, monitoring, review, recording, and reporting of risks.

The process is sequential, but continuous and an integral part of an organization (see above). Within an organization, many appropriately adapted applications of a risk management process can exist to meet the respective internal or external context. Risk management processes can be applied at the strategic, operational, program, or project level:

- Internal and external **communication** and **consultation:** Communication promotes awareness and understanding of risks. Consultation involves obtaining feedback and information to support decision-making.

- **Scope, context** and **criteria:** The purpose of defining the scope, context, and criteria is to adapt the risk management process to enable effective risk assessment and appropriate risk treatment. They include defining the scope of the process and understanding the external and internal context.
- **Risk assessment:** A holistic process, described in three basic steps. The process is systematic, iterative, and collaborative, to be conducted based on the knowledge and views of stakeholders.
  - **Identification** of risks: Finding, recognizing, and describing risks that can help or hinder an organization in achieving its goals. This can be done with a wide range of methods.
  - **Analysis** of identified risks: Understanding the risks, including uncertainties depending on the goal of the analysis. Analysis techniques can be qualitative or quantitative and should be based on reliable information. It can be difficult to quantify highly uncertain events. The analysis provides the basis for evaluation to decide whether and how risks should be treated and with which suitable strategies and methods. The effectiveness of existing controls can be considered.
  - **Risk evaluation:** In risk evaluation, the results of the risk analysis are compared with the established risk criteria to determine where additional measures are needed, where further analysis is required, consideration of risk treatment options, …
- **Risk treatment:** The goal of risk treatment is the selection and implementation of possible options to address the risk. The process is iterative in the following steps:
  - Formulation and selection of risk treatment options;
  - Planning and implementation of risk treatment;
  - Evaluation of the effectiveness of this treatment;
  - Decision on whether the remaining risk is acceptable;
  - If not acceptable, carry out further treatment;
  - Possible options include:
    - **Avoidance** of the risk;
    - **Taking** or **increasing** the risk (the latter in case of opportunities);
    - **Elimination** of the risk source;
    - Changing the likelihood of occurrence;
    - **Changing** the **consequences;**
    - **Sharing** the risk (e.g., through contracts, purchasing insurance);
    - **Retention** of the risk;
  - The process and its results are documented, for example, in a **risk treatment plan.**
- **Monitoring** and **review:** The purpose is to ensure and improve the quality and effectiveness of process design, implementation, and results. This is done through continuous monitoring and periodic reviews.
- **Documentation** and **report:** The risk management process and its results should be documented and reported through appropriate mechanisms. The recording and reporting aim to.

7.1.4 Risk Criteria

The definition of criteria for determining a risk level/risk value is very important for the application of a risk management process. The organization must determine the level and type of risks it can or cannot take in relation to its objectives. It must also define criteria to assess the significance of the risk and support decision-making processes. The risk criteria must be aligned with the risk management framework and tailored to the specific purpose and scope of the activity under consideration. The risk criteria should reflect the organization's values, objectives, and resources and be consistent with risk management policies and statements. The criteria should be defined taking into account the organization's obligations and the views of stakeholders.

In general, the following can be considered for the determination of risk criteria (among other things):

- the nature and type of **uncertainties,** that can affect the results and objectives (both tangible and intangible),
- **Consequences** (both positive and negative) and the occurrence probability/frequency (engl. ***"Likelihood"***), which should be defined, observed, and measured,
- time-related factors,
- consistency in the use of measurements,
- determination of the level of risk,
- consideration of combinations and sequences of multiple risks,
- ...

Examples from the Automotive Sector

Functional Safety [ISO26262]: the risk (for determining the ASIL (Automotive Safety Integrity Level)) is determined by the parameters:

- **Severity:** Estimation of the extent of damage to one or more persons that can occur in a potentially dangerous event
- **Exposure:** Condition of an operating situation that can be dangerous when compared to the examined fault state
- **Controllability:** Ability to avoid a specific damage or injury through timely reactions of the involved persons, possibly with the support of external measures

In functional safety, occurrence probabilities can be calculated.

Cybersecurity [ISO21434]: the risk value is determined by:

- **Severity**/extent of the **damage** caused by an attack (related to the four categories: Safety, Finance, Operability, Data Protection)
- **Attack feasibility** ◀

In information security, occurrence probabilities cannot be calculated as attackers act unpredictably. One must infer occurrence likelihood/frequencies from empirical observations. For example, if observed attacks in recent times mostly occurred via a back-end, it can be inferred that the next attacks will preferably happen via this route.

7.2 Automotive TARA according to ISO/SAE 21434

As a concrete example of a risk assessment process, the so-called TARA process (Threat Analysis and Risk Assessment [ISO21434]) from the automotive sector will be described. It serves to identify risks, assess the identified risks, and thus support the decision of risk treatment. The objective of the risk assessment is to associate/determine a corresponding **risk value** to the **threat scenarios**.

The process can be applied to different architectures and elements at different stages of development, e.g., at the system, software, or hardware level.

The process is divided into seven steps, each of which is described in the following subsections.

- Section 7.2.1: Identification of the values (assets) to be protected,
- Section 7.2.2: Identification of threat scenarios,
- Section 7.2.3: Determination of the severity of impact,
- Section 7.2.4: Analysis of attack paths,
- Section 7.2.5: Determination of the feasibility of attack,
- Section 7.2.6: Assessment of the risk,
- Section 7.2.7: Risk treatment decision

7.2.1 Identification of Values to be Protected

Unlike in functional safety, in information security/cybersecurity, it must first be identified which values/assets need to be protected and which protection objectives are to be achieved. A crucial role is played by the perspective of the respective stakeholders. A freshly baked sand cake has a very high value for a child, whereas for the parents it is rather low. Depending on the perspective (e.g., of the driver, pedestrian, vehicle manufacturer, fleet manager, etc.), different values/assets to be protected need to be identified. Characteristics of the values to be protected are corresponding protection objectives. These can be: **Confidentiality**, **Integrity** and **Availability** as well as others (see Table 7.2). The table shows the possible consequences of failing to achieve a corresponding protection objective.

Table 7.2 Characteristics Protection Objectives

Protection Objective	Exemplary Impact if Not Achieved
Authenticity	Received messages cannot be checked to see if they come from a trusted, authorized source or were sent unauthorized by an attacker
Integrity	A recipient cannot detect tampered message contents. Man-in-the-middle or replay attacks are easily possible
Non-Repudiation	After an attack, a sender cannot be proven (anymore) for sent fake/ tampered messages, and it remains unclear who really sent the messages
Confidentiality	It can be easy to gain unauthorized access to confidential information
Availability	Functionality and services can be denied. Access to databases is blocked, backup files can be deleted
Privilege Elevation	An attacker has unlawfully obtained privileged rights and exercises them

For applicable protection objectives, corresponding damage scenarios are identified. If no corresponding damage scenario can be found for the combination of value/asset and protection objective, the protection objective does not need to be pursued further.

Values to be protected can include, among others:

- Functionality
- Safety objectives
- Software
- Personal data
- Sensor data
- Components
- Communication channels
- Messages
- …

Depending on the value, different protection objectives need to be analyzed. For data and secret keys, confidentiality must be ensured in particular, while for communication channels, integrity plays a major role.

7.2.2 Identification of Threat Scenarios

After the identification of damage scenarios, corresponding threat scenarios are identified. Possible threat scenarios lead to the corresponding damage when realized. Damage scenarios and threat scenarios are in an n:m relationship with each other, i.e., a realized threat can trigger multiple damages, a damage can be threatened by different scenarios.

Threats are identified regardless of their feasibility or possible occurrence. Threats can be directed at a protection goal as well as directly at a value. If a value or protection goal is compromised, the corresponding associated damage can occur.

An important contribution can be made by already known security vulnerabilities. The exploitation of security vulnerabilities can always also represent a threat.

For the automotive sector, the UNECE Regulation No. 155 [UNECE-155] (Sect. 5.2.7) prescribes threat scenarios that must be considered for homologation. These are to be evaluated as further sources in a TARA. Seven threat families are given along with possible security vulnerabilities and countermeasures in a tabular format:

- **Back-end servers** in connection with vehicles in the field:
  - Through unauthorized physical or logical access, services, the back-end itself, or the vehicle can be attacked via the back-end server.
- **Communication channels:**
  - As a man-in-the-middle attack on the mobile network between back-end server and vehicle, data can be manipulated, deleted, or overwritten through spoofing attacks or Sybil attacks up to denial-of-service attacks. Unauthorized accesses and actions can also be carried out with corresponding privileges.
- **Update procedures:**
  - After an attack on the back-end server, the update procedure can be manipulated. Invalid/falsified updates can thus be loaded onto vehicles. The activation or performance enhancement of features can occur without authorization.
- **Human activities:**
  - Attackers can facilitate attacks through corresponding actions. Innocent victims are enticed and corresponding actions can enable attacks by, for example, not following defined security measures (e.g., after phishing attacks).
- **External connections:**
  - Any external communication possibilities offer attack opportunities: OBD II (On-Board Diagnosis), infotainment, radio keys, Wi-Fi, Bluetooth, …
- **Vehicle data/code:**
  - Vehicle owner-related personal data can be read out bypassing surveillance systems. Vehicle data/code can be manipulated or deleted, vehicle parameters can be changed.
- **Security vulnerabilities that are not sufficiently hardened:**
  - Too short cryptographic keys or outdated cryptography can be broken, known unpatched security vulnerabilities can be exploited, open ports could be compromised.

The UNECE regulation table also assigns 68 examples of security vulnerabilities and attack methods to the threat families. Further tables list possible countermeasures both in the vehicle and from outside to prevent the threats and link them with the relevant threats.

7.2.3 Determining the Severity of Impact

In the first step of the risk assessment, possible damages were identified (see Sect. 7.2.1). In this (third) step, the severity of the damage is determined. The corresponding categories must be defined according to the risk definition. In the TARA process in Automotive, the following damage categories are evaluated:

- **Functional Safety:** a safety-relevant function no longer works as specified
- **Finances:** the stakeholder suffers financial damage due to the attack
- **Operational Safety:** the car can no longer be used (without restrictions)
- **Data Protection:** personal data is published without authorization

For each stakeholder and damage category, the extent/severity is determined. For this purpose, appropriately adapted evaluation tables must be set up. For effects related to health/danger to life and limb, the evaluation in functional safety is referred to. The severity of damage due to a realized **threat** is to be evaluated the same as due to a **hazard.** For the affected stakeholder, the cause of the damage does not matter in terms of the amount of damage in the end.

The severity is assigned one of four possible levels in each category.

7.2.4 Analysis of Attack Paths

Once the threat scenarios are known, attack paths can be created and analyzed in the next step. Various methods can be used for this:

- **Brainstorming:** Mixed teams of developers, hackers, and subject matter experts analyze which threat scenarios threaten values and protection goals and thus cause damage based on architectures, history, known vulnerabilities, and attacks.
- **Attack Trees** [Sch99]: Setting up an attack tree is similar to setting up a fault tree for functional safety. These can be created in two ways:
  - **Top-down:** Various paths and possibilities are modeled by derivation from the top-level threat. A safe can be opened, for example, by guessing the combination, welding it open, extorting the combination, etc. What is necessary in terms of knowledge, tools, etc. can be attributed in the tree.
  - **Bottom-up:** If you know the vulnerabilities of the object under consideration, an attack tree can be developed from the bottom up by combining the exploitation of various vulnerabilities. You can get to the contents of a safe if the front door is left open, the safe was not properly locked, etc.

This step is a crucial one, albeit not an easy one. Knowledge about attack methods, available tools, necessary knowledge are essential if all possible attacks are to be covered. Overlooking an attack path can be enough for an attacker to carry out a successful attack.

Here too, there is an n:m mapping: A threat can be realized in various ways by attacks, an attack can realize several threats.

The feasibility of an attack initially plays no role and is only evaluated later. This step is about analyzing as many of all possible attack paths as possible.

7.2.5 Determining the Feasibility of Attacks

There are different methods and criteria for determining the feasibility of an attack. The corresponding ISO standard for IT security [ISO18045] (consistent with Common Criteria [ISO15408]) describes possible methods and evaluation schemes. One method is the evaluation of attack potential. Proposed factors (which were then similarly adopted for the corresponding method in TARA) are:

- **Execution time:** (Calendar) duration needed for an attack from planning to successful execution;
- **Expertise:** Knowledge and expertise required to successfully carry out an attack;
- **Knowledge:** Required knowledge about the object to be attacked;
- Window of **opportunity** with two dimensions:
  - How long do you have to be directly near the object?
  - From what distance (e.g., over the Internet or directly from the car) can attacks be successfully carried out?
- **Tools:** Type of tools needed for the attack (standard, bespoke, …).

Possible evaluation options for the factors are listed in Table 7.3.

Table 7.3 Evaluation factors for attack paths

Factor	Explanation	Example values
Execution time	Duration required by attackers for planning and execution of an attack	Less than a day, less than a week, …
Expertise	Knowledge and technical expertise required	Layperson (can follow a step-by-step guide from the Internet), several attackers with different levels of expertise
Knowledge	Knowledge about the object to be attacked	Information is publicly visible (e.g., via the Internet), necessary information is classified as secret
Opportunity	Combination of the length of a time window for a possible attack and the distance from which an attack can be launched	Unrestricted temporal and spatial access to the object to be attacked
Tools	Bespoke tools required for the execution of the attack	Standard tool easy and inexpensive to obtain, self-developed bespoke tool, …

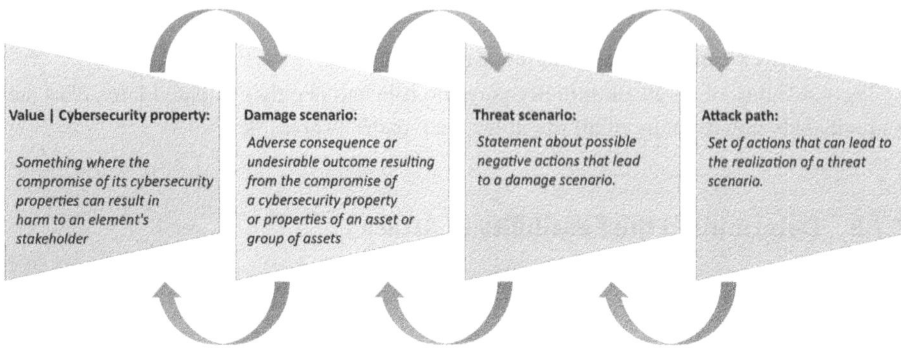

Fig. 7.1 Relationship and Information Flow

The **factors are to be evaluated independently** of each other, even though they are not independent in practice. For example, expertise or hardware/software can be a substitute for execution time. More efficient tools simplify an attack and reduce the necessary execution time. The values are derived from the observation of attacks as they occurred. Further possible methods are mentioned in the standard.

In the end, the feasibility of the attack is converted into one of four levels (depending on the evaluation table).

It becomes difficult with an attack scenario (which consists of many actions) with the propagation of attributes. Required times can add up, knowledge and tools cannot be aggregated so easily. Whether a lot of knowledge and simple tools or little knowledge but complicated required tools make an attack appear more likely is not easy to evaluate.

Figure 7.1 shows the information and argument flow:

- From left to right: A value/asset has security objectives/properties (Cybersecurity Properties). From these, damage scenarios are developed by considering what possible consequences could be if values or security properties are compromised. In the next step, threat scenarios are derived from this. Attack paths are identified for these.
- From right to left: In the end, attack paths realize threats, which invoke the damage that occurs when assets or security properties are compromised.

7.2.6 Risk Assessment

The definition of risk for Automotive consists of the combination of **severity/impact** of the **damage scenario** and **feasibility of attack.** The two values are combined according to a **risk matrix** or formula into a **risk value** between one and five.

The distribution of risk values in the tables can vary. The risk value for high damage and high feasibility of attack corresponds to the highest, a risk value for negligible damage and very unlikely feasibility of attack to the lowest value.

7.2.7 Risk Treatment Decision

Based on the risk value, the final step is to decide which option for risk treatment is chosen. There are four options given (see Sect. 5.2.5.2):

- **Risk Reduction:** A control, a cybersecurity goal, or a corresponding organizational measure is to be specified and implemented.
  - Example: It is decided to introduce sufficient encryption for a communication channel.
- **Risk Sharing:** The risk is delegated or, for example, insured.
  - Example: A fleet manager decides to insure the non-usability of his vehicles due to an attack.
- **Risk retain:** The risk is retained. The justification for retaining it is specified and must be regularly checked for the validity of the argument.
  - Example: Correspondingly strict encryptions cannot be broken in a realistically conceivable time, further measures should not be introduced.
- **Risk Avoidance:** The risk is avoided by removing the source of risk.
  - Example: A communication channel, such as Bluetooth, is deactivated, attacks via Bluetooth are no longer possible, the risk is avoided.

7.3 Security Risk Assessment according to ISA/IEC 62443

As mentioned in Sect. 5.2.4 Volume 3-2 of the **ISA/IEC 62443** [IEC62443] describes the **security risk assessment** for **system design**. This is done in two main steps:

1. **High-Level Cybersecurity Risk Assessment:**
   - **Identification** of the **subject of consideration** and its values to be protected
   - Setting a **target security level** based on a risk matrix with the dimensions **impact** and **probability of occurrence**
   - **Subdivision** of the subject of consideration/values into **zones and channels**. In particular, safety-critical (in terms of safety) values are grouped into safety-critical zones. If not separable, the entire subject of consideration is to be classified as safety-critical. Furthermore, temporarily connected devices, wireless communications, and devices with untrusted networks are identified.
2. **Detailed Cybersecurity Risk Assessment:**
   - Determination of the **remaining risk** and security level for the individual zones and channels

At the end of step 1, a detailed architecture is created that includes, among other things, logical and physical boundaries, a list of all physical and logical access points, connections between zones, a list of all values and consequences in case of compromise, etc. Each zone and each channel is assigned a target security level.

To derive security requirements, assumptions, and boundary conditions, a **detailed risk assessment** is carried out for each zone and channel in the second overarching step.

The approach described in the standard is a **threat-centered one:**

- Identification of **threats:** Description of a threat source, capability, threat vector, and potentially affected values
  - Example: Authorized maintenance personnel access a process control zone with an infected laptop.
- Identification of **security gaps:** To successfully realize threats, security gaps are exploited. Therefore, security gaps in the corresponding values must be identified to understand attack vectors. A security gap analysis can be carried out using appropriate information sources.
- Determination of **consequences** and **impacts.** Each threat scenario is examined to determine the consequence and impact if the threat is realized.
- Determination of a ***"Likelihood"*/probability of occurrence** (before the implementation of countermeasures). Each **pair of threat and security gap** must be examined to determine the likelihood of the threat being realized before the implementation of countermeasures. The likelihood is divided into five values—from **almost certain** (more than 1 × per year) to **very unlikely** (less than 1 × per 100,000 years).
- Calculation of an untreated **security risk** (before the implementation of countermeasures). For the examined pairs, the corresponding security risk is determined from the impact and likelihood (before the implementation of countermeasures).
- Determination of a **target security level** for each zone and channel
- Identification and examination of **existing countermeasures**
- **Redetermination** of likelihood and impact
- Calculation of the **residual risk**

If the residual risk is too high (above the tolerable risk), further countermeasures must be defined until the residual risk can be accepted.

The safety requirements derived at the end include:

- Description of the subject of consideration
- operational environment
- Threat landscape (summary of information about threats, causes, threat vectors, and trends)
- necessary security functions
- tolerable risks
- regulatory functions

Conclusion

The determination of a risk level is based on the consideration of the combination of threat and security gap and their evaluation regarding the likelihood of occurrence and impact for each zone and channel.

7.4 Risk assessment according to ISO/IEC 27005

As indicated in Sect. 5.2.5.2, the **ISO/IEC 27005** deals with risk management of information security.

The crucial content (see also Sect. 7.3) is the definition of how to deal with identified risks, the so-called risk treatment options. Using the example *"infected malware is installed on a laptop after the owner unknowingly plugged in an infectious USB stick"*, the four possible options will be explained.

- Risk-**Modification:** The level of risk should be controlled by the introduction, removal or modification of controls so that the residual risk can be reassessed as acceptable. For this purpose, for example, the **ISO/IEC 27002** [ISO27002] contains appropriate controls.
  - Example: The management decides that employees are not allowed to take their laptops home in order to reduce the risk of catching viruses via an infected, unnoticed USB stick (e.g. at home).
- Risk-**Retention:** The decision to retain the risk without further measures should be made depending on the risk assessment.
  - Example: The management decides that the USB interface does not need to be blocked by employees. The risk and its consequences of being attacked via this interface are accepted.
- Risk-**Avoidance:** The activity or condition leading to the particular risk should be avoided.
  - Example: The management instructs its IT department to logically and physically disable the USB interfaces on the employees' laptops. This eliminates the risk of unknowingly catching viruses via an infectious USB stick.
- Risk-**Sharing:** The risk is shared with another party who can deal with the respective risk most effectively depending on the risk assessment.
  - Example: The management decides to take out a cybersecurity insurance that covers the financial damage after infection of the laptop due to an infectious USB stick. In this case, the responsibility (and the damage) is covered (at least) with money.

These four options are typical for the treatment of security risks and are similarly proposed in all common security standards/guidelines.

7.5 Risk assessment according to NIST SP 800-30

The NIST standard **NIST SP 800-30** [NIST800-30] describes the execution of risk assessments and a generic risk model (the risk factors are mentioned in brackets):

1. Threat **source** (attacker capabilities, intent, …). They initiate the
2. Threat **event** (sequence of activities, scenarios, …). It is exploited (with corresponding likelihood) by a
3. **Vulnerability** (severity, penetration degree (in the context of predisposing measures (e.g., document classification, compliance with technical standards, …)), scope of the affected), effectiveness (of countermeasures) and thus leads to the
4. **Adverse impact:** (risk as a combination of impact and likelihood)

At the end of the chain is the organizational risk for operation (mission, functions, image, reputation), the organizational ability, individuals, other organizations, etc.

The standard **NIST SP 800-39** considers risk management hierarchically on three levels [NIST800-39]:

- Level 1: **Organization** (more strategic risks)
- Level 2: Mission, **Business processes** (e.g., securing business process resilience)
- Level 3: **Information systems** (more short-term/tactical risks)

Traditional risk management systems mainly focus on level 3. At this point, there is a risk for level 1, such as endangering a business goal due to an adverse impact on the information security level.

The described approach of a risk assessment process is very similar to the detailed risk assessment process from ISA/IEC 62443 [IEC62443] (see Sect. 7.3).

Step 1: **Preparation**

- Preparation of the risk assessment: Definition of the context (organization, policies, methods, determination of risk factors, …).

Step 2: **Execution**

- Identification of **threat sources,** that are relevant for organizations.
- Identification of **threat events,** that could be generated by these sources.
- Identification of **vulnerabilities** within organizations, that could be exploited by threat sources through certain threat events, as well as the predisposing conditions that could influence a successful exploitation.

- Determination of the **likelihood,** that the identified threat sources initiate specific threat events and the likelihood that the threat events are successful.
- Determination of **adverse impacts** on the operation and assets of the organization, individuals, etc., resulting from the risk.
- Determination of the **information security risks** as a combination of the likelihood of exploitation of vulnerabilities by a threat and the impacts of such exploitation, including all uncertainties associated with the risk determinations.

Step 3: **Communication** of the results

- Communication of the results of the risk assessment and
- Dissemination of information developed in the course of conducting the risk assessment to support other risk management activities.

Step 4: **Monitoring** of risk management

- Ongoing monitoring of risk factors identified in risk assessments and understanding of subsequent changes to these factors and
- Updating the components of risk assessments that reflect the monitoring activities of organizations.

The standard also suggests a classification of occurrence likelihood from less than once in 10 years to 100 times per year, as well as the success probability of an attack from almost always to highly unlikely. Both are then combined into an overall occurrence likelihood—from **occurs very rarely and has very rarely an impact** to **occurs very frequently and has very frequently adverse effects.** This overall likelihood can then be combined with the amount of damage (impact height). Damage categories mentioned in the standard are: damage to…

- Business processes (mission, business functions, services, …)
- Values to be protected (physical, property, information, …)
- People (life and limb)
- Organizations (finances, relationships, …)
- Nation

At the end of the standard, a risk template is described that summarizes the previous topics (with an example in brackets):

- **Threat Event** (Authorized privileged user inadvertently discloses critical/sensitive information)
- **Threat Source** (Faulty actions of individuals in the performance of their daily duties)

- Characteristics of the threat source:
  - **Attacker's Ability**: from sophisticated expertise with many resources and opportunities for coordinated attacks to very limited resources, expertise, and opportunity.
  - **Intent:** from attempting to undermine, seriously hinder, or destroy a central mission or business function, a program, or a company to attempting to seize, disrupt, or deface the organization's cyber resources without concern for the discovery of attacks or the disclosure of information.
  - **Objective:** from focus on specific high-value or mission-critical information, resources, supply streams, or functions, specific employees or positions to focus only possibly on specific organizations or classes of organizations.
- **Relevance:** from confirmed: the threat event was anticipated to possible; the threat event was mentioned somewhere.
- **Likelihood** of an attack: from very high: very likely that the threat event will materialize to very low: the threat event is very unlikely.
- **Vulnerability** and **predisposing conditions:** Need to handle information (how it is created, transmitted, stored, processed, and/or displayed) in a certain way due to its sensitivity.
- **Severity** and Penetration: from very high: The vulnerability is disclosed and exploitable, and its exploitation could lead to serious impacts to very low: The vulnerability is not of concern.
- **Success Probability** of an **Attack:** from very high: If the threat event is initiated or occurs, it is almost certain that it has negative impacts to very low: If the threat event is initiated or occurs, it is highly unlikely that it has negative impacts.
- **Overall Likelihood:** from very low to very high.
- Severity/Level of **Impact:** very high: It is expected that the threat event has several severe or catastrophic negative impacts, to it is expected that the threat event has a negligible negative impact.
- **Risk:** from very high a threat event has several severe or catastrophic side effects to very low, a threat event is expected to have negligible negative impacts.

7.6 Risk Assessment according to HEAVENS

HEAVENS (HEAling Vulnerabilities to ENhance Software Security and Safety) [HEAVENS16] was a Swedish research project (2013–2016) aimed at identifying security vulnerabilities in automotive E/E systems.

The project defines methods along with tools for conducting the security assessment. The assumed scenario of HEAVENS can be defined as follows.

> **Owners** (of values to be protected) demand **countermeasures,** to increase the protection of their **values,** with which the **risk** is minimized, which is present due to **vulnerabilities** that can be exploited by the **threats,** emanating from **sources of threat** (e.g., attackers) (thus becoming a **security gap**).

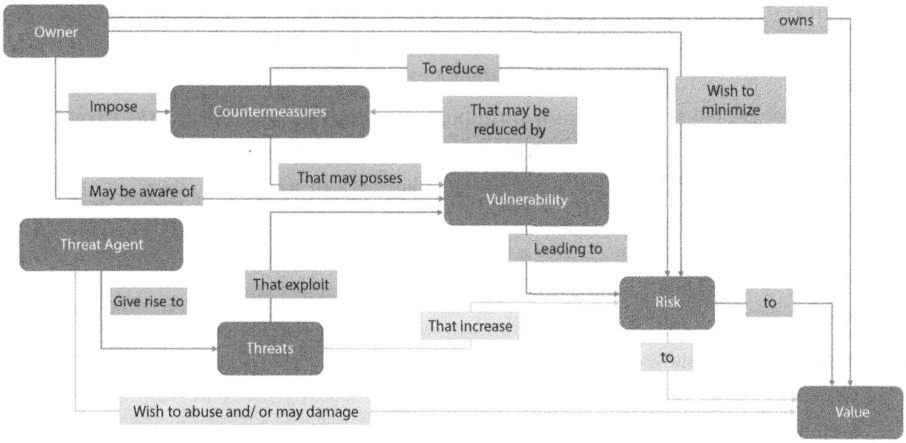

Fig. 7.2 Relationships in HEAVENS

Figure 7.2 provides a graphical overview of the individual relationships of the terms.

The goal was to create a **HEAVENS security model** based on **state-of-the-art methods,** from other domains, to derive security requirements for E/E systems in the automotive industry. The focus was on threat analysis and risk assessment.

Another project goal was to investigate the interplay of functional safety and security in the context of automotive E/E systems. The security objectives considered were **confidentiality, integrity, availability, authenticity, authorization, non-repudiation, privacy** and **timeliness.**

Various methods and models for threat modeling and risk assessment were evaluated: MS-SDL, TRIKE, OCTAVE, P.A.S.T.A, SINA, STRIDE, DREAD, CIA, CVSS, EVITA, TVRA, SECTRA, ….

While the MS-STRIDE model [STRIDE02] (see Sect. 7.7) was evaluated as a suitable threat model for automotive, the associated MS-DREAD model for risk assessment was ruled out as unsuitable. The EVITA [EVITA09] model has created a risk assessment scheme for automotive systems [EVITA09a]. Common Criteria [ISO15408] (see Sect. 5.2.8) was also a basis. The advantages of HEAVENS are:

- Equally applicable to a **wide range of road vehicles,** e.g., cars and commercial vehicles.
- Takes into account a variety of **stakeholders** (e.g., OEM, fleet owners, vehicle owners, drivers, passengers, etc.).
- **Threat-centered** model, realized by applying Microsoft's STRIDE approach in the context of automotive E/E systems.

- Use of only a **handful of generic threat categories** instead of thinking about virtually endless possibilities of attacks and attack techniques that can be associated with a value to be protected.
- The model provides a direct **mapping** between **security attributes and threats** during the threat analysis. This facilitates visualization and early estimation of the technical impacts (confidentiality, integrity, availability) of a specific threat on a specific value to be protected.

The derivation of security requirements is done in four steps:

1. **Definition** of the subject matter/use cases.
2. **Threat analysis:** threats, values to be protected, security attributes are identified for the subject matter.
3. **Risk assessment:** a security level is determined from the threat analysis, the impact, and threat level.
4. **Security requirements:** high-level security requirements are derived from the results of the threat analysis and risk assessment.

7.6.1 Threat Analysis

For the threat analysis, the **MS-STRIDE** model (Sect. 7.7) is applied. It is advisable to consider threats before vulnerabilities/weaknesses in threat analysis and risk assessment (e.g., in a TARA (see Sect. 7.2)). A TARA is usually carried out during the concept phase and there may not be detailed information (e.g., about the implementation) about the object to be evaluated. On the other hand, weaknesses can be found during product development and implementation (i.e., implementation weaknesses) and the configuration of a system (e.g., configuration weaknesses). As a result, it is almost impossible to discuss weknesses during the concept phase that relate to the specific implementation. In the context of the automotive industry, however, it is worthwhile to consider information about existing vulnerabilities gaps (such as the MITRE databases [CAPEC]). There is an n:m mapping between threats and weaknesses. A vulnerablity can lead to several threats, a threat can arise from different vulnerabilities and weaknesses.

7.6.2 Risk Assessment

The risk assessment is intended to classify the threats. To do this, the value and threat pairs of a use case are identified accordingly. A security level is assigned to all value-threat pairs. Security level should be understood as a measure of the strength of security measures for a security value in order to achieve a security level. The risk assessment consists of three steps:

1. **Threat Level:** EVITA [EVITA09] and Common Criteria [ISO15408] use the same five parameters. OWASP [OWASP] (suitable for web applications) uses eight other models accordingly similar. For HEAVENS, four are selected:
   - Expertise
   - Knowledge about the subject matter
   - Window of opportunity
   - Necessary equipment

   The HEAVENS model uses different scales and removes attack duration (because not seen as a priority for the threat level and proportional to the other parameters). The scale contains four levels for each of the four parameters. For each value-threat pair, the respective level values (0–3) are added together to be mapped into a five-level model for the threat level.
2. **Impact Level:** Various standards use different types of assessment. OWASP [OWASP] uses, for example, four technical impact categories and four business process-oriented impact categories. The latter can be seen as consequences of the technical ones. The four technical ones correspond to the security attributes, the four business process-oriented ones to the security objectives. HEAVENS uses, similar to EVITA [EVITA09a], the four impact categories: functional safety, finances, operability, and privacy and laws. These are classified differently depending on the stakeholder (vehicle manufacturer, fleet manager, vehicle owner, …). Each category is assigned four levels. The scale is not linear and goes for Functional Safety and Finances from 0, 10, 100 and 1000, for Operational and Privacy and Laws from 0, 1, 10, 100. Thus, functional safety and finances outweigh/override operability and data protection. In the end, the levels for each category are summed up and mapped onto five impact levels from *low* to *critical.*
3. **Security Level:** OWASP combines occurrence probability and impact level to end up in three levels *low, medium* and *high.* EVITA distinguishes between security levels for non-functional security levels and functional security levels. In the latter case, both the severity of the impact and the controllability of functional safety are taken into account. In the end, there are three levels: *Minor, Major* and *critical.* HEAVENS crosses the five levels of threat with the five levels of impact. In the matrix, the cells are then assigned to the five security levels *QM, low, medium, high* and *critical.* The five security levels can be mapped accordingly to the five EAL (Evaluation Assurance Level) at Common Criteria.

7.6.3 Security Requirements

After conducting the threat analysis and risk assessment, the final part of the HEAVENS security model deals with deriving security requirements based on asset, threat, security attribute, and security level. If the assigned security level is only QM, there is no need to specify additional security requirements.

For a value to be protected (asset), there can be multiple threats and thus potentially multiple security levels, which are based on multiple threat levels for all threats associated with a value. One approach to determining a security level for the value as a whole is to consider the highest security level from all security levels for all threats associated with the value. An alternative is to consider the highest threat level along with the impact level to define the security level for the value.

Background Information

Currently, work is being done on a HEAVENS 2.0 version, which is then supposed to be compliant with TARA (as described in Sect. 7.2) of ISO/SAE 21434.

7.7 Threat Modeling: STRIDE

The **MS-STRIDE** model (Microsoft-STRIDE) is threat and attacker-centered. Each threat is associated with a corresponding set of values to be protected from the attacker's perspective. An advantage of such an approach is that the focus shifts from identifying each individual attack to the end results of possible attacks. It may be useful to think about threats in terms of what the attacker is trying to achieve, rather than thinking about seemingly endless variations of specific attacks and attack techniques. The STRIDE approach was therefore adopted in the HEAVENS project [HEAVENS16]. It is also the basis of the LINDDUN framework [LINDDUN] (see Sect. 3.6.2).

The advantage of the STRIDE method is the direct (unambiguous) assignment to security attributes (see Table 7.4).

The STRIDE threat model can be performed both per element/component and per interaction.

- Section 7.7.1: STRIDE-per-Element: Data flow diagrams as a basis
- Section 7.7.2: STRIDE-per-Interaction: Interactions as a basis

7.7.1 STRIDE-per-Element

The basis is a corresponding data flow diagram. This shows a process that communicates with a data store on one side and a user on the other. An assumed trust zone can include the process and data store. The STRIDE threats can be applied to all identified elements. Depending on the element, different STRIDE threats may be relevant (see Table 7.5).

For all threats, the corresponding elements can be listed. If different elements are parts of the same attack, the same topics may become relevant at multiple points.

Table 7.4 Assignment between STRIDE threats and security objectives

STRIDE Threats	Description	Security Objective	Example
Spoofing	Attackers pretend to be someone or something else	Authenticity/Actuality	Messages from a fake sender
Tampering	Attackers alter data during transmission or in a data store, attackers can also alter functions—implemented in software, firmware or hardware	Integrity	Corrupt data or code, flashed malware, altering, injecting, tampering messages, manipulating, configuration change
Repudiation	Attackers carry out actions that cannot be traced back to them	Non-Repudiation	Repetition, fake messages, denial of message transmission and reception
Information Disclosure	Attackers gain access to data in transmission or in a data store	Confidentiality/Privacy	Eavesdropping, interception, wiretapping, unauthorized procurement
Denial-of-Service	Attackers interrupt the legitimate operation of a system	Availability	Shutdown, Denial-of-Service, Jamming
Privilege Elevation	Attackers carry out actions they are not authorized to do	Authorization	Unauthorized appropriation (keys, certificates, back-end databases), gaining root access

Table 7.5 Assignment of STRIDE threat and data flow diagram element

Element Type	S	T	R	I	D	E
External Entity	X		X			
Data Flow		X		X	X	
Data Store		X	X	X	X	
Process	X	X	X	X	X	X

7.7.2 STRIDE-per-Interaction

The significance of this approach is that tuples such as origin, target, interaction, and the threats against them are enumerated in the threat enumeration. The aim of this is to reduce the number of things a modeler has to consider. In the end, it seems likely that STRIDE-per-Element and STRIDE-per-Interaction will lead to the same number of

Table 7.6 STRIDE-per-Interaction Table

Element	Interaction	S	T	R	I	D	E
Process	Process has an outgoing data flow to the data store	X			X		
Data flow (Commands)	Crosses the system boundary		X			X	X
Data store (Database)	Process has an outgoing data flow to the data store		X	X	X	X	
External Interactor	External interactor passes input to process	X		X	X		

threats. The threats with the STRIDE-per-Interaction approach may be easier to understand. The STRIDE threats that apply to the interaction are listed in Table 7.6.

The difference between the two STRIDE variants is that the STRIDE-per-Interaction approach is complex without a reference diagram (e.g., architecture diagram) at hand. STRIDE-per-Element is also easy to understand for beginners if the diagrams are simple enough to understand well.

STRIDE-per-Element can also be applied to complex systems and is usually carried out via brainstorming. STRIDE-per-Interaction can be performed with tool support, but it does not really scale.

7.8 Summary

▶ **Risk assessment processes** can have **different orientations**:

- **Value/Asset-oriented** [ISO21434], i.e., initially, values to be protected are identified from the stakeholder's perspective
- **Threat-/Security gap oriented** [NIST800-30, IEC62443, ISO27005]
- **Risk treatment oriented** [ISO31000]
- **Attacker oriented** [NIST800-115]

An **occurrence likelihood** can include different factors: occurrence likelihood of the event, success probability of an event, height/severity of the impact. Usually, occurrence likelihood and severity of the impact are included.

Other important points and **distinguishing features** of the different methods:

- **Security levels** are not defined in every standard. When they are defined, they can have different meanings.
- Standards sometimes lack specifications for the **implementation quality** of the derived security requirements. Theoretically, requirements that specify important con-

trols in terms of risk reduction—behind which high impacts are hidden—can be realized and implemented without great care.

- The **effectiveness** of security controls is difficult to prove. Risks can indeed increase when security controls are implemented. Technical measures like whitelists can be hacked themselves, secret keys can be read out unauthorized.
- **Security levels** can change at any time if they are calculated from the occurrence likelihood or a risk value that depends on it.
- **Risk assessments** must be **monitored** over the entire lifetime of a product. The arguments for accepting or sharing a risk can quickly become invalid.
- Some standards explicitly include **functional safety**. In such cases, consistency checks between a hazard analysis and risk assessment and a threat analysis and risk assessment can be performed (see Chap. 4):
  - Functional safety objectives and security objectives must be consistent
  - Hazards and damage scenarios must be consistent
  - Individual events that can lead to a hazard from the perspective of functional safety are to be analyzed as protectable targets of attacks
  - Vulnerabilities can endanger functional safety as individual errors.

References

[CAPEC] ***„Common Attack Pattern Enumeration and Classification“***. Link: https://capec.mitre.org/. accessed: 18.04.2021

[EVITA09] ***"E-safety vehicle intrusion protected applications“.*** Link: https://www.evita-project.org/. accessed: 23.04.2021

[EVITA09a] ***„Security requirements for automotive on-board networks based on dark-side scenarios“,*** 2009. Link: http://www.evita-project.org/. accessed: 23.04.2021

[GPfSoIOT19] ***„GOOD PRACTICES FOR SECURITY OF IOT – Secure Development Lifecycle“***, ENISA, November 2019. Link: https://www.enisa.europa.eu/publications/good-practices-for-security-of-iot-1. accessed: 23.04.2021

[GPoSC19] ***„ENISA GOOD PRACTICES FOR SECURITY OF SMART CARS“,*** ENISA, November 2019. Link: https://www.enisa.europa.eu/publications/smart-cars. accessed: 23.04.2021

[HEAVENS16] ***„HEAVENS: HEAling Vulnerabilities to ENhance Software Security and Safety“***. Aljosha Lauterbach, Chalmers Mafijul Islam, Volvo AB. Released, March 18, 2016. Link: https://autosec.se/wp-content/uploads/2018/03/HEAVENS_D2_v2.0.pdf. accessed: 23.04.2021

[IEC62443] ***„New ISA/IEC 62443 standard specifies security capabilities for control system components“;*** ISA.org home page: https://www.isa.org/intech-home/2018/september-october/departments/new-standard-specifies-security-capabilities-for-c. accessed: 18.04.2021

[ISO15408] ***„Information technology – Security techniques – Evaluation criteria for IT security –“,*** Common Criteria, ISO/IEC 15408 Band 1–3

[ISO18045] ***„Information technology – Security techniques – Methodology for IT security evaluation“***; ISO/IEC 18045

[ISO21434] ***„Road Vehicles Cybersecurity Engineering",*** International Standard ISO/SAE 21434:2021

[ISO26262] ***„Road Vehicles – Functional Safety***"; International Standard; ISO 26262–2nd edition

[ISO27002] ***„Information technology – Security techniques – Code of practice for information security controls***"; ISO/IEC 27002

[ISO27005] ***„Information technology – Security techniques – Information security risk management***"; ISO/IEC 27005

[ISO31000] ***„Risk management – Guidelines***"; DIN ISO 31000

[LINDDUN] ***„LINDDUN: a privacy threat analysis framework***"; Link: https://people.cs.kuleuven.be/~kim.wuyts/LINDDUN/LINDDUN.pdf or https://www.linddun.org/. accessed: 23.04.2021

[NIST800-30] ***„Guide for Conducting Risk Assessment***"; NIST SP 800-30; Link: https://www.nist.gov/privacy-framework/nist-sp-800-30. accessed: 10.04.2021

[NIST800-39] ***„Managing Information Security Risk: Organization, Mission, and Information System View***"; NIST SP 800-39. Link: https://www.nist.gov/privacy-framework/nist-sp-800-39. accessed: 10.04.2021

[NIST800-115] ***„Technical Guide to Information Security Testing and Assessment***"; NIST SP 800–115

[OWASP] ***„OWASP***". Link: https://www.owasp.org/index.php/Top_10-2017_Top_10. accessed: 23.04.2021

[Sch99] ***„Attack Trees***"; B. Schneier, Dr. Dobb's Journal, December 1999. Link: https://www.schneier.com/academic/archives/1999/12/attack_trees.html. accessed: 17.04.2021

[STRIDE02] ***„The STRIDE Threat Model";*** 2002; https://msdn.microsoft.com/pt-br/windows/desktop/ee823878. accessed: 23.04.2021

[UNECE-155] ***„Addendum 154 – UN Regulation No. 155";*** Link: https://unece.org/sites/default/files/2021-03/R155e.pdf. accessed: 18.04.2021

IT Service Management

8

The **IT Service Management** includes methods that are necessary to achieve the best possible support of business processes by the IT organization.

Information security in the company…

- ensures the preservation and **continuity of the company**
- **avoids, reduces** or **transfers risks**
- prevents and/or **limits damages**

This is not primarily about the security of a product in the field, such as securing secret keys in control units in the product itself. There are generic standards and norms for the implementation of information security. Requirements (controls) must be evaluated and adapted to the company:

- **Control mechanisms** for specifications must be implemented
- Processes must be **documented** and lived
- **Emergency processes** must be tested and documented
- **Responsibilities** must be installed
- **Effectiveness** of information security must be measured and reported

Company obligations include the reliable, timely and comprehensive securing of IT systems as well as the initiation, implementation, operation and maintenance of an early risk detection system:

- **legally:** operational/service agreements, control through contracts, terms and conditions etc.
- **organizationally:** responsibility, accountability, usage guidelines, policies etc.
- **technically:** virus protection, archiving, filters, back-up etc.

T. Liedtke, *Information Security*, https://doi.org/10.1007/978-3-658-45711-2_8

In an IT strategy, the company goals defined in the corporate strategy are related to IT and described in detail. The creation of an IT strategy makes sense wherever IT represents a significant factor of production.

In a policy for an ISMS (Information Security Management System) or CSMS (Cybersecurity Management System), the scope and goal of a management system are defined. The following applies:

- **Compliance:** Rules and procedures provide clarity and transparency about what is to be complied with in which situations: IT-Security (e.g. guidelines, concepts), Incident Management Process, Business Continuity (Emergency Management, Crisis Management), Risk Management (Vulnerability Management), Compliance Management (e.g. Data Protection), Asset Management, Supplier Management
- **Enabling:** The assignment of responsibilities clarifies who is responsible for what in an organization: Roles CISO (Chief Information Security Officer), DPO (Data Protection Officer), IT-SiBe (IT Security Officer), ...), Structures (Security Department), Tasks (Job Descriptions), Competencies (Escalation Matrix)
- **Securing:** Assignment of appropriate resources ensures that processes can be lived and pursued accordingly.

An ISMS/CSMS takes care of processes at the organizational level. At the core is the handling of risks and the protection of corresponding values:

- **material** values (e.g. real estate, vehicles, employees, ...),
- **intangible** values (e.g. information, applications, ...)

The core components of a management system are document, process control and steering. For Information Security Management Systems, information flow control is added.

The requirements from laws, industry-specific standards and best practices require verifiable regulations of information security. Corporations demand a proven ISMS from service companies in the context of the supplier relationship (e.g. by means of ISO/IEC 27001 certificate). Without verifiable documentation (regulation), there is personal liability of the management (board) and can be sanctioned as organizational fault.

The **IT Governance** regulates the interaction and shared responsibility between the department and IT:

- **Planning** of tasks, competencies, and responsibilities
- **Control** of planning and control processes in IT
- Development of the **IT concept**
- Determination/coordination of the **IT architecture**

The **IT Compliance** describes the adherence to legal, internal company (IT Governance), and contractual regulations in the area of the IT landscape.

Implementation of measures in the areas of:

- **Information security** (Archiving, Backup, Business Continuity Management, …)
- **IT security** (Securing the protection objectives, technical measures, …)
- **Data protection** (Informational self-determination, rights of those affected, etc.)

The **IT Controlling** includes:

- Control
- Measurement (**KPI** – Key Performance Indicator)
- Leading discussions away from purely financial and budget discussions towards a **qualitative, strategic** discussion of the use of IT
- Use of an **IT metrics system** for controlling management processes
- **IT Scorecard** with the following views:
  - **Financial**-oriented,
  - **Customer**-oriented,
  - **Process**-oriented,
  - **Innovation/Capability**-oriented

Various perspectives in IT controlling (also **Business-Service-Management**) are:

- Total **C**ost of **O**wnership (**TCO**)
  - Selection of the continuity strategy must be made considering the economic circumstances
  - Consideration of the acquisition costs as well as the costs of later use over the entire lifecycle of the investment
  - Goal: consider hidden costs
- Total **B**enefit of **O**wnership (**TBO**)
  - Effects of the acquisition of IT/TC components
  - Effects such as improvement of customer service or improvement of decision making
- **V**alue **o**n **I**nvestment (**VOI**)
  - **The additional value**, generated by realizing the benefit, which includes non-monetary or long-term results
  - **Intangible** benefit (competence, ability to respond to changes, compliance, …)
- **R**eturn **O**n **I**nvestment (**ROI**)
  - Statement on the **return** of the invested capital within a **defined period**
- **R**eturn **O**n **S**ecurity **I**nvestment (**ROSI**)
  - Return calculation on the capital invested in **information security**
  - Determination of whether the costs for security measures are in a **reasonable ratio to risk reduction**

On the next level after a policy is a concept that prescribes the implementation in an organization operationally:

- Establishment of **decision criteria** (term, orientation towards the company strategy, …)
- **Establishment of standards** (e.g. ITIL) to improve integration capability
- **Enforcement of methods** (system development, documentation, change management etc.)

8.1 Motivation (Embedding)

For an **ITSM** (IT Service Management) there exist various frameworks. Known standards/norms are:

- **ITIL** (IT Infrastructure Library) [ITIL] (see Sect. 8.2.1):
  - Developed by the **OGC** (Office of Governance Commerce) in Norwich (England) on behalf of the British government
  - Worldwide de-facto standard for Service Management
  - Contains a library of good ITSM practices
- **COBIT** (Control Objectives for Information and related Technology) [COBIT] (see Sect. 8.2.2):
  - Collection of best practices (framework) for the management of information technology (IT), created by the Information Systems Audit and Control Association (**ISACA**) and the IT Governance Institute (**ITGI**)
  - Incorporates IT Service Management into its control objectives for support and delivery.
  - Since Cobit V4.1: SPICE-compliant assessment model

Both standards are described in Sect. 8.2.1 and 8.2.2 respectively.

Other standards relevant in this context are:

- **ISO/IEC 20000** [ISO/IEC20000]:
  - The first international standard for IT Service Management
  - Published in 2005, by ISO/IEC JTC1 SC7 (based on BS 15000)
  - Requirements for IT Service Management Systems
  - Companies can certify their IT organization processes according to the requirements of the standard. The first normative part of the standard sets minimum requirements for service management
  - It includes a process for Information Security Management and is aligned with ITIL.

- **ISO/IEC 15504**—Part 8 (see Sect. 5.2.8) [ISO15504]
  - An exemplary assessment model for IT Service Management
  - Use of ISO 20000-4 as a process reference model
- **ISO 20000-PAM**
  - ISO 15504-compliant process assessment model for ISO 20000 (PAM)
  - Use of ISO 20000-4 as a process reference model
  - Covers all SMS requirements (Security Management System) of ISO 20000-1:2011
  - Since 2014: intacs verified and accepted PAM
- **CMMI** for Services (CMMI-SVC):
  - Developed by the Software Engineering Institute (published in Feb 2009)
  - One of three CMMI constellations: Development/Procurement/Services
  - Maturity Framework for Service Management (not IT-specific)
- Microsoft Framework (**MOF**)
  - A series of guides designed to help IT professionals establish and implement reliable, cost-effective services

8.2 ITIL and COBIT

As mentioned at the beginning of Chap. 8, ITIL and COBIT are two well-known **ITSM** (IT Service Management systems). They will be described in this subsection.

- **ITIL:** Service orientation/**process landscape** focuses more on **work steps** and the responsibilities of individual process managers and processors
  - Framework for service management processes
  - Primarily helps the **IT manager and technical staff in operations** to understand their tasks and responsibilities in service management
- **COBIT:** Governance approach **bird's eye view** of IT service management
  - Goal-driven **framework for executives** that is **less** interested in the **process details.**

▶ **COBIT 5.0** sets its requirements for the ITIL processes. COBIT represents the engine, ITIL rather the transmission in a company.

8.2.1 ITIL—IT Infrastructure Library

ITIL (IT Infrastructure Library) is a **best practice model** for the introduction and operation of an IT Service Management (ITSM). The goals are:

- Systematic introduction to the promotion of the quality of IT services
- Standardization of terms **(glossary)**
- IT services must meet defined **quality objectives (service level)**

ITIL is a de facto standard in Europe. It serves as a guide to align a technology-oriented organization to be **process-**, **service-** and **customer-oriented**.

In ITIL v4, a total of 34 practices are described in three groups:

- 14 **general** management practices
- 17 **service-**management practices
- 3 **technical** management practices

Incident and Service Continuity Management can be found in the group of service management practices. Information Security Management is located in the group of general management practices and consists of the following sub-processes:

- **Design of security controls:** The goal is to design appropriate technical and organizational measures to ensure that all values, information, data, and IT services of a company are always protected in terms of their confidentiality, integrity, and availability.
- **Security testing:** Ensuring that all security mechanisms are regularly tested.
- Processing of **security incidents:** Detecting and defending against attacks and breaches of information security, and minimizing damage in the event of security breaches.
- **Security review:** Checking whether the security measures and procedures are still in line with the risk assessments from a company perspective and whether the corresponding measures and procedures are regularly kept up to date and tested.

8.2.2 COBIT—Control Objectives for Information and Related Technology

COBIT (Control Objectives for Information and Related Technology) is a globally recognized reference model and is established in many, especially larger, companies. It is a control framework for the implementation and proof of effective IT governance: COBIT was developed by the IT Governance Institute (ITGI) and Information Systems Audit and Control Association (ISACA) and was originally intended as a guide for IT auditors. It is about controlling IT from a business perspective and developing a model to ensure compliance with legal requirements (Compliance).

COBIT defines six basic principles for the governance system and the management of corporate IT:

- **Fulfillment** of **requirements,** to create value for stakeholders
- **Coverage** of the entire company **end-to-end**
- Application of a uniform, integrated **holistic approach**
- **Separation** of **governance** and **management**
- **Dynamic governance system**
- Tailored to the **needs** of **businesses**

Design factors are the respective strategy, size, role of IT, compliance requirements, and risk situation of the company.

In total, there are 40 governance and management objectives. They are equivalent to each other.

COBIT supports a process capability scheme based on CMMI (Capability Maturity Model Integration) from 0 to 5.

A focus area describes a specific governance topic that needs to be considered in a special way. Cybersecurity is an example of such a focus area.

8.3 27k—Information Security Management System

As described in Sect. 5.2.5, information security management is also part of an integral management system of a company. The ISMS can be assessed and certified according to **ISO/IEC 27001**.

Since the [ISO27001] primarily focuses on the **protection of business processes** of a company, interfaces and subsets to other values worth protecting must be carefully defined—such as software development, which also has to deal with risks of the product to be developed (during and after development). For this purpose, the clauses and controls for a policy and its guidelines as well as for development are relevant.

The **ISO/IEC 27005** [ISO27005] provides specifications for a risk analysis and management (see Sect. 5.2.5.2 and 7.4).

Depending on the business process, further volumes of the standard series must be considered, e.g. the **ISO/IEC 27034** [ISO27034] for application security.

8.4 IT Baseline Protection Compendium

For over 25 years, the **IT Baseline Protection** has been a method, guideline, recommendation, and globally recognized standard in one. It is applicable to all institutions that want to secure their IT systems and data networks and thus their business or administrative processes according to the **state of the art** in times of digitization. The **IT Baseline Protection Compendium** [BSI200-1] is a tool for information security. Together with the **BSI standards**, it forms the basis for all those who want to deal comprehensively with the topic of information security.

IT Baseline Protection Modules form the basis of the IT-Baseline Protection Compendium. Since 2021, the topics of automated and networked driving as well as web applications have also been included as new IT-Baseline Protection modules. The IT-Baesline Protection Compendium can be the entry point into an information security management system.

Influencing factors are: organization, personnel, technology, infrastructure, and compliance.

In the **first part,** 47 possible so-called **elementary threats** are explained. These include, for example, fire, water, natural disasters, up to malware, sabotage, social engineering, and data loss. These threats are:

- intended for use in **risk analysis,**
- always product-neutral and as technology-neutral as possible,
- compatible with comparable international catalogs and standards (see, for example, ISO/IEC 27005 [ISO27005]).

The **second part** contains six process modules: ISMS, organization and personnel, concepts and procedures, operation, detection, and reaction.

The **third part** contains four system-oriented modules: IT systems (e.g., servers, IT systems), Industrial IT (e.g., ICS components), networks (e.g., wireless networks, network components, …) and communication, infrastructure (e.g., general building, general vehicle, …).

The modules each contain a description of the component under consideration, procedures and IT systems, as well as specific threats and concrete requirements to secure the target object. Each module also describes who is responsible for its implementation.

Requirements are each marked as to whether they are a **basic** requirement, **standard** requirement, or a requirement for **increased protection needs**—a kind of tiering in three levels. Requirements are marked as **MUST-** and **SHOULD-** requirements.

As potential damages are assigned to the usual categories :

- Loss of **availability**
- Loss of **confidentiality** of information
- Loss of **integrity** (correctness) of information

The individual modules address typical processes of business processes and areas of IT use, such as emergency management, client-server networks, … The IT-Baseline Protection Compendium reflects the state of the art. This means what is technically advanced at the respective time and, on the other hand, what has proven to be suitable in practice.

The requirements listed in the IT-Baseline Protection Compendium should be met in order to achieve an appropriate level of security. The basic requirements represent the minimum of what is reasonably to be implemented in terms of security precautions. However, adequate security according to the **state of the art** is only achieved with the implementation of the **standard requirements.**

For certification according to ISO/IEC 27001 [ISO27001] based on IT-Baseline Protection, the basic and standard requirements must be met for the selected scope.

To model a complex **information network** according to IT-Baseline Protection, the appropriate modules of the IT-Baseline Protection Compendium must be selected and implemented. All relevant security requirements are thus collected. For this, all processes, applications, and IT systems must be recorded, or the **structure analysis** and usually a **protection needs determination** must be available. Based on this, an IT-Baseline Protection model of the information network is created, which consists of various, possibly also multiple used IT-Baseline Protection modules and includes a mapping between the modules and the security-relevant aspects of the information network.

8.4.1 BSI Standards for Implementation

Four BSI standards describe the implementation:

- **Management systems for information security** (ISMS): BSI standard 200-1 [BSI200-1] describes how an information security management system (ISMS) can be established. A management system includes all regulations that ensure the control and guidance of the institution and thus contribute to the achievement of objectives. A management system for information security therefore determines which tools and methods the management level of an institution can use to transparently guide tasks and activities aimed at information security.
- **IT baseline protection methodology:** BSI standard 200-2 [BSI200-2] represents a methodology for effective management of information security. This can be adapted to the requirements of institutions of various types and sizes. It is implemented through the three approaches ***"Standard protection"***, ***"Basic protection"*** and ***"Core protection"***. The methodology is based on the BSI standard 200-1 management systems for information security (ISMS) and thus also on the **ISO/IEC 27001** [ISO27001].
- **Risk analysis based on IT baseline protection:** With the BSI standard 200-3 [BSI200-3], the BSI provides an easy-to-use and recognized approach that institutions can use to manage their information security risks appropriately and purposefully.
- **Business Continuity Management:** The BSI standard 200-4 [BSI200-4] offers an individually adaptable, resource-saving and goal-oriented methodology to build and operate your own **BCMS** (Business Continuity Management System).

▶ The **Basic protection** (against gross negligence); simplified entry is a basic initial protection; specifically tailored to SMEs (small and medium-sized enterprises). The **Standard protection** corresponds to the implementation of a comprehensive security process according to BSI 200-2 on the basis of which an ISO 27001 certification is possible. The **Core protection** means the protection of outstanding, particularly vulnerable business processes (***"crown jewels"***) with a focus on a small, but very important information network with in-depth protection.

The phases of the security process are:

- **Initiation of the security process:** The management level must initiate, steer, and control the security process. This requires strategic guiding principles for information security and organizational conditions, i.e., how a functioning security process is structured and which organizational structures are sensible for this. A rough estimate of the value of information security and identification of the **critical business processes** ("crown jewels") is carried out.
- **Creation of the information security guideline:** A fundamental basis for the design of the security process is the guideline for information security. It describes the security objectives and the level of security the institution aims for, what the motivation for this is, and with which measures and structures this should be achieved. All employees should therefore be familiar with and understand the contents of the security guideline.
- **Establishment of a suitable organizational structure:** An organizational structure suitable for the size and type of the institution must be established for information security management.
- **Creation of a security concept:** After initiating the information security process, defining the security guideline and information security organization, the security concept for the institution is created. The basis for this can be found in the modules of the IT baseline protection compendium for typical components of business processes, applications, IT systems, and other objects according to the state of the art. These are thematically structured into modules so that they can be built upon each other. When applying IT baseline protection, a comparison is made between the security requirements from the relevant modules of the IT baseline protection compendium and the measures already implemented in the institution. Only if there is a significantly higher need for protection, a risk analysis must be carried out taking into account cost and effectiveness aspects. As a rule, it is sufficient to supplement the security requirements of the IT baseline protection compendium with correspondingly individual, higher-quality measures. For this purpose, a risk analysis based on IT baseline protection is described in BSI standard 200-3 [BSI200-3] as a simpler approach compared to traditional risk analysis methods.
- **Implementation of security concepts:** An adequate level of security can only be achieved if existing deficits are identified, the status quo is recorded in a security concept, necessary measures are identified, and these measures are consistently implemented.
- **Maintenance and continuous improvement of information security:** The goal of security management is to achieve the desired level of security and to maintain and improve it permanently. Therefore, the security process and the organizational structures for information security must be regularly checked to see if they are **appropriate, effective** and **efficient**. It is also necessary to analyze whether the measures of the security concept still **fit** the information network, whether they are **practical** and whether they have been **correctly implemented.**

▶ Methods of **protection requirement determination** include:

- **Inheritance:** A determined protection requirement inherits itself to the objects used for their processing, i.e., applications, IT systems, and other devices, rooms, and communication connections.
- **Cumulative effect:** The cumulative effect describes that the protection requirement of an IT system can increase if a higher total damage can occur through the accumulation of several (e.g., smaller) damages on an IT system. A trigger can also be that several IT applications or a large number of sensitive information are processed on an IT system, so that the total damage can be higher due to the accumulation of damages.
- **Maximum principle:** According to the maximum principle, the damage or the sum of the damages with the most severe effects determines the protection requirement of a business process, an application, or an IT system.
- **Distribution effect:** An application with a high protection requirement does not transfer this to a considered IT system because only insignificant parts of the application run on this IT system. Here, the protection requirement needs to be relativized.

Example

- **Inheritance:** A server room is assigned a high level of protection if servers, applications, and data with a high level of protection are physically located in this room.
- **Cumulative effect:** Almost all non-critical applications of a company run on only one server. The failure of each individual application is non-critical. However, a higher damage can occur if all non-critical applications fail simultaneously. The server's protection requirement is then rated higher than the individual applications.
- **Maximum principle:** A server runs an application with a high and one with a low protection requirement. The server is assigned a high level of protection.
- **Distribution effect:** Redundancies or the distribution of an application across multiple servers can keep the protection requirement of an affected server lower than the application itself. ◀

Example

The **modeling** will be demonstrated using an example (*italic* are the specific hints from the compendium):

1. The *Data protection/Privacy (CON.2)* is chosen as the building block.
2. The compendium **describes** and explains the building block and its objective.
3. The second section addresses the **threat situation** (e.g., *disregard, data access by third parties that do not serve the purpose of the original data processing, …*).

4. In the third section, **requirements** are divided according to
   - Basic requirements,
   - Standard requirements, and
   - Requirements for increased protection needs.
5. One of the **basic requirements**/measures is the *implementation of a standard data protection/privacy model.*
6. In another section, the **cross-table** with the assigned **elementary threats** is given:
   - e.g., poor planning or lack of adjustment.
   - This is (like all elementary threats) thoroughly motivated.
   - In this case, among others: If organizational processes that directly or indirectly serve information processing are not properly designed, this can lead to security problems. ◀

The **measures** are marked with a corresponding label:

- **A: Indispensable** standard security measures; implementation is required for all three levels of IT basic protection qualification.
- **B: Most important** standard security measures; implementation is required for the advanced level and for the certificate.
- **C:** Measures **required beyond a certificate.**
- **Z:** Implementation of **additional** IT security measures to increase IT security, but not necessary for qualification according to IT basic protection.

In certain cases, an **explicit risk analysis** must be carried out. For example, if the considered information network contains target objects that have a **high** or **very high protection requirement** in at least one of the three basic values of confidentiality, integrity, or availability. It is analyzed whether possibly additional security measures, which go beyond the IT basic protection model, need to be planned and implemented.

8.4.2 BSI Risk Analysis

The risk analysis consists of three overarching steps (see also Chap. 7):

1. **Identification** of risks
2. **Analysis** of risks
3. **Evaluation** or assessment of risks

The **BSI standard 200-3** describes the steps for risk analysis in detail:

- Step 1: Creation of a **hazard overview**
  - Compilation of a list of possible elementary hazards

  - Identification of additional hazards that go beyond the elementary hazards and result from the specific deployment scenario
- Step 2:
  - **Risk classification**
  - **Risk assessment** (determination of frequency of occurrence and damage amount):
    - **Frequency of occurrence** ranges from ***rare*** (event could occur at most every five years according to current knowledge) to ***very frequent*** (event occurs several times a month).
    - **Damage amount** ranges from ***negligible*** (damage effects are minor and can be neglected) to ***existential*** (damage effects can reach an existentially threatening catastrophic extent).
  - **Risk evaluation** (determination of the risk category):
    Impact and frequency of occurrence are crossed and mapped onto **four levels *low*** (the security measures already implemented or at least planned in the security concept provide sufficient protection) to ***very high*** (the security measures already implemented or at least planned in the security concept do not provide sufficient protection against the respective hazard). As a rule, low risks are more likely to be accepted, very high ones only rarely
- Step 3: **Risk treatment.** The four known options (see Sect. 7.2.7):
  - **Risk avoidance:** For example, exclude the cause of the risk
  - **Risk reduction:** Conditions that have contributed to the risk classification are modified (determination of security measures)
  - **Risk transfer:** Risks are shared with other parties
  - **Risk acceptance:** For example, the opportunities/consequences associated with the risk are perceived.
- Step 4: **Consolidation** of the **security concept**
  - **Integration** of the additional measures identified as a result of the risk analysis into the security concept

For the consolidation of the security concept, it is suggested:

- **Suitability** of the security measures to ward off the hazards
- **Interaction** of the security measures
- **User-friendliness** of the security measures
- **Appropriateness**/quality assurance of the security measures

8.5 The IT Security Officer

An information security organization consists of various roles. Depending on the size of the company, these are more or less explicitly defined and divided among a corresponding number of people:

- **C**hief **I**nformation **S**ecurity **O**fficer (**CISO:** Head of Information Security)
  - Responsible for the company-wide organization of IT security/Information Security
  - Responsible for IT compliance
  - Responsible for IT risk management
  - Responsible for emergency management
- IT Security Officer (**IT-SiBe**)
  - Responsible for the technical security of IT
  - Responsible for compliance and implementation of IT security guidelines
- IT-**Risk Manager**
  - Responsible for the identification, evaluation, and organization of IT risks
- IT-**Compliance Manager**
  - Responsible for the comprehensive and permanent compliance with requirements of the legislator and the company
- IT-Security **Auditor**
  - Checks the effectiveness of security guidelines/policies through audits and the monitoring of key figures

An **IT Security Officer** should be appointed at every institution that uses information technology (IT) for its task completion. It can be performed by a single person, a group of people, externally or part-time. Its appointment depends on the size of the company, the available resources, and the desired level of security. The main task of the IT Security Officer is to advise the company management on tasks related to IT security and to support their implementation.

The tasks of an **IT security officer** are listed below as examples:

- prepares the **management's perception** of the **importance of IT,** the desired IT security level and the company-wide IT security objectives, formulates them and brings about a decision
- **reports** to the management **about** the **status quo** of IT security
- **advises the management** on IT security issues
- develops and formulates the **IT security policy** and **obtains** the **approval of the management** thereafter
- **communicates** the agreed **IT security policy** to all affected employees of the company
- issues **guidelines** and **regulations,** on how IT security should be achieved in the company
- **supports** the **application of basic IT protection** and the **conduct of risk analyses** for the creation of the IT security concept

- **coordinates** the **IT security objectives** with the company's IT deployment objectives and aligns them with the IT strategies of the individual business areas
- **defines** the **tasks for IT security** for the subordinate area
- **reviews** the created **IT security concepts** for correctness and traceability
- **prepares the company decision** on costly IT security measures to be taken **and** brings about a decision
- manages the resources available for IT security in terms of money and working time
- monitors the progress of the implementation of IT security measures
- **coordinates controls** of the **effectiveness** of IT security measures in ongoing operations

References

BSI200-1 Information Security Managaement System (ISMS), Link: https://www.bsi.bund.de/SharedDocs/Downloads/EN/BSI/Grundschutz/International/bsi-standard-2001_en_pdf.pdf?__blob=publicationFile&v=2. accessed: 25.04.2021

[BSI200-2] IT-Grundschutz Methodology. Link: https://www.bsi.bund.de/SharedDocs/Downloads/EN/BSI/Grundschutz/International/bsi-standard-2002_en_pdf.pdf?__blob=publicationFile&v=2. accessed: 25.04.2021

[BSI200-3] Risk Analysed based on IT-Grundschutz. Link: https://www.bsi.bund.de/SharedDocs/Downloads/EN/BSI/Grundschutz/International/bsi-standard-2003_en_pdf.pdf?__blob=publicationFile&v=2. accessed: 25.04.2021

[BSI200-4] Risk Analysed based on IT-Grundschutz. Link: https://www.bsi.bund.de/SharedDocs/Downloads/EN/BSI/Grundschutz/International/bsi-standard-2003_en_pdf.pdf?__blob=publicationFile&v=2. accessed: 25.04.2021

[BSIGK] ***„IT-Grundschutz-Kompendium; BSI (Bundesamt für Informationstechnik)“***. Link: https://www.bsi.bund.de/DE/Themen/Unternehmen-und-Organisationen/Standards-und-Zertifizierung/IT-Grundschutz/IT-Grundschutz-Kompendium/it-grundschutz-kompendium_node.html. accessed: 25.04.2021

[COBIT] ***„COBIT“***; Link: https://www.isaca.org/resources/cobit. accessed: 10.04.2021

[ISO20000] ***„Information technology – Service management“***

[ISO15504] ***„Information technology - Process assessment“***

[ISO27001] ***„Information security management systems – Requirements“;*** ISO/IEC 27001

[ISO27005] ***„Information technology – Security techniques – Information security risk management“;*** ISO/IEC 27005

[ISO27034] ***„Information technology – Security techniques – Application – security“;*** ISO/IEC 27034

[ITIL] ***„ITIL“;*** Link: https://www.axelos.com/best-practice-solutions/itil. accessed: 10.04.2021

Appendix: Control Families 9

In the **NIST SP 800-53R5** [NIST800–53R5], 20 control families are described. In Table 9.1, these are listed along with appropriate keywords for topics to be considered for the corresponding control family. They can be considered general, so that the listed security controls can be mapped (bi-)directionally to other standards. For example, to the security controls of the **ISO/IEC 27001** [ISO27001] or to functional and security requirements of the **Common Criteria** [ISO15408].

Examples of mapping to controls of other standards:

- ISO/IEC 27001: Policies for information security (A.5.1.1) and all guidelines and procedures (XX-1).
- Common Criteria: Functional requirement for security audit automatic response/security alarms (FAU_ARP.1) and response to errors in audit processing (AU-5).

The illustrations work in both directions.

T. Liedtke, *Information Security*, https://doi.org/10.1007/978-3-658-45711-2_9

9.1 Control families for Security and Privacy

Table 9.1 Control families for Security and Privacy

Control Family	Number of Control Extensions	Examples (lists are not exhaustive)
Access Control	25	• Policies and procedures address the controls to be implemented in the system or organization, such as a risk management strategy • Account management: Definition of types, specification of authorized users, … • Access enforcement: Enforcement of approved permissions for logical access to information and system resources • Information flow enforcement: Enforcement of approved permissions to control the flow of information • Separation of duties: Definition of system access rights to enable separation of duties • Least privilege
Training and Awareness	6	• Policies and procedures • Training and awareness: practical examples, insider threat, social engineering, threat situation: environmental control • Role-based training, training evidence, feedback
Audit and Accountability	16	• Event logging, audit records, response to errors in the audit logging process • Review, analysis, and reporting of audit logs • Protection of audit reports, timestamps, non-repudiation, retention, report generation
Assessment, Authorization, and Monitoring	9	• Information exchange, exchange authorization intra- and inter-organization • Continuous monitoring: trend analyses, risk monitoring, consistency analyses • Planning of activities and milestones • Penetration tests: independence, red team operations
Configuration Management	14	• Baselines: Automation support for accuracy and timeliness, maintenance of configurations • Change control: Documentation, testing, automated responses, reviews for system changes, cryptography management • Impact analyses: separated test environments, verification of controls • Access restriction for changes: Privilege restriction for production and operation • Settings: automated management • Least functionality: periodic reviews, prevention of program execution, compliance with registration • Configuration management plan • Software usage restriction (e.g., open source)

(continued)

Table 9.1 (continued)

Control Family	Number of Control Extensions	Examples (lists are not exhaustive)
Planning for the Unexpected	13	• Plan creation: Capacity planning, resumption of operational and business functions, business continuity, alternative processing • Training • Testing the plan • Alternative storage, Alternative production, … • Telecommunication backup • System Backup: Testing reliability and integrity, … • System recovery • Safe mode • Alternative backup measures
Identification and Authentication	12	• Device identification and authentication: Multi-factor authentication, Individual and group authentication • Identification management • Authentication management: Passwords, Public-Key Infrastructure, Biometric access, Expiry of accesses, … • Identification of cryptographic modules • External authentications • Service identification • Identity proofs: Supervisors, address confirmations, externally confirmed identities, …
Incident and Response	9	• Training • Testing: Automation, Continuous Improvement • Handling, Monitoring, Reporting: Operational continuity, Automatic system shutdown, Insiders, Correlations to external organizations, Supply chain organization, Integrated event handling team, Behavioral analysis, Security Operation Center, Public relations • Event monitoring • Event reporting: Automated reports, associated security gaps • Response to information overload: Training: Measures for afterwards, …
Maintenance	7	• Control: Automation • Maintenance tools: Tools, media, prevention of unauthorized theft, …, restricted use of tools, authorization concept, … • Non-local maintenance: Logging, authentication and separation of maintenance sessions, … • Maintenance personnel: Security clearances for classified systems • Preventive and predictive maintenance

(continued)

Table 9.1 (continued)

Control Family	Number of Control Extensions	Examples (lists are not exhaustive)
Media Protection	8	• Access, • Labeling • Storage: Access restriction • Transport • Recovery: Review, approval, tracking, non-destructive techniques • Usage
Physical and Environmental Protection	23	• Access authorization • Access control: System access, • Transmission control • Output devices • Monitoring of physical accesses • Guest accesses • Power and cabling • Emergency exits, emergency power, emergency lighting • Fire protection: Fire detectors, … • Environmental controls: Monitoring with alarm function • Water damage protection, • Delivery and disposal • Alternative production sites • Location of system components • Information breaches • Asset monitoring and tracking • EMC protection • Component labeling
Planning	11	• System Security and Privacy plans: Functional architecture • Rules of conduct: Usage restriction for social media and external websites/applications • Operational concept, • Security and Privacy architectures • Central management • Baseline Tailoring

(continued)

Table 9.1 (continued)

Control Family	Number of Control Extensions	Examples (lists are not exhaustive)
Program Management	32	• Information Security Plan • Resources for Information Security and Data Protection • Activity Plan and Milestone Planning • System Inventory • Performance Measurement • Critical Infrastructure Plan • Data Protection Reports • Authorization Processes • Process Definitions • Insider Program • Testing, Training, Monitoring • Threat Awareness • Protection of Controlled, Unclassified Information on External Systems • Data Protection Plan • Dissemination of Information on the Data Protection Program • Record Keeping of Disclosures • Personally Identifiable Information, Quality Management • Data Governance Committee • Data Integrity Committee • Minimization of Personally Identifiable Information Used in Testing, Training, and Research • Complaint Management • Data Protection Reporting • Roles of Program Management in Risk Management • Supply Chain Risk Management Strategy • Continuous Monitoring Strategy
Personnel Security	9	• Personnel Screening, Termination, Transfer • Post-Employment Requirements • Access Rights • Sanctions
Processing of Personal Data and Transparency	8	• Authorization to Process Personal Data • Processing Purposes • Consent: Revocation, … • Special Categories of Personal Data
Risk Assessment	10	• Security Categories • Risk Assessment: Supply Chain, Dynamic Threats, Predictive Analyses, … • Vulnerability/Security Gap Monitoring and Scanning: Breadth and Depth Analysis, Privileged Accesses, Trend Analyses, Review of Historical Audit Reports, … • Technical Monitoring of Countermeasures • Data Protection Impact Assessment • Criticality Analyses • Threat Hunting

(continued)

Table 9.1 (continued)

Control Family	Number of Control Extensions	Examples (lists are not exhaustive)
System and Service Acquisition	23	• Resource Allocation • System Development Lifecycle: Management of Production Environments • Acquisition Process: Development Methods, Techniques, Practices, Use of Information Assurance Tools, Continuous Monitoring Plans for Security Controls, … • Security and Data Protection Engineering Principles: Clear Abstraction, Partially Ordered Dependencies, Minimized Sharing, Reduced Complexity, Trusted Components, Hierarchical Trust, Least Privilege, Secure Standards, Procedural Rigor, … • External System Services • Development Configuration Management: Integrity Verification, Trusted Distribution, … • Development Testing: Static Code Analysis, Threat Modeling, Independent Verification, Manual Code Reviews, Penetration Testing, Attack Surface Reviews, Dynamic Code Analysis, … • Development Processes, Standards, Techniques: Quality Metrics, Security and Privacy Tracking Tools, Criticality Analyses, Continuous Improvement, Event Tracking Plans, Automatic Vulnerability Analysis • Developer Training • Security Architectures • Custom Testing of Critical Components • Developer Screening
System and Communication Protection	51	• Separation of system and user functions: HW separation, … • Isolation of security functions • Information in shared system resources • Protection against Denial-of-Service: Limiting the ability to attack other systems, … • Resource availability • Protection of boundaries: Access points, external telecommunication services, rejection as standard, access only in exception, Fail Secure, … • Transmission confidentiality and integrity: Cryptographic encryption, … • Trusted paths • Cryptographic key management • Transmission of security and privacy attributes • Public-Key Infrastructure certificates • Mobile codes • Session authorization • System partitioning • Operational security • Wireless connection protection • Sensor capabilities and data • User restrictions • System time synchronization • HW-based protection

(continued)

Table 9.1 (continued)

Control Family	Number of Control Extensions	Examples (lists are not exhaustive)
System and Information Integrity	23	• Error correction: automated patch management tools, automated SW and firmware updates • Malicious code protection: Updates for privileged accesses, testing and verification, … • System monitoring: Intrusion detection systems, automated tools for real-time analysis, testing of monitoring tools, privileged users, … • Security alarms, alerts, directives • SW, firmware and information integrity • Spam protection • Error handling • Preventive error avoidance • Memory protection • Fail-safe procedures • Information diversity
Supply Chain Risk Assessment	12	• Risk management plan • Controls and processes: Limitation of damage • Acquisition strategies, tools, methods • Supplier evaluation and reviews • Notification agreements • Inspections • Component authenticity: Anti-counterfeiting training, configuration controls for component service and maintenance • Component disposal

References

[ISO15408] ***„Information technology – Security techniques – Evaluation criteria for IT security –“,*** (Common Criteria), ISO/IEC 15408 Band 1–3

[ISO27001] ***„Information security management systems – Requirements“***; ISO/IEC 27001

[NIST800-53R5] ***„Security and Privacy Controls for Federal Information Systems and Organizations“;*** NIST SP 800-53 Revision 5. https://csrc.nist.gov/publications/detail/sp/800-53/rev-5/final. accessed: 18.04.2021

Glossary

Ad-Blocker A program that ensures that advertising contained on websites is not displayed to the viewer. Such advertising can occur in various forms, for example as images, videos, text inserts, and pop-ups.

Anonymization By deleting a sufficient number of attributes, the data can no longer be assigned to any person.

Attack surface The totality of all existing vulnerabilities of a technical system/device/network (see also attack vector). Example: Bluetooth interfaces, windows, doors. …

Attack vector Possible attack path or attack technique that an unauthorized intrusion can take to compromise a foreign computer system (see also attack surface). Example: Security gap in firewall, open door, ….. .

Authenticity Protection objective: No imitation of something or someone else. Example: Authenticity can be broken with identity theft.

Authorization Protection objective: Not being able to acquire capabilities (e.g., performing an action) without permission (only being allowed to do what one is authorized to do).

Availability Protection objective: Timely availability for authorized instances/redundancy. Example: Network, Internet provider. Risk: Loss of information.

Backdoor Program that is deposited in a recognized vulnerability and allows access from outside.

Backdoor A covert method for bypassing normal authentication or encryption in a computer, a product, an embedded device (e.g., a home router), or its embodiment (e.g., part of a cryptosystem, an algorithm, a chipset, or even a "homunculus computer"—a tiny computer within a computer, as found in Intel's AMT technology). Backdoors are most commonly used to secure remote access to a computer or to gain access to plaintext in cryptographic systems. From there, they can be used to gain access to privileged information such as passwords, damage or delete data on hard drives, or to transmit information within networks.

Business Continuity Management (BCM) Strategy, plans, and actions to protect activities or processes—whose interruption would cause serious damage or devastating losses to the organization (such as operational disruptions)—or to enable alternative procedures.

T. Liedtke, *Information Security*, https://doi.org/10.1007/978-3-658-45711-2

Black-Hole-Attack A place in the network where incoming or outgoing data traffic is silently discarded (or "dropped") without informing the source that the data has not reached the intended recipient. The black holes themselves are invisible and can only be discovered by monitoring the lost data traffic.

Bluetooth Industry standard for data transmission between devices over short distances using radio technology (WPAN).

Bot (from robot) Runs on networked computers, whose network connection as well as local resources and data are available without the owner's consent.

Botnet Group of automated malicious programs, known as bots.

Browser-Fingerprinting The attempt to use data about device fingerprint or machine fingerprint, which is collected via the software and hardware of a remote computer device for the purpose of identification, for identity determination.

Brute-Force-Method Method of raw force, which is based on trying out all possible cases. Example: A password is spied out by trying all possible combinations of letters.

Bug (Programming Error) Programming error, software error, or software anomaly, which leads to erroneous behavior of computer programs due to inconsistencies or incorrect implementation of a specification.

Bug-Bounty A "bounty program" for software bugs is an initiative to identify, fix, and publicize errors in software by offering material or cash prizes for the discoverers.

CEO Fraud (also "Fake President") A scam in which companies are manipulated into transferring money using false identities.

Compromise of a computer system Unauthorized intrusion into a computer system in order to take it over or at least misuse it for one's own purposes.

Confidentiality Protection objective: Secrecy/no availability for unauthorized persons/ access control. Example: public/internal/confidential/secret. Risk: Espionage.

CRC—Cyclic Redundancy Check Method for determining a check value for data in order to detect errors during transmission or storage.

Credential Proof of authorization (identification technology): the identity of another system or user is confirmed to a system. Often: user recognition in connection with an authentication feature. Example: knowledge and possession (User-ID, password and biometric thumbprint, token password, …).

Credential Stuffing Attack methods in which already stolen or known passwords from other applications are used.

Cross-Site-Scripting (XSS) Refers to the exploitation of a computer security vulnerability in web applications by inserting information from a context where it is not trusted into another context where it is considered trustworthy. An attack can then be launched from this trustworthy context.

Crypto-(Ransom-)Trojan See Ransomware attack.

Cyberattack Targeted attack on computer networks of a (critical) infrastructure from the outside.

Cyber Kill Chain Describes cyber attacks. Consists of several stages that describe the attacker's increasingly deeper penetration.

Cyber Security Protection of the processing of electronic data in the cloud. Often used in two words in the British language area, then has the same meaning as Cybersecurity in one word.

Cybersecurity The totality of all technologies, processes, and procedures designed to protect digital assets, such as networks, computers, programs, and data from attacks, damage, or unauthorized access. Or: The state in which values to be protected are sufficiently protected against threat scenarios. When written as one word (mostly in the American language area), electronic information/data is meant as the target of attack. Subgroups include IT security, IoT security, information security, and OT security.

Darknet Peer-to-peer overlay network, whose participants manually establish their connections with each other.

Data minimization A fundamental principle of privacy. As few personal data as possible should be collected and processed. Access rights should be defined as strictly as possible and the number of people with access to personal data should be strictly limited.

DDoS Attack (Distributed Denial-of-Service) Multiple computers simultaneously attack a website or an entire network infrastructure in combination (botnets). This can, for example, lead to the failure of the servers.

Deep Web Hidden Web; the part of the World Wide Web that is not discoverable in a search using normal search engines.

Defect (error) Specific errors: Something wrong in the software code (e.g., caused by a design problem), hardware failure, misconfiguration.

Degradation Condition or transition of a system into a state with reduced functionality, performance, or both.

Drive-By-Attack Hacked web servers of reputable websites redirect users to websites with malicious code, which then attempt to infect the computer of an unsuspecting user.

Dumpster Diving Technique used to find information that can be used to carry out an attack on a computer network. Searching the "trash" for obvious treasures, such as access codes or passwords written on sticky notes. A phone list, calendar, or organizational chart can help an attacker gain access to the network using social engineering techniques.

Emergence Possibility of the formation of new properties or structures of a system as a result of the interaction of its elements.

Ethical Hacker/ Ethical Hacking Computer security expert who specializes in penetration tests and other testing methods that ensure the security of a company's information systems.

Eval-Function A special function for metaprogramming, which, for example, instructs an interpreter to evaluate a code fragment written in the programming language itself, which exists as a data object, and to use the result of the calculation accordingly.

EVITA EU research project, launched in 2008 with the aim to design, verify, and prototype an architecture for vehicle on-board networks. It defines, among other things, the four impact categories used in automotive (functional safety, finance, operability, privacy) in risk models and provides assessment tables for attack assessment for automotive based on IT standards.

Fail-Close In the event of a hardware/power failure at the limit protection mechanism, any communication over the limit of the control system should be prevented.

Fake President (CEO Fraud) See CEO Fraud.

Fault Injection Testing technique that helps understand how a virtual/real system behaves when it is stressed in an unusual way.

Flaw—Deficiency (Weakness) Type of defect that is instantiated in the software code due to an error or oversight in the design phase.

Freshness Protection objective that ensures replayed messages are recognized as such in a replay attack.

Functional Safety (also abbreviated as FuSa) Refers to the part of a system's safety that depends on the correct function of the safety-related system and other risk-reducing measures. Functional safety does not include, among other things, electrical safety, fire protection, or radiation protection.

Fuzz Testing A type of testing where large amounts of random data (usually in an automated or semi-automated manner) are input into a system to search for weaknesses and vulnerabilities (e.g., failures and coding errors).

Hack Creative solution for a technical problem.

Hardening of Computers The security of a system is increased by using only dedicated software that is necessary for the operation of the system, or by removing all software components and functions that are not absolutely necessary for the program to fulfill its intended task.

HEAVENS Research project in the automotive sector from 2013–2016. Evaluation of various state-of-the-art methods for risk assessment and derivation of a HEAVENS risk model. Based, among other things, on MS-STRIDE and EVITA.

Honeypot A facility designed to distract an attacker or enemy from the actual target or draw them into an area that would otherwise not have interested them—e.g., in the form of a decoy target.

Industrial Automation and Control Systems Collection of personnel, hardware, software, and policies involved in the operation of the industrial process and can affect or influence the safe and reliable operation.

Identity theft Misuse of another person's personal data. A perpetrator uses the foreign identity for theft and fraud.

Implementation attack Directly targets the hardware and software and uses physical properties to break mathematically secure methods, such as AES, 3DES or RSA.

Thus, through active error injection, the execution of an algorithm can be disrupted and secret data can be extracted.

Information Security Properties of information processing and storing (technical or non-technical) systems that ensure the protection objectives of confidentiality, availability, and integrity.

Information Security Management System Establishment of procedures and rules within an organization that serve to permanently define, control, monitor, maintain, and continuously improve information security.

Integrity Protection objective: Correctness, completeness, authority to modify. Example: Maintenance, changes (Risk: Manipulation).

Interveneability Protection objective: An affected person can intervene against processing, edits can be withdrawn.

Intrusion-Detection-System Tool that actively monitors data traffic to and from IT systems or networks for the detection of attacks directed against a computer system or network.

Intrusion-Prevention-System Tool that actively monitors data traffic to and from IT systems or networks and provides functions that can fend off a detected attack.

IP-Spoofing Sending of IP packets with a spoofed sender IP address.

Island Mode Prevents communication across the boundary of the control system. Key to security breaches when they are discovered within the control system or when an enterprise-level attack occurs.

Keyless-Entry Feature that allows a vehicle to be opened without a key. The key only needs to be in the vicinity of the vehicle for this to work.

KRACK: Key Reinstallation Attack In this attack, a NONCE, although it should only be used once, is used again. This is what happens when breaking the WPA2 protocol.

Likelihood See occurrence frequency.

Linkability Protection objective: Different data are stored in such a way that they cannot be linked/connected with each other. Example: electricity consumption values at a provider with the water consumption in the municipality.

Linkage Attack Attempt to re-identify individuals in an anonymized data set by combining this data with background information.

Malware Software (such as viruses, worms, etc.) that can infiltrate computer systems and cause disruptions or damage there (see also malicious software).

Malware See Ransomware.

Man-in-the-Middle-Attack An attacker inserts themselves into a communication taking place between two stations (PC, control units, etc.). The attacker pretends that their malicious packets come from a trusted computer.

Millionaire's Problem Two millionaires want to know who is richer. However, they do not want to inadvertently find out any further information about their mutual wealth.

Non-repudiation also Traceability Protection goal: Not being able to claim not to have done something (not responsible). Example: Log files can prove activities. In data protection often used inversely, here the deniability is a necessary part of anonymization.

NONCE (number) used only once A combination of numbers or letters that is used only once in the respective context.

Online-Proctoring Term for digital formats of exam supervision, which are intended to enable secure and reliable exams to be carried out regardless of location (e.g., from home).

Occurrence frequency (likelihood) The occurrence frequency is a weighted risk factor based on a (subjective) analysis of the frequency of occurrence that a particular threat can exploit a particular vulnerability (or a series of vulnerabilities). The risk factor for occurrence frequency combines an estimate of the frequency of occurrence that the threat event is triggered with an estimate of the probability of impact (i.e., the probability that the threat event leads to adverse effects). In risk management terminology, the word **Likelihood** is used to denote the chance of something happening, regardless of whether it is objectively or subjectively, qualitatively or quantitatively defined, measured or determined, and described in general terms or mathematically.

Over-the-top content Refers to the transmission of video and audio content over internet access, without an internet service provider being involved in the control or distribution of the content.

Pepper To further complicate dictionary and brute-force attacks, the password can be combined with a string chosen and kept secret by the server before the hash value is calculated. It is usually the same for all passwords on a server.

Permission Fact The processing of personal data is only permitted if a permission fact exists.

Penetration Test A group of testing methods used to find weaknesses in a system that can be exploited by an attacker to take control, gain privileged access, disclose privileged data, or simply cause a system malfunction. Penetration tests often involve real attacks on real systems and data, using the same tools and techniques employed by actual attackers.

Personal Data All information relating to an identified or identifiable natural (living) person.

Phishing Large volumes of emails are sent randomly to recipients to get them to click on harmful links or disclose confidential information.

Phreaking Refers to a subculture of hackers who deal with security mechanisms of telephony, particularly with the manipulation of telephone connections.

Presumption of prohibition Basic, preventive data processing prohibition.

Privacy Protection of the right to informational self-determination. Protection of personal rights in data processing and also protection of privacy.

Privacy-by-Default By default, the more privacy-friendly settings are set in software and devices.

Probability See. Probability of occurrence.

Probability of occurrence Measure, expressed as a number between 0 and 1, where 0 stands for impossibility and 1 for absolute certainty. Can be calculated mathematically. The total population is known.

Profiling Useful creation of a complete personality profile for specific purposes. The creation is done by merging data and then analyzing and evaluating it for specific purposes.

Programming error See Bug.

Protection requirement Level of information security to be achieved.

Pseudonymization Names are replaced by pseudonyms. Personal data can only be recovered using a translation list (pseudonyms).

Ransomware A subtype of malware (malicious software), also known as extortion trojan, ransomware, crypto trojan, or encryption trojan.

Ransomware Attack Software sometimes also referred to as encryption trojans. It initiates a blackmail based on data that is indecipherably coded for the user. Ransomware sneaks into the system until the user is horrified to find that his computer is locked. There are two types in this case:

- Screenlockers lock the screen;
- File-Encrypters encrypt the data on the computer and take children's photos, text files, and important folders hostage.

Relay Station Attack Attack method using the bridging of radio signals between key and vehicle, on Passive Keyless Entry and Start Systems.

Roll-Jam-Technique Attack method using a jamming device (Jammer). For example, it is used for vehicle theft.

Salt A randomly selected string of characters that is appended to a plaintext before its further processing (e.g., input into a hash function) to increase the entropy of the input.

Sandbox generally refers to an isolated area within which any action has no impact on the external environment.

SCADA (Supervisory Control And Data Acquisition) Monitoring and controlling technical processes using a computer system.

Side-channel analysis/attack Based on a passive measurement, e.g., the power consumption or the EM radiation of a circuit. After applying analog and digital preprocessing methods, tools are used that can implement attacks. Example: Circuits for recovering the side-channel signal of contactless smart cards and the GIAnT, an FPGA platform for implementing implementation attacks.

Social Engineering Social Engineering involves interpersonal influences with the aim of eliciting certain behaviors in individuals, for example, to persuade them to disclose confidential information, to purchase a product, or to release financial resources.

SOTIF Safety of the Intended Functionality is a subfield of technical product safety, which deals with the hazards of technical systems. At the heart of SOTIF is the indefinite question of how to specify, develop, verify, and validate an intended function so that it can be considered sufficiently safe.

Spear-Phishing A sinister type of cyber attack. Fraud attempts via email against organizations with the aim of gaining unauthorized access to confidential data. Unlike phishing attacks, the recipients are carefully researched and selected beforehand. The emails are personally tailored to make them appear credible.

Stakeholder Person or organization that can be affected by the damage of a value to be protected. Example: User of a product, manufacturer, distributor of products.

Stakeholder (representative of interests) S. Representative of interests.

State of the Art Refers to the best performance available on the market of a subject to achieve an object. The subject is the IT security measure; the object is the legal IT security objective.

Statement of Applicability (SoA) Customized application for an information security management system according to ISO/IEC 27001, in line with an organization's business processes.

Sybil Attack Attack on peer-to-peer networks by creating spoofed identities. Example: Attack of a vehicle by other previously manipulated vehicles.

Threat Analysis and Risk Assessment Risk assessment method in the automotive sector, based on an initial item definition, which is carried out at the beginning of a project.

Threat Hunting Threat Hunting is a proactive method for improving Cyber Security. It proactively searches for potential threats in networks and IT environments.

Threat Intelligence Network Network that proactively distributes global threat information (e.g., about Zero-Hour/Zero-Day attacks).

Tracker Attack An attacker can isolate a single individual by performing multiple aggregate queries (e.g., AVG() and SUM() in SQL) on a dataset. Most interfaces for aggregate queries are naive and only block queries with small result set sizes. This function alone is not sufficient to maintain privacy.

Transparency (engl. Transparency) An important protection objective for personal data: the processing of personal data is transparent to the person concerned. They are aware of what is being done with their data.

Trustworthiness The characteristic of a person or company that conveys to others the trust in the qualification, the skills, and the reliability of this entity to fulfill certain tasks and to assume assigned responsibilities.

Vulnerability Security gaps in computer systems that exploit a weakness.

Vulnerability Scanning Detection of already known security vulnerabilities/weaknesses.

Water-Holing Attack Frequently visited websites outside of an organization are manipulated to gain access to the infrastructure within an organization through them.

Weakness A technical or organizational deficiency that allows a threat to become a hazard, and thus can become a security vulnerability.

Whaling Particularly intense attack on individuals. The fraudulent messages sent appear to come from someone who is particularly high-ranking or influential in their company.

Zero-day Exposure Time span between the discovery of a security vulnerability and the provision of a solution to close it (e.g., through a software patch).

Zero-Hour Attack/Zero-Day Attack Attack that occurs in the same hour/on the same day that the vulnerability being exploited in the corresponding software is discovered.

SPRINGER NATURE

GPSR Compliance

The European Union's (EU) General Product Safety Regulation (GPSR) is a set of rules that requires consumer products to be safe and our obligations to ensure this.

If you have any concerns about our products, you can contact us on ProductSafety@springernature.com

In case Publisher is established outside the EU, the EU authorized representative is:

Springer Nature Customer Service Center GmbH
Europaplatz 3
69115 Heidelberg, Germany

The manufacturer's authorised representative in the EU is Springer Nature Customer Service Centre GmbH, Europaplatz 3, 69115 Heidelberg, Germany. If you have any concerns regarding our products, please contact ProductSafety@springernature.com

Printed and bound by CPI Group (UK) Ltd, Croydon, CR0 4YY
30/09/2026
02225566-0020